GRETCHEN BECKER, a magna cum laude and Phi Beta Kappa graduate of Radcliffe College, Harvard, is a writer and editor specializing in medical books. She was diagnosed with type 2 diabetes in 1996 and is a longtime participant in several diabetes e-mail lists on the Internet. She lives on a small farm in Halifax, Vermont, where she also raises sheep and makes hats from their wool. Becker can be reached via e-mail at gretchen@sover.net.

GRETCHEN BECKER

THE FIRST YEAR™
TYPE 2
DIABETES

A PATIENT-EXPERT GUIDE
FOR THE NEWLY DIAGNOSED

ROBINSON
London

www.constablerobinson.com

First published in the US by Marlowe & Company,
an imprint of Avalon Publishing Group, Inc, 2001

First published in the UK by Robinson,
an imprint of Constable & Robinson Ltd, 2004

Publisher's Note: This book is not intended to be a substitute for medical
advice or treatment. Any person with a condition requiring medical
attention should consult a qualified medical practitioner
or suitable therapist.

ISBN 978-1-84119-804-0

Printed and bound in the EU

10 9 8 7 6 5 4

TO ALL MY FRIENDS ON THE DMLIFE,
LC-DIABETES, AND WORLD MAILING LISTS,
FROM WHOM I HAVE LEARNED SO MUCH.

Contents

CONTENTS

DIABETES IS increasing across the world. Already close to one in ten of the world's population either has diabetes or are likely to develop it during their lives. The prevalence of diabetes is predicted to double over the next 15 years and most of this increase will be in type 2 diabetes.

This 'epidemic' of diabetes represents a serious and increasing challenge for societies and health care systems worldwide. However, each individual faced with the diagnosis of diabetes faces an equally formidable challenge.

In the days, weeks, months and years following a diagnosis of diabetes, there is so much to learn, so much to deal with. A wealth of facts to accumulate – about the disease itself, and the various treatments available. A host of skills to acquire – how to monitor blood glucose (sugar) levels, and how to watch out for and detect early signs of complications. We all know that diligent control of blood glucose levels can offer excellent protection against those complications, yet this goal remains, even with the range of treatments at our disposal, no easy task. To achieve such control requires the full and active participation of the patient, constantly balancing diet, lifestyle and treatment to steer a course between the short-term consequences of a blood glucose level that has fallen too low, and the long-term damage caused by running too high a level for too long. There are few other conditions which make such demands.

And there are more subtle adjustments that need to be made. The diagnosis of diabetes brings with it significant mental and emotional challenges. On the one hand, there are the inevitable concerns about the future, and the new demands of managing a condition that requires constant vigilance and attention. On the other, there is the need to ensure that such concerns do not destroy the spontaneity and pleasures that make life worth living.

Hopefully, most people with diabetes will find that the coterie of health care professionals that they encounter following the diagnosis of diabetes (a team that includes their GP, practice nurse, diabetes specialist nurse, dietitian, consultant diabetes specialist, podiatrist, ophthalmologist, and others!) will provide much of the guidance they require. Some will have access to structured education programs, whilst others will glean information and support from friends, relatives, community groups or the Internet.

But every person living with diabetes – and anyone living with someone living with diabetes – will find Gretchen Becker's wonderful book an invaluable complement to those other sources of information. *The First Year – Type 2 Diabetes* carries the reader through that first year after diagnosis, dispensing solid scientific background and sensible practical advice, throughout instilling confidence that the challenge of dealing with diabetes is a manageable one. The book is infused with Gretchen's own experiences of coming to terms with the diagnosis of diabetes. She can walk the reader 'step-by-step' through the highs and lows, through the obstacles and the challenges, simply because she's been there herself. And though she pulls no punches, the message is definitely upbeat – information means empowerment, and empowerment means better control of your diabetes, and fewer problems in the future.

If there is a better guide to living with diabetes, I've not found it. I know that my patients with type 2 diabetes – not just those newly-diagnosed, but anyone wanting a 'refresher' course – will find in this book a valuable companion.

Introduction

DIABETES, PERHAPS more than any other chronic disease, must be managed largely by you, the patient. This is because everything you do affects your blood sugar levels. Most especially, every morsel of food you eat has a major effect. Exercise, or its lack, also plays an important role.

Other life situations can affect blood sugar levels as well. These include physical stress such as getting the flu and emotional stress such as losing a job. Medications can also make your blood sugar go either up or down.

Doctors and nurses can guide you in your quest for normal blood sugar levels, but they cannot be at your side 24 hours a day. You may not see them for weeks or even months at a time. Thus to gain good control, you must take charge and learn to do a large part of the management of your diabetes yourself. To make wise daily decisions about the myriad factors that can affect your blood sugar levels, you need knowledge.

Diabetes is an immensely complex disease that affects every system in the body. To make things even more complex, type 2 diabetes comes in many forms. A treatment that works wonderfully for someone else may not work at all for you.

Your doctor, and even a complete 'health care team', cannot control your diabetes without your help. Learning how diabetes works and then working with your doctor to figure out which of the many treatments available will be best for you is extremely important if you want to obtain normal blood sugar levels, and this is the best way you can reduce your chances of ever developing complications.

You have a lot to learn, and no one expects you to learn everything at once. It takes time before you can absorb it all. I know. I have type 2 diabetes myself.

What happened to me

The first sign – I realized later – that something was wrong was in late summer 1995, when I noticed the black fly bites I'd scratched in May when working on my sheep farm in Vermont had still not healed. That autumn, some strange pink algae persisted in growing in my toilet, despite numerous cleanings with chlorine bleach. I get my water from a spring, so I concluded there was a new type of algae in my water supply. I didn't feel sick, so I didn't worry about it.

The following January, I noticed I was thirsty a lot and attributed this to the fact that I use a lot of salt. Later I noticed I seemed to need to urinate a lot and attributed that to the fact that I drink a lot of coffee while I earn a so-called living copyediting medical books.

I got more and more myopic and attributed that to the fact I'd been spending 50 to 60 hours a week trying to edit a manuscript an ophthalmologist had sent to a publisher single-spaced, in tiny type. I guessed that he was trying to drum up business (and had succeeded in my case).

I started craving sweets. One day in April, I realized I was rushing through my dinner, not enjoying it as I usually did, so I could get to the big glass of fruit juice I usually drank at the end.

The next day I visited a friend, who offered me a cup of coffee. 'What I'd really like is a glass of water,' I said. 'I don't understand why I'm thirsty all the time.' She suggested I be tested for diabetes.

So I rushed home, where I had some of those tablets people used to use to test for sugar in urine. My mother had been diagnosed with diabetes some years before, so I'd kept them on hand to do periodic checks. Previously they had always stayed blue, meaning no sugar. This time, they turned deep brown.

Going to the doctor's office simply confirmed what I already knew. I had diabetes. The blood sugar test the nurse did gave a reading of 16.8 mmol/L, four hours after my last meal. 'Is that bad?' I asked, totally uninformed about what a normal blood sugar reading should be.

Later the nurse said, 'You're not terribly overweight, so we don't know if we'll have to put you on insulin or not,' which didn't cheer me up a lot. I'd never been seriously ill, so I was stunned. Now I had not only a disease, but an incurable one. I'd never be able to eat normally again. Maybe I'd have to have injections. I'd have huge medical bills, because I didn't have good medical insurance. (Of course, if I'd been living in Britain, this wouldn't have been a worry.) I didn't know how I'd cope.

But I wanted to know more. So I bought books about diabetes. Then I explored the Internet and found Rick Mendosa's website that linked to almost every page available on the Internet. I signed up for several e-mail mailing lists and read other people's accounts of their experiences, started asking them questions, and learned and learned. Now I would like to share some of this information with others.

How to use this book

Because I know what a shock it is to receive a diagnosis of diabetes and how much there is to learn, I have tried to break down the information into small bits that you can absorb slowly, starting with the most essential things you should know right away and then slowly moving on to the more subtle aspects of dealing with this disease. Sometimes I outline the bare essentials of a complex topic like diet in an early chapter and then later discuss it in more detail.

Ideally, you would get this book the day you were diagnosed, but it may take days or weeks before you find it or are ready to read about this disease. Whenever you get the book – or open it – start with Day 1 and work your way through it at your own pace.

The book is modelled after the classic approach to creating a fine oil finish on a piece of furniture, in which you oil the wood every day for a week, every week for a month and every month for a year. After that, you only need to touch it up every now and then.

So too, when you are diagnosed, there is so much to learn that you need to spend a little time every day learning about this disease. Then, as dealing with it becomes part of your regular routine, you can spend a little less time until eventually you'll only need to 'touch up' your knowledge every now and then.

Each day or week or month in this book is divided into a Living and a Learning section. The Living sections deal with the problems of living with this chronic disease. I hope the Living sections will help you to understand that you are not alone; that the emotional upheavals you'll probably go through are normal; that living with diabetes is sometimes hard, but it's possible to lead a rewarding life nevertheless; and that once you come to terms with having diabetes and get your blood sugar under control, you may find you feel better, have more energy and enjoy your food more than you ever have before.

The Learning sections explain some of the science of diabetes. Some of you may be more comfortable reading about science than others. If you've always liked science and technology, I hope you will appreciate the depth of the discussions in the later Learning chapters. There is material there you won't find in other popular books about diabetes.

Even if you are a technophobe, I hope you will read the Learning sections in Days 1 to 7, at least, because they include important information that you really should know, as well as the summaries at the ends of each section. Skimming the subheads in each chapter should also give you a general idea of what the chapter says. Later, as you get more comfortable with the science of diabetes, you can go back and read the rest of the Learning sections, or you can consult them for reference when you have a question about some aspect of diabetes. Terms in **bold** are defined in the glossary at the end of the book.

I will not prescribe

I am not a doctor, and I will not prescribe for you. I will not tell you which treatment I think is best or how much medication or vitamins you should take. Diabetes research is going on at a furious pace. New diabetes drugs and paraphernalia are appearing every year, and opinions on the effectiveness of vitamins and supplements sometimes seem to change from newscast to newscast. A medication or vitamin recommendation that seems best today might seem wrong in a couple of years.

Thus instead of giving you a lot of specifics that will soon be outdated, I've tried to give you enough background information about how diabetes, current drugs and current meters work so that you can understand what you read about new treatments, medications and supplies. As your knowledge about diabetes evolves, I hope what you learn from this book will enable you to keep up with the new advances, so you can work with your doctor to ensure that your own individual treatment plan evolves as well.

Because there are different philosophies about how to treat type 2 diabetes, rather than prescribing what you *should* do, I have tried to describe different approaches so you and your doctor can decide together which philosophy might be right for you.

Like many people in America, I started off on the American Diabetes Association exchange diet, and I lost 13.5 kilograms. However, I was hungry 24 hours a day, and my blood sugar levels continued to be above normal. So I gradually cut back on my carbohydrate intake and ended up on a low-carbohydrate diet. On this diet I stopped losing weight, but I also stopped being hungry all the time. My blood sugar levels are mostly in the normal range, and what weight I had already lost, I've managed to keep off for seven years.

I hope my own experiences haven't biased my discussions toward this dietary approach; what works for me might not work for you. There are no studies comparing the long-term effects of the various diabetic diets, so your choices must be based on conjecture about how a particular diet will affect you in the long term, as well as your own experience with its short-term effects.

Where the focus is

This book is aimed at people going through their first year with type 2 diabetes. Most of you will not require insulin injections in your first year. Although I discuss the pros and cons of insulin therapy for people with type 2 diabetes, I do not go into the details about different types of insulin and how to inject them. For the same reason, I focus on preventing diabetes complications instead of details of how to treat them. If you can use the knowledge in this book to maintain near-normal blood sugar levels, I hope you will never get major complications. If you already have early signs of them, I hope you can reverse them with good control.

I have assumed that you are an intelligent person who wants to take an active part in your treatment rather than just accepting your doctor's prescription without understanding the reasons behind it. I have also assumed you have already received – or will very soon receive – from your doctor or a nurse the very basic instructions or pamphlets usually given to patients just diagnosed with type 2 diabetes. Rather than simply repeating in a parrot-like fashion the information you'll get from these professionals or pamphlets, in the first few days I focus on some of the things you probably *won't* be told, some of the emotional upheavals you'll undoubtedly go through, some of the challenges you'll face. Later, when I hope your emotions have become more stable, I go back and review some of the basic things you were probably told in those first meetings, just to make sure you've absorbed them all.

If for some reason you did not receive any of the basic instructions after your diagnosis, you might want to go right to Month 2 and read through the 'diabetes ABCs'. Then you can go back and review them later, when your emotions have settled down.

Throughout this book I emphasize the need to use a home meter to learn what your blood sugar levels are. In fact, I mention testing so often you may begin to think I have shares in a test strip company. I don't. I just care about your health.

I have quoted comments from real people who are living with type 2 diabetes, although their names may have been changed to preserve their privacy. As you read these comments, keep in mind that what works for one person may not work for you. But sometimes reading about what someone else has gone through strikes a chord and makes you realize that your own feelings and reactions are normal. I hope it helps.

Keep on learning

By the end of your first year with diabetes, I hope you will understand where you can go to continue this learning process as well as share your knowledge with others, and how to evaluate the announcements of diabetes news in the popular press.

If you have access to the Internet, the excellent section by Internet diabetes expert Rick Mendosa will provide you with a guide to using that immense resource to increase your knowledge about diabetes, learn about advances in treatment as they occur and share experiences with other people living with diabetes.

Diabetes is a chronic genetic disease that today is incurable. The good news is that it can be controlled. With knowledge and care, most people with type 2 diabetes can live near-normal lives for many years. It has been said that the best way to live a long life is to get a chronic disease, because it makes you take care of yourself. Many people who take charge of their type 2 diabetes find this to be true. They lose weight, start exercising, eat healthy foods and feel healthier and more energetic than they have in years. I certainly do.

This is not to say that a diagnosis of type 2 diabetes means unmitigated joy. There are obvious sacrifices involved, especially isolation from sharing 'normal' food with friends and family, and some people do suffer handicapping side effects. So I am sorry that you have become a member of the 'Type 2 Diabetes Club', but I welcome you to our worldwide community. Remember, you now have diabetic 'brothers and sisters' all over the world who understand what you are going through. You are not alone.

THE FIRST YEAR™

Type 2 Diabetes

living

It's Not
Your Fault

YOU'VE JUST been diagnosed with type 2 diabetes. If you're like most people, you're probably in a state of shock. At the first consultation, your doctor probably told you a lot of things about diets and drugs and insulin and glucose and carbohydrates and blood tests and avoiding this and doing that, and you probably came out of the office with your head spinning, not remembering much of what the doctor said.

Don't worry, you're not alone. Most people feel that way.

If no one in your family ever had diabetes, and especially if you're thin and thought diabetes only happened to fat people, you're probably especially puzzled. 'What did I do wrong? Why is this happening to me?'

Sometimes a diagnosis comes like a thunderbolt on a sunny day. Sophie C. consulted a doctor about a toenail fungus, and he drew some blood for routine tests. 'Next day the phone rang, and my doctor informed me quite bluntly that I was diabetic,' she said. 'Talk about a slap in the face! I was scared out of my mind. There must be some mistake here. I wasn't blind, my feet weren't gangrenous. No family history of the disease, no warning signs (that I knew of at the time), not a clue.'

Or maybe you were expecting a diagnosis someday. You've got relatives with diabetes: your grandmother had diabetes and died from gangrene in her foot. Your father got it when he was 65 and died from a heart attack a few years later. If you're also overweight, maybe you figured someday you'd get diabetes yourself. But you probably figured 'someday' would be far in the future, when you were old. Not today. Not now. 'I'm not ready yet.'

Whether you expected it or not, a diabetes diagnosis is a shock.

Getting diabetes is not your fault

There's so much to learn, but you can't learn it all at once. Trying to accept the diagnosis is enough for your first day. Here's what you should remember as you deal with this: Getting diabetes is not your fault.

A lot of people may tell you that if only you'd eaten less sugar, or eaten less fat or exercised more, or eaten more fibre, or smoked less, or done none of the things that 95 per cent of people do, you wouldn't have got diabetes. Especially if you're overweight, since most people with type 2 diabetes have a problem with weight, people will suggest that it's your fault that you got diabetes because you let yourself get fat.

There is no question that type 2 diabetes is *associated with* obesity. Therefore, most people assume that the excess weight *causes* the diabetes. But here's something to think about: It's possible that diabetes causes obesity.

You need the genes

To get diabetes, you need to have diabetic genes. One of the causes of your diabetes is a poor choice of ancestors. People without those genes can spend their lives lying around eating chips and watching TV and they'll probably get fat. But they won't get diabetes.

Having the genes, however, isn't enough to give you the disease. Even if you have diabetes genes, if you live in an environment where you don't get a lot to eat and you do hard physical labour all day, you still probably won't get diabetes. Some people think the diabetic genes are **thrifty genes** that make your body use its food more efficiently, meaning that you can gain more weight with less food. In times of famine, this comes in handy, and when food was extremely scarce, your ancestors probably fared better and had more children than other families who didn't have those genes.

But when your family moved to a different country or into a different type of lifestyle where food was plentiful and machines did all the work, those diabetes genes weren't so handy after all. When food is limited, it doesn't matter how hungry you are. You can't eat enough. When food is readily available, having a good appetite can be a disaster.

Diabetes may cause hunger

Having diabetes genes may affect the appetite. Alex E. described the time someone brought some scrumptious pastries to work. A thin person walked in, looked at the pastries, and said, 'Oh my, those look good. I wish I were hungry so I could try one.' Alex was flabbergasted. He was hungry all the time and thought everyone else was too. Only after he learned to control his blood sugar levels did his hunger abate and he learned what normal hunger is like.

Some people find that they get ravenously hungry when their blood sugar is fluctuating rapidly. You may have had poor blood sugar control for years before you were diagnosed with diabetes. This means that after every meal, your blood sugar went abnormally high. Then it came down again. This may have triggered intense hunger, which would make you eat again. Then the roller coaster would repeat. No wonder you put on a little weight.

'All my life I was hungry! The more "healthy" my diet, listening to all the diet gurus, the more hungry I became,' said Linda C.

You can't change your genes

So it may have been those diabetes genes that made you hungry. The hunger made you eat. The thrifty genes were especially efficient in turning that food into fat. And the fat made it harder for you to exercise. So you had another snack instead.

I've probably already told you more about diabetes than you wanted to know right away. But for now, just remember this. To get diabetes, you need to have diabetes genes. There's nothing you can do to change your genes.

Your diabetes is not your fault.

IN A SENTENCE:

> *Diabetes is not your fault.*

learning

What Is Diabetes?

DIABETES IS an incredibly complicated disease that comes in many flavours. Later, we'll discuss some of those exotic flavours. But for now, we'll stick with the two basic groups, called **type 1** and **type 2 diabetes**.

Type 1 is autoimmune

Type 1 diabetes, which used to be called *juvenile diabetes*, or **insulin-dependent diabetes mellitus (IDDM)**, is usually, but not always, diagnosed in children and young adults. It is an **autoimmune disease**, meaning that for some reason, the immune system has mistaken its own **pancreas** for foreign tissue and destroys the cells that produce **insulin**, which is a **hormone**. As a result, people with type 1 diabetes produce almost no insulin and must take daily insulin injections.

Type 2 means insulin resistance

Type 2 diabetes, which is what you have, used to be called *adult-* or *maturity-onset diabetes*, or **non-insulin-dependent diabetes mellitus (NIDDM)**, sometimes popularly called *old-age diabetes*, because it is usually, but not always, diagnosed in older people. Today, more and more younger people, even children, are being found to have type 2 diabetes. Because this book is about type 2 diabetes, whenever I say just *diabetes*, unless I specify otherwise, I am referring to the type 2 variety.

Type 2 diabetes is probably *not* an autoimmune disease, and you probably don't have less insulin than normal. In fact, you may have *more* insulin than normal. The problem is something called **insulin resistance (IR)**.

Insulin lets glucose into cells

Before we discuss IR, let's go back and try to understand what insulin does. Like a car that needs energy to run and uses petrol as an energy source, your body also needs energy to function and uses a sugar called **glucose**. When you eat food, the body converts much of that food into glucose. The glucose is taken up by the brain and the muscles to make you think well and run fast, both useful characteristics if you're trying to avoid being eaten by a sabre-toothed tiger or hail a taxi in London.

The brain doesn't need insulin to take up that glucose, but the muscles do. In the presence of insulin, the muscles produce what are called **glucose transporters** – which you can think of as little boats that carry glucose passengers – to ferry the glucose across the cell membrane into the cell. Without enough insulin, the cell doesn't produce enough transporters, so a lot of the glucose can't get into your muscle cells. The glucose just builds up in the bloodstream and causes all kinds of problems.

If you're thin, you may be one of the minority of people with type 2 diabetes who for some unknown reason simply don't produce enough insulin. In this case, your IR may be normal.

If you're overweight, it's more likely that you're producing plenty of insulin, but you've got IR. For some unknown reason, the insulin just doesn't work very well. The body (which is generally much more intelligent than we are) recognizes this and produces more insulin to compensate for the IR. But after many years, the cells in the pancreas that produce the insulin (called **beta cells**) can't keep up with the demand and eventually get 'exhausted', not able to produce all the insulin you need. Then your blood sugar (**blood glucose**) level rises, and that's usually when you're diagnosed with diabetes.

The drinks machine analogy

If you like analogies, think of muscle cells as drinks machines. If you want a drink, you put money (insulin) into the machine and a can of fizzy drink (glucose transporters) comes out.

Thomas is a single father who just got fired from his job. He's thirsty and he finds a functioning drinks machine, but he simply has no money to put into the machine, so he can't get a drink. Thomas is like the thin person with type 2 who just isn't producing enough insulin (money), even though the glucose-transporter factory (the drinks machine) is working well.

Rhoda, on the other hand, is wealthy. She has all the money she needs, because she prints her own money on a machine in her basement. She's thirsty, finds a drinks machine, puts in some money and discovers that the machine is broken; no can comes out. But Rhoda is in luck for today. She discovers that if she puts in £25, she can get a drink out of the machine. Getting money is no problem for her, so she keeps using the drinks machine because it's near where she works.

Rhoda is like the overweight person with IR. She can produce plenty of money (insulin), but the machine (her glucose-transporter factory) is broken. For a while, things work all right for Rhoda. When she needs a drink, she just prints more money.

Then one day, Rhoda's money-printing machine (her insulin-producing beta cells) starts wearing out. Every day, she's got less and less money (insulin). Finally, she doesn't have enough money for even one drink. Now she's like the person with IR whose beta cells are exhausted.

Focus on the basics

No one yet understands exactly how all these processes work, but scientists are working hard on the problem. Later, we'll discuss some of the details. For now, it's enough just to understand the basics: **Diabetes is a disease of insulin deficiency, in either quantity** (the beta cells don't produce enough) *or* **quality** (you've got plenty of insulin, but it doesn't work very well). **As a result, your blood glucose levels are too high**.

There are many ways to treat type 2 diabetes. For now, trust your medical team to make the best choice for you and don't worry about all the whats and whys. You've probably gone for many months, maybe even years, with high blood glucose levels, but with no treatment at all. Now almost any treatment will improve your situation. You've got a lot to learn in the days ahead, so concentrate on becoming informed and let your medical team lead the way.

IN A SENTENCE:

> *Diabetes means you don't have enough (in quantity or quality) insulin to keep your blood glucose levels in the normal range.*

living

Is It All
a Mistake?

I SUSPECT most people with diabetes have the same fantasies.

In the first fantasy, you're sitting at the kitchen table surrounded by diabetes paraphernalia and lists of food choices called *exchanges* that you got from the nurse. You're trying to understand what insulin resistance (IR) is, and you can't remember if your doctor said you had too much of it or too little. You're wondering if you'll have to have injections.

Then the telephone rings.

'Hello? Is this Mr Bigappetite? This is Dr Birdwhistle's receptionist. There's been a mistake here at the lab. They mixed up your lab results with Mr Bigape E. Tight's. Your blood sugars were fine. You don't have diabetes after all.'

Unfortunately, that fantasy is not likely to come true. Your diabetes is real. And it's not like the flu or a bad case of bronchitis. It doesn't go away. Someday in the future, they'll discover how to cure diabetes. But that day isn't here yet. Your diabetes is going to be with you for a long, long time.

You want it to go away

Diabetes doesn't show. You don't have any obvious outward signs like a high fever or black warts on your nose or joints that scream when you move. Many people feel perfectly healthy once they've got their blood glucose levels under control. So it's easy to fantasize that your diabetes might have gone away. In this fantasy, you're standing at the checkout in the supermarket. You smile as you see a copy of the latest edition of your local newspaper, with your picture on the front. The cover story says, 'Middle-aged diabetic miraculously cured.'

There is a picture of you, eating a chocolate fudge sundae. 'It was the oddest thing,' you are quoted as saying. 'After dinner last night, I had a bite of this strange Tibetan chocolate, and the next day my blood sugar stayed normal no matter what I ate. Then this morning, I discovered I'd lost weight.' Doctors confirmed your recovery. 'We can only say it's a miracle,' says Dr Charge A. Lott.

This second fantasy never comes true either. Unfortunately, your diabetes is here to stay.

You can be diagnosed with or without symptoms

You may have been diagnosed because you weren't feeling well. Many people feel tired when their blood glucose level is high. High blood glucose levels can cause constant thirst and frequent urination. It can cause recurrent yeast infections. It can also cause problems with the lens of your eyes, so that you have to change the prescription for your glasses too often. Some of you may have had elevated blood glucose levels for five or ten years before you were diagnosed. If that is the case, you may have had more severe symptoms, such as sores that wouldn't heal, numbness or tingling in your arms or legs, problems with your kidneys or damage to the retina of your eyes. You may even have had a heart attack before you were diagnosed.

If you've had any of these symptoms of diabetes, it may be easier for you to believe that you do, in fact, have this disease, especially when the symptoms disappear, or at least stop getting worse, after you get your blood glucose levels under control.

But you may have been diagnosed on the basis of a random blood glucose test during a physical exam or screening at a health fair when you were feeling perfectly fine. Then someone pricked your finger and tried to tell you that you've got diabetes.

How can you believe that when you're feeling so good? Surely it must have been a mistake. No one in your family has diabetes. You've always eaten healthily. So admittedly, you don't run the London Marathon every year, and you don't lift weights every day. But you're reasonably fit and reasonably active. You thought diabetes only happened to overweight people who never went far from the TV remote control. How could this happen to you?

It must be a mistake. Maybe the machine was broken. Maybe that nice woman doing the test wasn't properly trained. Or maybe it was just because you had been eating sweets before you took the test and probably when you eat regular food again everything will be back to normal. Right? Unfortunately, wrong is the right answer here.

Acceptance is difficult

Accepting that you have diabetes is difficult for anyone, even if you had obvious symptoms when you were diagnosed. One day, you're just like everyone else. Then suddenly everything is changed. You're different. Simple things that you've always taken for granted are now suddenly forbidden to you – probably forever.

How do you deal with this sudden curtain falling down on the world as you knew it? The easiest way is to deny it. They think you're going to stop eating almost everything that tastes good? No way.

Taking tablets is easy. But changing your entire way of living is more difficult. 'I went through the various phases of being unable to imagine giving up my favourite foods, or feeling cheated that certain foods would be taken from me, or that I had a right to these foods and it was unfair for this disease to treat me this way and even a little, "I'm strong, these high blood glucoses won't hurt me,"' said Edward A.

But acceptance leads to control

Accepting your diagnosis as soon as possible is absolutely the best thing you can do for your control of this disease, because there's both bad news and good news about type 2 diabetes. Diabetes is incurable. That's the bad news. The good news is that it is controllable. And the most important agent in that control is you.

Of course it's not easy. Acceptance takes time. But once you are able to accept the fact that you really do have type 2 diabetes, a condition that won't ever go away, you can start taking control. In many cases, you will eventually feel healthier and more energetic than ever before.

That first step may be one of the hardest to take, and it normally takes a while to fully accept this new way of life. The front page of the newspaper fantasy will probably be with you for years to come. But acceptance is the key. Acceptance allows you to dump all the unnecessary baggage of pretending and blaming and resenting and wasting your energy looking for medical mistakes or miracle cures.

You know that diabetes is not your fault. It's simply one of those bad breaks. You've got it, and it's not going to go away. Now you can focus on learning more about this complicated disease so that you can control it well and lead a happy, rewarding life.

IN A SENTENCE:

> *Accepting that you have diabetes is the first step towards controlling it.*

learning

Measuring Your Blood Glucose Levels

THE BEST thing you can do is to get a blood glucose meter. Right away. Now. There are many different kinds of meters and subtle differences among them that I'll discuss later. But for now it doesn't really matter what kind of meter you get. What matters is that you get a meter and that you *use it*.

A *simple meter may be best to start*

Strips are available free on a National Health Service (NHS) prescription but you will have to buy a meter. Adequate ones will cost less than £25 and they are available in all good chemists. Alternatively the practice or hospital diabetes nurse will advise you.

Some meters offer fancy extras. If you're a gadget freak, you'll want to check these out right away. If you're visually impaired, look for a meter with a large display. There are also talking meters as well as little gizmos that help you aim the drop of blood onto the strip when you can't see it very well.

Otherwise, a simple meter is just as good, especially to start with. The important thing at this point is not the bells and whistles in the meter. The important thing is to get a meter, learn how to test and do it every day.

Every meter operates slightly differently, so of course you'll need to read the instruction manual for your own particular meter before you actually do a test. Or your doctor, nurse or diabetes educator may show you how to use it.

Pricking your fingers is a minor annoyance

Some aspects of testing are pretty much the same no matter which meter you have. Testing your blood glucose (which from now on I'll call **BG**) requires you first to obtain some blood. This means that you must puncture your skin. Ouch. Yes, it does hurt a little. And yes it does take a few days before you stop worrying about the pain. I remember the first time I tested my blood. I knew that all I had to do was press this little button on my finger-pricker and it would do all the work for me. I did a few dry runs pricking imaginary fingers in the air. Then I put the pricker on my finger and . . . and . . . finally I closed my eyes and clicked, and ouch, a little hurt and then it was done.

It doesn't take long to realize that pricking your fingers is one of the minor annoyances of having diabetes. When you're starting out, it's the anticipation that hurts the most. And certain types of finger-prickers hurt more than others. The best kinds are the ones you can adjust for different depths. At the lowest setting, you hardly feel a thing.

Blood is usually easy to get

But wait. Let's go back a minute. Before you prick your finger, wash your hands in warm water. This not only reduces the number of germs on your fingers, but it ensures that you don't have any traces of sugar on your fingers that might interfere with the test, and it's also easier to get blood from warm hands. Then dry your hands thoroughly. Extra moisture on the skin could dilute the blood and give a wrong result. Don't use an **alcohol** wipe. If you don't get it all off, the alcohol might interact with the test materials and cause false results.

After you've pricked your finger, wait a second or two, and then gently squeeze out a little blood and let it drop onto the test strip. Your meter will start working, and in less than a minute you will know what your BG level is.

The best place to prick your fingers is on the side of the tips, close to the nail (but not too close, or the blood will run all over the nail and won't drop onto the strip). The fingers are less sensitive there.

Many people rotate their fingers, using a different finger every day, so each finger has several days to heal before being used again. This is a sensible method, but I find that my ring finger and little finger are the easiest to get blood from, and I tend to use them day after day.

The instructions to your meter will tell you to make sure to use a fresh **lancet** every time you test, but many people use the same lancet for days, weeks or even months without changing. It seems that people usually build up immunity to the germs on their own skin, and infections from used lancets are rare although they can occur. For the same reason, it's not absolutely essential to wash your hands before lancing your fingers to test, but if you're near a bathroom, it certainly doesn't hurt and reduces the chances of contaminating the blood sample with something on your fingers that might affect the test. Of course, to avoid getting infected with hepatitis, AIDS or other viruses, you should *never* use a lancet that has been used by anyone else.

Use a few tricks when the blood won't flow

Sometimes blood is easier to get than other times. Anything that increases your circulation, such as exercise or a hot bath, makes the blood run out more easily. That's a good time to use your 'bad' fingers – the ones that don't bleed as well. Sometimes you may have difficulty squeezing a drop of blood out, especially if your hands are cold. If this happens, try warming your hands in hot water. If that's not enough, try swinging your arms to push the blood into the fingertips. Then, after you've pricked a finger, hold your hand well below your heart, the lower the better, and relax your hand for a few seconds before you try to squeeze some blood out. Don't worry. You'll get the hang of it pretty quickly.

Although 'milking' the finger by grasping it at the base and squeezing towards the tip can help, it's best to avoid getting blood this way if you don't have to, as it can force nonblood fluids (called **interstitial fluid**) into the drop, and this sometimes affects the results. If all else fails, try putting a rubber band on your finger like a tourniquet to build up pressure at the tip. Needless to say, you'll want to take it off as soon as possible.

Test as often as you can

Once you've learned how to measure your BG level, you'll want to do it (OK, you *should* do it) frequently. This is especially important early on, when you're learning how your body reacts to various things like the foods you eat and the exercise you get. We're all different, and we all live under different circumstances. No book and no doctor and no diabetes nurse can tell you exactly how your particular body is going to react to your particular diabetes treatment plan. Only by testing as often as you can will you be able to learn about your own particular physiology.

If your BG strips are provided by your general practitioner (GP) on an NHS prescription, there may be a limit of, say, 50 per month. If you feel the need for more, discuss it with your GP who is likely to be sympathetic if you put forward a good case.

The best times to test depend on your situation

When should you test? Most people like to do it as soon as they get up in the morning. This is called a **fasting** test, and it sometimes gives a very approximate indication of how good your control was on the previous day. Other common times to test are one and two hours after a meal, which tells you how high your BG level goes when you eat particular foods; before the next meal, which tells you whether the BG rise that usually follows a meal has come down to the starting point before the next meal; before and after exercise; at bedtime and any time you feel that something is wrong.

This sounds as if you have to test yourself almost ten times a day. You might learn a lot by testing this often but it would be unreasonable to keep it up for long. **Continuous monitors** that test BG levels every few minutes have been developed and are becoming available. The first ones are too expensive for general use, but the prices will undoubtedly come down.

When the number of strips is limited, you can rotate the testing times to get additional information. For instance, on Monday, test first thing before eating and before lunch. On Tuesday, test first thing before eating and after supper. On Wednesday, test before and after exercise. If your diet and exercise patterns are pretty regular, eventually you'll get a sense of how various factors affect your BG levels.

Here's some good news. After a year or so of this intensive testing, you'll get a very good sense of how your body reacts to various influences, and unless you are taking insulin, you won't have to test as often. I often don't test at all for days, and then I do a detailed test of some new food or exercise pattern.

Advanced meters are being developed

New meters seem to be coming out almost every month. More and more allow you to get blood from less sensitive parts of your body (such as the arms) as well as the fingers.

Because most people don't really enjoy punching holes in their fingers and the market is huge, companies are working fast and furiously to develop *noninvasive meters* that will allow BG testing without drawing blood. One approach is to measure the BG level in interstitial fluid. This method uses patches to absorb the fluid, and then either you read the patch with a meter or a watchlike device gives readings for many hours. Other creative ideas include using a sensor implanted in a contact lens.

Some meters on the market today test **ketones** (see Day 5) as well as BG levels. One tests for **lipids** (see the box in Month 6), ketones and glucose, with more tests planned for the future.

But don't wait for all the new gadgets. The important time to do a lot of testing is *now*, as soon as you can. The sooner you get into the habit of knowing what your BG level is, the sooner you will begin to learn how to control this major inconvenience called diabetes.

IN A SENTENCE:

Testing your blood glucose levels regularly is the best way to learn how to control your diabetes.

CONVERTING GLUCOSE VALUES
BETWEEN MMOL/L AND MG/DL

To convert units exactly, divide mg/dL by 18.016, or multiply mmol/L by 18.016. To approximate, simply use 18 as the conversion. The following table has done some of these conversions, rounded off (see page 60).

MMOL/L	MG/DL	MMOL/L	MG/DL
1.7	30	2	36
2.8	50	3	54
3.9	70	4	72
4.4	80	5	90
5.0	90	6	108
5.6	100	7	126
6.7	120	8	144
7.0	126	9	162
7.2	130	10	180

7.8	140	198	11
8.3	150	216	12
8.9	160	234	13
9.4	170	252	14
10.0	180	270	15
10.6	190	288	16
11.1	200	324	18
13.9	250	360	20
16.7	300	396	22
22.2	400	450	25
27.8	500	540	30
33.3	600	631	35

DAY **3**

How Do I Tell My Friends and Colleagues?

SEVERAL DAYS after your diagnosis, you probably still haven't accepted this new way of life emotionally. Accepting a chronic disease is a lot like accepting the death of a good friend. It takes a lot of time. In this case, the good friend is someone you've known all your life: your former nondiabetic self. Before you can fully accept your new condition, you need to take some time to mourn your loss.

But as you go through the slow process of acceptance, you need to deal with the other people in your life. Your closest friends and relatives have probably already heard about your diagnosis. But what about your casual friends? Should you tell them? If so, how? Should you tell your colleagues at work? Will it affect your job security if you do?

Some people tell everyone

Of course we're all different and have different life situations. Some people are very up-front about their condition. I try to tell everyone. Well, maybe not everyone. I don't walk down the street taking total strangers by the collar and informing them that I have type 2 diabetes. But if it's relevant – for example, if someone invites me to dinner and I want to make sure they know in advance that I won't be able to eat certain foods because of my condition, not because I hate their cooking – then I tell them. This comes in very handy if I do, in fact, hate their cooking.

As a freelance writer and editor, I told my primary client because I wanted the client to understand that I could no longer spend 50 or 60 hours a week at a computer terminal; I needed some time to exercise every day. My disclosure had little effect on our working relationship. Not everyone has the freedom to be so forthright in a business situation.

Some don't want to tell

Some people find it difficult to communicate their condition with the rest of the world. Katherine G., who was diagnosed on the basis of a random blood test when she was feeling perfectly fine, said, 'When I was diagnosed I went through all the stages of emotions. First I was sure there had been a mistake with the blood test. Then I tried to keep anyone from finding out and asked Frank not to mention it to any of the children. I had guilt feelings. What had I done wrong? I got angry and wanted to smack every over-weight person I saw. I refused to attend meetings where all those diabetics talked about their problems, since I didn't belong with that group. I didn't want anyone seeing me go into the Diabetic Centre. I wouldn't use the local library to get books about diabetes, so I went to the library in another town. I worried that I'd passed on the genes to my children and grandchildren. I had nightmares about being blind, in a wheelchair because I had no feet, and being wheeled in to use a dialysis machine.'

It may be especially difficult to accept a diagnosis of a chronic disease if you've always been the strong one in the family, the one who coped when things got rough, the healthy one who took care of other people when they got sick. Now all of a sudden someone tells you that you're the 'sick' one, even if you're feeling perfectly OK. If you tell the rest of the family what's going on, will you lose your long-standing role in the family? Is your life going to totally change?

Many men are raised to think that men should always be strong and soldier on no matter how much they hurt. You may see illness as a type of unmanly weakness and want to deal with it by pretending it doesn't exist. If so, you naturally wouldn't find it easy to broadcast your new vulnerability to the world.

Whether to tell your employer depends on the circumstances

Deciding whether to tell people at work that you have a chronic disease is even more difficult than telling family and friends. If you are taking diabetes drugs or insulin that might make your blood glucose (BG) levels go too low (see Week 3), it would be wise to let someone at work know this, so they would understand if you suddenly started acting differently or needed to interrupt work in order to have a snack. If you operate dangerous machinery and are taking medication that could make your BG levels go so low that you could pass out and hurt other people, then of course you have a moral obligation to inform your employer. And if asked outright if you are diabetic, it's not wise to lie.

If there's no reason your employer needs to know about your diabetes, you may feel a 'don't ask, don't tell' approach makes sense. You may worry that letting your employer know that you have an expensive chronic disease will jeopardize your career. The employer may worry that you will take a lot of sick days. Or your employer may think everyone with diabetes spends a lot of time away from their work giving themselves injections.

It's illegal to discriminate against people with diseases like diabetes. But we all know that unscrupulous employers can get around the laws by inventing excuses to lay you off or to make your life so unpleasant that you decide to resign. If you're the only breadwinner in the family, deciding whether or not to tell your employer about your diabetes is not an easy decision.

The 'diabetes police' can be annoying

Although the consequences of telling your friends might not be as serious, they can also cause problems. For example, people who know about your diabetes may assume the role of 'diabetes police'. Most people think that people with diabetes can't eat any sugar, but that other foods, including bread and potatoes, are fine. So they'll watch you like a hawk. After watching you slug down a plate of potato salad sandwiches on buttered white bread without comment, if you reach for a tiny cookie, they'll say, 'Are you allowed to eat that?' as if you weren't able to take care of yourself.

Sometimes the diabetes police take an even more active role. A friend told me about Loretta, who had type 1 diabetes and 'had an insulin reaction, stopped at the corner shop, grabbed a chocolate bar and began munching it down, muttering to the shop assistant that she was diabetic and was having a reaction. The shop assistant leaped on her and grabbed the chocolate bar, screaming, "Diabetics aren't supposed to have sugar!"'

People deal with the diabetes police in different ways. Some simply ignore them. Some explain. My favourite is the woman who turns to the person interfering and says, 'That's odd. You don't *look* like my mother.'

If you don't tell your friends and co-workers that you're diabetic, you won't need to worry about the diabetes police. But then when sugary treats are served at office breaks and social gatherings, you'll have to either risk your health by eating things that aren't good for you or risk hurting your friends' feelings by turning down their delicious offerings.

If you're overweight, you can always say you're on a diet – which of course you are – and simply refuse to give in when everyone says, 'Oh come on, one bite won't hurt you.' They may all hate you for your strong willpower, but at least you won't let the food hurt you. If you're thin, that excuse won't help.

As someone once said, 'I always tell the truth, because that way I don't need to remember what I said.' It's always easier to be truthful. But if you're worried about keeping your job, it may not always be possible to take the easy route.

There is no one right way to decide when to tell your friends and colleagues that you have diabetes. Like the disease itself, this decision is complex and different for each of us. You have to take charge and make the decision that is best for you.

IN A SENTENCE:

> *How to tell friends and colleagues about your diabetes is as individual as you are.*

learning

How Does Food Affect My Blood Sugar?

WHEN MOST people think of diabetes, they think of **sugar**. People with diabetes can't eat sugar; anything else is OK. I'm not surprised by this narrow view of diabetes, because it's what I thought before I was diagnosed.

The sad truth is that almost every type of food you put in your mouth will affect your blood glucose (BG) levels one way or another, and it's important to understand how.

There are three types of food

There are basically three major classes of food: fat, protein and carbohydrate. You probably know quite well what **fat** is. It's that greasy stuff that tastes so good and seems to leap directly from the plate onto your thighs or stomach. To be more specific, fat includes solid fats like butter, margarine and vegetable shortening; oils like olive oil; and hybrids like soft margarine.

Fat is composed of long, water-insoluble molecules called **fatty acids** attached to a small molecule called **glycerol** (known as *glycerin* in pharmaceutical preparations). The glycerol is shaped like the letter *E*, and when three fatty acids are attached to the glycerol (one on each arm of the *E*), the resulting fat is called a **triglyceride** (sometimes called *triacylglycerol*; it means the same thing). This is one of the blood lipids that is usually measured when you have your blood fat level measured. Fat contains 9 calories per gram (cal/g).

Protein foods are meat and fish, eggs and cheese. Most meats and cheeses also contain a lot of fat, so if you want to limit your fat intake, you'll have to limit your intake of fatty meats and most cheeses as well.

Proteins are composed of long chains of **amino acids** strung together like Christmas tree lights and then moulded into three-dimensional shapes. Proteins are made up of many different kinds of amino acids. Protein contains 4 cal/g.

Carbohydrate foods include both starchy foods, such as bread, rice, beans and potatoes, as well as sugars (see the box Understanding Sugars, Other Sweeteners and Bulking Agents), such as **sucrose** (table sugar), **lactose** (milk sugar) and **fructose** (a sugar found in honey and fruits).

The starchy foods contain **polysaccharides**, which are composed of long chains of sugars; when you digest polysaccharides, they are broken down into the sugars they contain. Some people call polysaccharides *complex carbohydrates*, but this term can be misleading (see Month 10). Sometimes the chains form a lot of branches, and the degree of branching can affect how quickly they are digested. Sugars, like amino acids, come in many types, and the types of sugars in the carbohydrates can also affect how quickly they will raise your BG levels. Carbohydrate contains 4 cal/g.

Fibre is the portion of carbohydrate that humans are unable to digest. Much of the fibre is *cellulose*, a main component of plant cell walls. Ruminants such as cows and sheep can eat grass, and bacteria in their rumen – one of their four stomachs – digest the cellulose for them. Having only one stomach, we are unable to digest cellulose, and much of the fibre passes right through us.

Some of the fibre in humans can be digested by bacteria in the *colon* that convert the fibre to fatty acids and gas, a phenomenon often observed when a person eats a lot of beans. Fibre contains very few calories; the number depends on how much of the fibre the colonic bacteria are able to digest.

Most foods are mixed

Many foods contain a combination of food types. For instance, beans, rice and grains contain a lot of carbohydrate, but they contain protein as well. Eggs, nuts and tofu have a lot of high-quality protein, but they also contain fat. Even lean meats may contain several grams of fat per serving.

Cream contains a lot of fat but has some protein and carbohydrate as well. Fruits and vegetables are mostly carbohydrate, but vegetables also contain some protein and fat and even fruits contain trace amounts.

Today, knowing the exact composition of the food you eat is pretty simple. Food labels tell you how much of each type of constituent is in most of the food you buy. Nutritional tables are available in books or, if you have Internet access, on numerous sites on the Internet (*see* For Further Reading).

If you do have a computer, there are numerous nutritional software packages that will not only determine how much of each constituent is in the various foods you use, but also keep track of the total amounts you've had each day and alert you if you've had too much or too little of a nutrient that is important to your diet.

Carbohydrate has the greatest effect

The food that has the greatest effect on BG levels is carbohydrate. This is true whether you have diabetes or not. The BG levels of people without diabetes also rise after they eat a carbohydrate-containing meal. The difference is that their BG levels only go up a little, maybe 1.5 **mmol/L** (millimols per litre – the units with which BG levels are expressed) after a meal containing a lot of carbohydrate. Then their pancreas secretes just the right amount of insulin, and their BG levels come down quickly.

The BG levels of people with diabetes increase a lot more than that. Some people might see their BG levels increase 5.6 or even 11 or more mmol/L after eating a lot of carbohydrate. The pancreas tries to put out enough insulin, but it can't. Or it secretes a lot of insulin, but because of insulin resistance (IR), the **effective insulin** (meaning the amount that can actually have an effect despite the IR) is insufficient.

Without enough effective insulin, your BG levels not only go up higher but take longer to come down. It is this long-term increased BG level that causes diabetic complications, and that is what you want to control with your diabetes treatment.

Fibre is important too

Fibre has a large effect on how fast the carbohydrate raises your BG levels. There are two types of fibre, soluble and insoluble. The **insoluble fibre** is a lot like sawdust. It doesn't dissolve in water and pretty much just goes right through you, absorbing water and adding a lot of bulk. Insoluble fibre, although it has a healthy effect on elimination, is thought not to make much difference to how quickly your BG level goes up after a carbohydrate meal.

The **soluble fibre** forms a gummy solution that slows down the speed of digestion of carbohydrate. It has a big effect on how quickly a carbohydrate meal will raise your BG levels. It is also thought to decrease **cholesterol** levels (see the box in Month 6). Soluble fibre eaten at one meal can even decrease the rate at which your BG level increases at a later meal. Soluble fibre is a very good food for people with type 2 diabetes, and many of the traditional remedies for the disease, such as fenugreek, guar gum, prickly pear (nopal), barley and aloe, are very high in soluble fibre. Soluble fibre is also found in oat bran, flaxseed and many fruits.

Fibre is considered a carbohydrate, but unlike other carbohydrates, it isn't broken down into sugars in the human small intestine. Thus when you want to know how much **effective**

carbohydrate – the amount that your body will convert to sugar – a food contains, you should check the label. A hypothetical ice cream flavour called Garlic Ripple with Sawdust Chunks might contain 34 grams of total carbohydrate and 14 grams of fibre.

In the UK, Europe and Australia the fibre has already been subtracted on food labels. The label for Garlic Ripple with Sawdust Chunks would list 20 grams of carbohydrate and 14 grams of fibre. However, the rules for food labelling are different in North America, Africa and Asia, where you will need to subtract the fibre from the total amount of carbohydrate to get the amount of carbohydrate that will make your BG level go up. It is important to remember this when you are reading food labels on imported food.

Protein and fat have smaller effects

Protein also affects your BG levels. This is because some of the protein we eat, usually estimated at 40 to 60 per cent, is converted to glucose in the liver. This conversion takes time, so a pure protein meal will not only cause a lower increase in your BG levels, but the increase will be much longer after eating, usually four to six hours. Some people with type 2 diabetes still produce enough insulin to cover slowly released sugars. If so, you might not see any increase in your BG levels at all after a small protein meal.

Fats eaten by themselves won't cause an increase in your BG levels. But who wants to eat a meal consisting of chunks of butter swimming in olive oil with cocoa butter for dessert? Eaten with other foods, however, fats have an effect on your BG level.

First, fats decrease the rate at which the stomach empties. This means that if you eat carbohydrate, which might make the BG level peak in 60 minutes if you ate it alone (see Figure 5) but add some fat, the BG level might peak at 90 minutes instead.

Some people find that eating a little fat with carbohydrate not only delays the peak but makes it lower. Their BG level never goes as high when they add the fat. Other people say that just a little bit of fat makes their BG levels go much higher, perhaps by increasing IR. Sometimes this effect can still be seen with a higher fasting level the next day. Because different people react differently to fat, the best way to find out how fat affects your BG levels is (alas) to prick your fingers a few extra times after you've eaten fatty meals to see if the fat makes your BG go up or go down.

Alcohol reduces blood glucose levels – sometimes too much

Alcohol is neither a fat, a protein, nor a carbohydrate, but it does contain 7 cal/g. If you're following an **exchange diet** (see Day 4), alcohol is usually counted as a fat.

People used to say that anyone with diabetes should never drink alcohol. This is because alcohol can lower BG levels, and if you are taking insulin or **sulphonylureas** (see Week 3) that can make your BG levels go too low, the alcohol can increase the effect and paralyze the mechanisms that normally bring the BG levels back to normal.

However, if you are not taking these drugs, small amounts of alcohol such as a small glass of red wine with a meal may help moderate the BG-raising effects of the meal as well as possibly having heart-protecting actions. Note that the important word here is *small*. Excessive drinking is not a good idea when you have diabetes of any kind.

Knowledge is power

In Month 9, I discuss in more detail how you can get actual numerical values for your after-dinner BG tests. You probably don't want to get that fancy right away. For now, you should just know that all these foods interact and will affect your BG levels after a meal, and as usual, the best way to find out how your favourite foods affect your own BG levels is to test, test and test again.

All this finger-pricking and testing of foods may sound depressing. Granted, it's inconvenient, and it does hurt a little bit. But the rewards are immense. Knowing from the beginning just how you react to the various foods you eat is the best way you can keep your BG levels as close to normal as possible and avoid any of the complications that occur in people whose BG levels are uncontrolled.

Trust me. Your BG levels matter. Take charge, test and learn. Knowledge is the best weapon you have against diabetes.

Understanding Sugars, Other Sweeteners and Bulking Agents

HERE is a list of most of the sweeteners you will encounter. Refer to this list whenever you see an unfamiliar name on a list of ingredients and wonder what it is.

○ **Sugars.** The names of sugars end in -*ose*, but not everything ending in -*ose* is a sugar (for example, cellulose, which is insoluble fibre). They include single sugar units called **monosaccharides**. The most common of these are *glucose, fructose* and **galactose.** They also include sugars made of two sugar units, or **disaccharides**. These include *sucrose*, or common table sugar (made of glucose and fructose); *lactose*, milk sugar (made of glucose and galactose) and *maltose* (made of two glucose units).

Most sugars contain 4 cal/g, the same as **starch**. They are carbohydrates, and the calories should be counted in your diet plan.

Fructose, a natural sugar found in fruits and vegetables, is **metabolized** (broken down) slightly differently from glucose and doesn't raise BG levels as quickly. However, it has the same number of calories, and it tends to increase triglyceride levels more, especially if eaten in excess.

Sucrose, also a natural sugar found in fruits and vegetables, contains half glucose and half fructose. Hence table sugar won't actually raise your BG levels quite as fast as 100 per cent glucose.

Carob powder, a chocolate substitute, contains 75 per cent sucrose, glucose and fructose.

○ **Other names.** Often the word *sugar* is not mentioned in a list of ingredients, but sugar-containing syrups are. These include *honey, corn syrup, high-fructose corn syrup, rice syrup, molasses, treacle, sorghum, turbinado, starch syrup, malt extract* and *maple syrup.* You can assume these will affect your BG levels the same as sugars. Processed starches such as *corn-starch, potato starch, wheat starch* and *tapioca starch* will also raise your BG levels at least as fast as sugar.

○ **Fructooligosaccharides.** The fructooligosaccharides are short chains of fructose found in onions and asparagus. They are not broken down in the small intestine, so they are eaten by bacteria in the colon, where they are supposed to stimulate the growth of favourable bacteria.

Longer chains of fructose are called *inulin*, which is found in Jerusalem artichokes. Inulin has often been recommended as a good food for people with diabetes because like the fructooligosaccharides, it isn't broken down in the intestines and doesn't raise BG levels. Many people confuse the words *inulin* and *insulin* and will tell you to eat Jerusalem artichokes because they're full of insulin. Even if they were, insulin would be destroyed in the stomach.

○ **Dextrose. Dextrose** is just another word for glucose. So too, *levulose* is an older term for fructose. (These terms come from the fact that solutions of these sugars rotate polarized light in a particular direction. When you break down sucrose into a 50:50 mixture of glucose and fructose, the mixture is sometimes called *invert sugar*, because the direction that a solution rotates polarized light is inverted in the process.) Another name for glucose is *grape sugar*, because grapes contain a lot of glucose.

○ **Bulking agents.** Many artificial powdered sweeteners are so intensely sweet that you only need tiny amounts, and it would be difficult to pour such small amounts. Hence the manufacturers add *bulking agents.* One such agent is glucose (usually listed as *dextrose*). You may think it odd that sugar substitutes contain glucose, but the amounts are relatively small, usually less than 1 gram. If your diet includes a lot of carbohydrate, this amount is negligible. However, if you're on a **low-carbohydrate diet**, it may be significant, and you should use liquid or tablet sweeteners instead. Some tablets also contain bulking agents, so check the labels.

Another common bulking agent is *maltodextrin*. This is simply starch (a polysaccharide made of glucose) that has been partly broken down into smaller units, but not completely broken down into glucose. However, it will raise your BG levels about the same as glucose or starch. It does not taste sweet. *Polydextrose* (see later) is also a common bulking agent.

The 'measure-for-measure' sweeteners that let you substitute one teaspoon of the sweetener for a teaspoon of sugar usually have the most bulking agents.

○ **Sugar alcohols.** When you treat sugars with hydrogen, you can reduce their aldehyde or ketone groups to alcohol groups. If you don't remember from chemistry courses what this means, don't worry about it. It's not important. What is important is that when you do this, the resulting **sugar alcohols** are *metabolized* (broken down and converted to energy) slightly differently from the sugars, so they don't raise your BG levels quite as fast and have fewer calories. They are not intoxicating, like ethyl alcohol, the formal name for booze.

The names of many sugar alcohols end with *–itol*. Common ones are **sorbitol** (or *glucitol)*, *xylitol, mannitol* and *lactitol*, made from *glucose, xylose, mannose* and *lactose*, respectively.

The number of calories and the amount the sugar alcohols raise your BG levels vary with the different ones. Most of them are considered to have from 2 to 3 cal/g, but some of them (for example, sorbitol) have as many calories as sugars (4 cal/g).

Some sugar alcohols have names that don't tip you off to what they are. These include isomalt, polydextrose and HSH, all carbohydrates that have been treated to produce some sugar alcohols.

Isomalt is a combination of glucose-sorbitol and glucose-mannitol. It is used as a sweetener and bulking agent and works synergistically, meaning the two agents acting together have a greater effect than the sum of their effects when used alone, with aspartame and acesulfame K (see later). It has about 2 cal/g.

Polydextrose is made by reacting glucose and sorbitol in the presence of citric acid. It contains a complex mixture of glucose units connected by bonds that aren't broken down easily by human digestive **enzymes**, so it has fewer calories (1 cal/g) than other carbohydrates. It is not sweet and is used as a bulking agent.

Hydrogenated starch hydrolysate, or *HSH*, is another carbohydrate alcohol. It's made by partially breaking down starch and then adding hydrogen to make various monosaccharides, disaccharides and polysaccharides containing sugar alcohols. The different ones have different degrees of sweetness. HSH has about 3 cal/g.

When carbohydrates aren't broken down in the small intestine, they keep moving through your digestive tract, and as they do, they draw in water. For this reason they can act as laxatives if you eat a lot of them. Bacteria in the colon can break down some carbohydrates that human digestive enzymes can't, and the result is gas. Most of the sugar alcohols result in gas and diarrhoea if you eat too much of them. Some sugar alcohols occur naturally in fruits, especially plums – which is why prunes are a traditional laxative.

○ **Other sugar substitutes.** Sweeteners available in shops include the following. They are used in such tiny amounts that the calories are negligible. All intense sweeteners are food additives and are required by law to undergo safety testing before being approved for use. The government then sets Acceptable Daily Intakes (ADIs), which are the maximum amount of each type of sweetener considered to be safe for daily use. Diabetes UK recommends using a wide variety of products containing different kinds of sweeteners to reduce the risk of exceeding ADIs.

Acesulfame K is not metabolized and has no calories. It acts synergistically with *aspartame* and *cyclamate*, but not with *saccharin*. It is heat stable.

Aspartame is made from two amino acids linked together. It is primarily metabolized like other amino acids. Aspartame is synergistic with other sweeteners, especially acesulfame K, but it is not stable to heating and is not suitable for cooking. Some people do not tolerate aspartame well and say their BG levels go up when they use it. *Cyclamate* is available in the UK but not in the United States, where it was banned in 1969 after some studies suggested it might be carcinogenic. It's often combined with saccharin.

Saccharin is one of the oldest (used since 1879) artificial sweeteners used. Early studies showed that high levels caused bladder cancer in rodents, and some countries have restrictions on its use. However, people with diabetes who have used it for years don't seem to have more bladder cancer than other people, and more recent studies have suggested that the sweetener is not dangerous at the amounts usually eaten.

○ **Bitterness.** Many of the artificial sweeteners have a bitter aftertaste when you use too much of them. One way to minimize this problem is to use smaller amounts of several different sweeteners together.

IN A SENTENCE:

Foods contain protein, fat and carbohydrate, and the carbohydrate has the greatest effect on your BG levels.

living

Networking with Others

BY NOW you may have begun to accept the fact that you really do have diabetes, and it's time for you to connect with other people who are in the same boat.

If you have access to the Internet, one of the best things you can to is to join one of the many Internet mailing lists or read the newsgroups that are now available. If you do not have Internet access either at home or at your local library, you will probably benefit from joining a local diabetes support group.

Start with the Mendosa site

In Month 12, Internet diabetes expert Rick Mendosa will guide you through diabetes resources on the Internet. The best place to start is his site: *www.mendosa.com/diabetes.htm.* Rick understands the problems of type 2 diabetes; he has diabetes himself. When he was first diagnosed, he learned so much from the Internet that he wanted to share his knowledge with others and created at his own expense what many feel is the best diabetes home page available today.

I like Rick's web pages because he focuses on information instead of fancy graphics or animated advertisements, so the pages download quickly. He also provides short reviews of the sites he has links to, which helps you decide which ones to visit.

If you have not yet tried the Internet and are considering getting a computer, you might try browsing at the library first to see how it works. Then if you like what you find – and I think you will – you can buy a computer to use at home. If money is a problem, look into getting a secondhand computer. Technology progresses so fast in the computer field that today's computers are often considered old hat before the ink on the cheque is dry, and fast-lane people who need to be on the cutting edge of technology often sell perfectly good used computers at good prices.

The World Wide Web has vast resources

There are four major ways you can use the Internet to get information about diabetes. The first is through the World Wide Web. Once you have access to the web, you can use Rick Mendosa's home page to link to all kinds of diabetes information including a number of international diabetes organizations such as the **Diabetes UK** pages; the Joslin Diabetes Center in Boston – one of the best diabetes treatment and research centres in the world; alternative medicine treatments; vitamin sources; PubMed, the US National Library of Medicine's free database of summaries of professional journal articles; and teaching resources in endocrinology, biochemistry and general medicine.

As you browse the Internet, you should keep in mind that there's a lot of incorrect information along with the good – for example, snake oil salespeople may try to sell you mysterious wonder cures at high prices. But this is no different from information available in print or on television. You wouldn't accept a report of alien invaders in a newspaper tabloid or an infomercial on a new weight-loss cream that is supposed to melt your stomach flab and make you rich and healthy while you eat chocolate sundaes and hot dogs. So too, you must evaluate the source of anything you find on the Internet.

Newsgroups provide support

Another resource is the Internet *newsgroups*. Newsgroups are like bulletin boards. People post messages, and if you sign up for a particular newsgroup – such as misc.health.diabetes or alt.support.diabetes – you can then see the titles of all the messages people have recently posted to the board. If one of the messages sounds interesting, you can click on it to *download* – meaning transfer it from a computer out in cyberspace somewhere to your own machine – and read it. If you wish, you can reply to the message, and everyone else will be able to see the title of your reply and read it if they wish.

E-mail lists are more private

The third resource is the *e-mail list*. With an e-mail list, you subscribe to the list and all the messages that everyone writes are sent directly to you, as part of your daily e-mail download. If you reply to a message, your reply is sent to everyone on the list. The e-mail lists are often more private and less vitriolic than the newsgroups because administrators may screen the subscribers and remove spammers – people who send the Internet equivalent of junk mail – or people who don't follow the rules of the list. Some lists are *moderated*, meaning someone reads every message before it is posted to make sure the list rules are followed.

Some of the e-mail lists have *archives* that you can search for information that was posted before you joined. Other lists prefer not to keep archives, which means your comments will not be available for the whole world to read forevermore.

Living in a rural area far from large academic libraries, I find the

World Wide Web a tremendous aid in obtaining background information about diabetes, learning the official medical explanations for various phenomena and reading about new research almost as soon as it is published.

The e-mail lists I belong to provide information that is often even more valuable. You can ask questions, and other people who have lived with diabetes longer than you have often provide interesting answers. Even if you don't ask questions yourself, other people often ask about things you were wondering about, and you can benefit from the answers.

Often the discussion centres around the inconveniences – or worse – of living with diabetes, and there's nothing like learning how other people cope with common problems to give you ideas about how to deal with the same problems in your own life. Just reading descriptions of how different people react to various foods, medications or types of exercise gives you a sense of how variable people's responses can be. What works for me might not work for you. On the lists we call it **YMMV** (Your Mileage May Vary).

One benefit of the lists is the instant feedback you can get. Someone with a serious problem might get a response within minutes. And people care about each other. On one list, a woman who had been depressed once posted a note asking how much insulin you'd need to inject to commit suicide. In less than 30 minutes, another list member managed to find out where she lived and sent an ambulance to her house in case she had actually tried such a thing. It turned out the action saved her life.

Another advantage of lists is the ability to vent. Everyone gets down in the dumps every now and then, or maybe angry at the health care system, or at the family who doesn't understand or whatever. Being able to vent your feelings and finding out that other people often feel the same way can be very therapeutic.

A fascinating aspect of these lists is their international membership. One list I'm on has had active members not only from the UK but also from the US, Canada, Romania, India, Australia, Scandinavia, Central America, Brazil, Belgium, Israel, and South Africa. One learns not only about diabetes but also about different approaches and recipes from different places in the world.

Chat rooms offer instant feedback

A fourth form of personal communication on the Internet is the *chat rooms*. In this case, you are communicating with people in 'real time', meaning that as you type, your message is posted for everyone to read. It also means you don't see the messages that were posted when Fido insisted that you take him for a walk, and you have to spend a lot of time sitting in front of the screen waiting for someone else to type an answer. If several people are chatting at once, it can get confusing. I'm too impatient to use this form of communication, but many people enjoy it.

Support groups offer personal contact

Internet websites, newsgroups, e-mail lists and chat rooms are great conveniences when you don't have transportation to get to public meetings or are shy about going to them and just want to read what other people are saying about diabetes on the various lists (reading without posting is called *lurking*, but it's not considered rude). But you might sometimes enjoy the social aspects of support groups given by your local hospital or other health care centre. If your area doesn't have one, you might think about organizing one yourself.

Usually such groups have a public speaker such as a doctor, diabetologist, **dietician** or **diabetes specialist nurse (DSN)** to talk on some aspect of diabetes, and then members can get together to chat and eat diabetes-friendly snacks.

Such support groups offer most of the benefits of on-line lists except for the instant feedback. Members may become good friends and can communicate by telephone, but it's obviously more difficult to ask a question of more than one member at a time except at the meetings themselves.

Magazines can also help

If you just want to read about other people with diabetes, you can subscribe to a diabetes magazine (see Month 12). *Balance*, the magazine of Diabetes UK, includes a list of people seeking pen pals, if you'd like to keep in touch with others through the mail.

Networking speeds up learning

Whether you choose to network online or at a local support group, such networking will in most cases speed up your learning about this complex disease, give you advice about where to go for more information, offer recipe suggestions no matter what diet approach you are taking, keep you in touch with the latest advances in diabetes research and, perhaps best of all, give you new friends who really understand what you're going through as you adjust to this new way of life.

IN A SENTENCE:

> *Networking with other people who have diabetes is one of the best ways to come to terms with the disease.*

learning

What Is a Diabetic Diet?

No one likes to diet. It's especially difficult in a society that seems to be focused on food. We expect to eat Often, Abundantly and Fast, which in a sense makes us all OAFs. Many of us have been duped by advertisers to think that we need to nibble on sweets, crisps and fizzy drinks all day and then wolf down restaurant meals or gargantuan pizzas before we settle in for an evening in front of the TV.

Even 'from-scratch' organic health-food restaurants often serve portions that are too large, and social gatherings may focus more on the gourmet food that is served than on interesting conversation with the dinner companions.

In such a land of abundant food and a constant barrage of media messages urging us to eat even more, it's difficult for anyone to try to limit calories. When you have *thrifty genes* that are ever so efficient at turning every extra calorie on the plate into fat on the stomach – and often an unusually large appetite to boot – this is even more difficult. But unfortunately, that's what you've got to do. **Limiting the amount you eat is one of the most important things you can do to control your type 2 diabetes.**

Controlling what you eat helps control your diabetes

That's the bad news. But wait! There's more! The good news is that carefully controlling what you eat will help you slim down and have a lot more energy. Many people say that after they started controlling their blood glucose (BG) levels through diet, they felt better than they'd felt in years. Many also find that when they get their BG levels under control, their formerly mammoth appetites become human-sized again.

Controlling what you eat may also allow you to remain on very low dosages of diabetes drugs or very minimal amounts of insulin, or off drugs and insulin altogether, for many years. In addition, research has shown that limiting food intake may increase your lifespan. It's not easy to do, but making the effort today will probably give you more tomorrows.

Diabetic diets differ

When you were diagnosed, your doctor or a dietician may have handed you a copy of a 'diabetic diet'. (Some people try to avoid the loaded word *diet* and refer to *food plans* instead. I don't like euphemisms. Diabetes isn't a 'suboptimal blood glucose control condition', it's a disease. And as far as I'm concerned, a specific eating plan is a diet. Why try to sugarcoat it? We're not dummies.) Or perhaps you've been scheduled to meet with a dietician, who may show you some rubber food to give you an idea of portion sizes and then write out a diet that is appropriate for you. (Actually, the rubber food is a good idea. After looking carefully at a lot of worn rubber hamburgers and orange juice, I wasn't sure I ever wanted to eat again.)

When comparing notes with someone else who has diabetes, or

reading one of the many diabetes diet books on the market, you may discover that the diet you've been given is quite different from the diet someone else with diabetes is following. What's going on here?

The fact is, people have been arguing about the best diet for diabetes for centuries, and they still can't agree. That is, they can't agree on the best composition of the diabetic diet. Unfortunately, one thing most people agree on is that type 2 diabetes is greatly helped by limiting the number of calories in your food.

No one ever said this disease was going to be easy.

Almost all the diabetic diet 'experts' agree that lean meats and fish, green leafy vegetables and other low-calorie, high-fibre vegetables such as cucumbers, broccoli, cauliflower, peppers, asparagus and cabbage are good foods to eat.

Then the various diet proponents begin to, well, I'll call it 'disagree', although the mention of a suitable diabetic diet often brings forth heated debates.

High-carbohydrate-and-fibre diet follows the Food Pyramid

There are four basic approaches to the diabetic diet. The first approach is the very low fat **high-carbohydrate-and-fibre diet**, sometimes called the *HCF diet*. The high-carbohydrate-and-fibre diet limits fat and emphasizes carbohydrates that are the least processed and contain a lot of fibre (about 40 or 50 grams a day), for example, whole grains instead of white flour; brown rice, beans or lentils instead of white rice; and starchy vegetables like corn and potatoes, in addition to the green vegetables mentioned earlier.

The high-carbohydrate-and-fibre diet is in accordance with the currently recommended **Food Pyramid** of the US Department of Agriculture (USDA), which many dieticians also recommend. It contains about 20 per cent protein, 70 per cent carbohydrate, and 10 per cent fat.

Carbohydrates are broken down in the intestine to produce sugars, mostly glucose, and a lot of glucose is what people with diabetes can't handle. So it may seem odd to prescribe what is essentially a high-sugar diet to a person who can't deal with sugar. Why would anyone want to do that?

There are several reasons behind this diet. First, a high fat intake may increase insulin resistance (IR), and a high carbohydrate intake may reduce IR. So if IR is your main problem, this diet may help.

In addition, people with diabetes are at greatly increased risk of **cardiovascular** disease, and in the general population (including people without diabetes), a low fat intake has been associated statistically with a reduced risk of cardiovascular disease. The high-carbohydrate-and-fibre diet usually makes your BG go higher after meals, but some people feel this is less important than its beneficial effects. Of the popular diet books, *The McDougall Program* and the Dean Ornish (*Eat More, Weigh Less*) vegetarian diets, the Pritikin diet and the *Choose to Lose* diet would be in this category.

Low-glycaemic index diet focuses on blood glucose increases

The second approach is the **low-glycaemic index diet.** This diet is similar to the high-carbohydrate-and-fibre diet in that it recommends low-fat, high-carbohydrate foods, but it allows a little more fat and limits the carbohydrates even more than the other **high-carbohydrate diets**, emphasizing those carbohydrates that have what is called a low **glycaemic index**.

The glycaemic index is a measure of how quickly foods raise your BG level. You might be surprised at some of the results. For instance, potatoes (which used to be called 'complex carbohydrates' and were thought not to raise BG levels very fast) in fact have a higher glycaemic index than table sugar. Of the popular diet books, the *Glucose Revolution* diet, the *Sugar Busters!* diet, and the French Montignac diet (*Eat Yourself Slim*) are in this category. Each of these diets specifies a slightly different percentage of nutrients.

Exchange diet allows a little of everything

The third approach is what used to be called the **ADA** (American Diabetes Association) **diet**. In recent years, the ADA has modified its position somewhat and now agrees that one diet isn't best for every patient. So I'll refer to this as the **exchange diet** instead.

The exchange diet is designed for a person who doesn't want or is unable to undergo a total change of food choices. Almost any food is permitted on the exchange diet, as long as the portion sizes and the number of portions per day are controlled. Each food is assigned to a category such as a fat, protein, starch, milk, fruit or vegetable group, and you are assigned a certain number of the various exchanges for each meal. For example, on a 1500-calorie exchange diet, you might be allowed two starch exchanges for lunch (in addition to meat, milk, fruit, vegetable and fat exchanges). One starch exchange would consist of one slice of bread or ⅓ cup of rice or a small potato. Each starch exchange is *approximately* equal to 15 grams of carbohydrate.

Like the previous diets, this one is relatively low in fat and relatively high in carbohydrate. But any kinds of carbohydrate can be used, including white bread, breakfast cereals and orange juice – all foods with high glycaemic index values. Nevertheless, because the number of calories is controlled on the exchange diet, many people are able to control their BG levels while continuing to eat (in small portions) their favourite foods at home or in restaurants. Many 'diabetic cookbooks' and 'diabetic foods' take this approach and tally the number of exchanges found in each portion, which is a convenience for the person without a lot of time to devote to preparing special food.

ADA exchange diets used to contain about 55 to 60 per cent carbohydrate, 10 to 20 per cent protein, and less than 30 per cent fat, but that can now be individualized. Current recommendations are 10 to 20 per cent protein, with the rest of the calories distributed between carbohydrate and fat, emphasizing **monounsaturated fat** (see the box in Month 6) depending on your needs. The popular *Zone* diet is actually a type of exchange diet in which exchanges are called *blocks*, and there is less carbohydrate (40 per cent) and more protein (30 per cent) than in the ADA exchange diet.

Carbohydrate counting works well when you use insulin

A variation of the exchange diet is called **carbohydrate counting.** With this approach, you are allowed a certain number of grams of carbohydrate for each meal. As with the exchange diet, you are not limited in what type of carbohydrate you choose to eat. You use tables to calculate the amount of carbohydrate in each food, but you don't need to keep track of the amount of protein and fat. So instead of being assigned two starch exchanges, one fruit exchange and one milk exchange, you might be assigned 57 grams of carbohydrate for lunch, and you would calculate how much carbohydrate there was in each food you chose.

This method is more accurate than the exchange method when you're trying to match your insulin injections to the carbohydrates you eat, so it is especially suited to thin people who are using insulin to control their BG levels. But because carbohydrate counting doesn't keep track of the amount of protein and fat you eat, it probably won't help you lose weight and would not be the best way to start if you are overweight when you are diagnosed.

Low-carbohydrate diet allows more fat

The fourth approach is just the opposite of the USDA Food Pyramid. This is the **low-carbohydrate diet**, which severely limits the intake of any kind of carbohydrate, either starch or sugar, but allows larger portions of both protein and fat.

For many years, a high-fat, low-carbohydrate diet was the standard way to treat diabetes. It worked. People who followed this diet were able to keep their BG levels down, and before insulin was discovered, it kept many people with type 2 diabetes alive.

The problem was that people with both types of diabetes are at higher risk of heart disease than people without diabetes. And because studies had shown that high-fat, high-carbohydrate diets increased the risk of heart disease, it was assumed that high-fat, low-carbohydrate diets would have the same effect. Thus it was decided to give people with type 1 diabetes less fat and more carbohydrate, and also more insulin to handle the additional carbohydrate load. Later, the high-carbohydrate diet was recommended for people with type 2 diabetes as well – even for those who were trying to control with diet alone.

Now some people believe that the original low-carbohydrate diet may be best for people with diabetes after all. Dr Richard Bernstein, the author of the *Diabetes Solution*, who has type 1 diabetes himself, is the main proponent of the benefits of this diet for people with diabetes. The Atkins and *Protein Power* diets are also low-carbohydrate diets but are designed primarily for people who want to lose weight, not specifically for people with diabetes. Thus their emphasis is more on the total amount of carbohydrate in the diet rather than whether or not that particular carbohydrate would raise your BG level.

Critics of these diets claim that their high fat content will increase the risks of heart disease, but many people on these diets see their lipid profiles improve. Almost all see a reduction in their BG levels, especially after meals, and recent research has suggested that **postprandial** (after-eating) BG levels are more important than **preprandial** (before-eating) BG levels in determining overall BG control.

Some people do find that their cholesterol levels increase on high fat, low carbohydrate diets. For such people, several modifications of the low-carbohydrate diet exist. The Ezrin diet (*The Type II Diabetes Diet Book*) is a low-fat, low-carbohydrate diet designed for weight loss. Another modification of the low-carbohydrate diet, the Goldberg-O'Mara diet (*GO-Diet*), emphasizes monounsaturated fats and low-glycaemic-index high-fibre foods, thus combining the concept of the benefits of a high-fibre diet with the benefits of a low carbohydrate diet. Very low carbohydrate diets can cause constipation, sometimes severe, and fibre helps prevent this.

Find the best diet for you

I discuss more of the pros and cons of the various diet approaches in Months 10 and 11. For now, what you should understand is that dietary recommendations for people with type 2 diabetes are highly controversial. What you eventually need to do is to find the diet that works best for *you*.

To start, the best approach is to try the diet that your doctor or your dietician recommends. Follow it carefully for a few months and test your BG levels when you get up in the morning and after eating various meals.

Then, when you've had time to absorb more information about diets and when you've seen how your own BG levels respond to the diet you're on, take stock (see Month 7). If your BG and lipid levels are well controlled on this diet and you're content with the food choices that you have, stick with it. It's a good diet for you.

If not, you might try another approach. As I mentioned before, type 2 diabetes is an incredibly complex disease, and we all have different life situations, economic situations, taste preferences and weight-loss needs. What works best for someone else may not work best for you.

The important thing for now is to accept the hard fact that you're going to have to be on some kind of diet (OK, call it a 'meal plan' or a 'nutritional minimization attack strategy' or an 'OOO' [OAF-overcoming orientation] if you prefer) for a long time.

If you can find a diet plan that works for you and follow it rigorously – well, most of the time, none of us are perfect – you will have accomplished one of the most difficult things you can do to control your diabetes. Diet (alas) is the key to control.

IN A SENTENCE:

> There is no single 'diabetic diet', and you need to find what works for you.

Tips on Reading a Food Label

MOST food labels indicate the total calories and the amounts of the three basic food classes (*protein, fat* and *carbohydrate*) as well as the percentage of your daily needs that a serving size should provide. Here are a few tips to make your reading of food labels more accurate. If this is more complex than you want to deal with right now, come back to it later when you've had more experience calculating your daily nutritional needs.

○ Sometimes the classes are broken down into subclasses, for example, total fat may be broken down into **saturated fat, polyunsaturated fat** and **monounsaturated fat** (see the box in Month 6). Sometimes not all the subclasses are listed.

To estimate the amounts, first add the grams of the subclasses. If the total grams of the subclasses don't equal the grams of the class, then something isn't listed. For example, with foods like margarine or crackers that list various types of fat, if the label says you have 10 grams of fat, including 5 grams of saturated fat, 2 grams of polyunsaturated fat, and 1 gram of monounsaturated fat, then there are 2 grams of something else. This is probably **trans fat** (see the box in Month 6). Many labels list only total fat and saturated fat. You can assume the rest includes monounsaturated, polyunsaturated and trans fats but you can't tell how much of each.

○ Multiply the grams of total carbohydrate and total protein by 4, and then multiply the grams of total fat by 9. Add them together. If this doesn't equal the total number of calories, something is probably missing.

Note that the numbers listed on the labels are usually rounded off. So if the food contained 8.4 grams of carbohydrate and 2.4 grams of protein, these would be listed as 8 grams of carbohydrate and 2 grams of protein, which you would calculate as $10 \times 4 = 40$ calories. But in fact the calories would be $10.8 \times 4 = 43.2$ calories. So small differences may be the result of rounding.

If you get a lot more calories than are listed on the label, this might be because the manufacturers don't have to include calories from the insoluble fibre. They do have to include calories from the soluble fibre (4 cal/g). You have no way of knowing how much of each is included.

If you get a lot fewer calories than are listed on the label, this could mean that the food contains something not listed on the label. For example, some of the 'low-carb' bars now being marketed don't list carbohydrates such as glycerol and other sugar alcohols (see Day 3, page 31) that they claim don't raise your BG levels.

As an example, one such bar lists 2 grams of carbohydrate, 22 grams of protein and 8 grams of fat. This would represent (24 x 4) + (8 x 9) = 168 calories. But the label lists 230 calories. This means 62 calories are not accounted for and must represent unreported carbohydrate. At 4 cal/g, this would be an extra 15.5 grams of glycerol and other sugar alcohols, both of which can be converted to glucose, albeit slowly, in the '2 grams of carbohydrate' bar.

○ American manufacturers calculate the carbohydrate content by the 'difference' method. This means they determine how much protein and fat it contains and assume that everything else is carbohydrate. In most cases this is pretty accurate. Sometimes it isn't.

For example, yoghurt is usually considered to have about 11 grams of carbohydrate per cup. But the bacteria that turn milk into yoghurt do so by converting a lot of the milk sugar (lactose) into *lactic acid*. Using the difference method, the lactic acid is calculated as a carbohydrate, but it doesn't raise your BG levels. Thus according to the authors of the *GO-Diet*, you can subtract 8 grams of carbohydrate per cup from the amounts listed on the food labels.

○ Manufacturers don't have to report small amounts of ingredients: less than 5 calories or less than 0.5 gram of carbohydrate, protein or fat per serving can be reported as zero. As long as you eat only the amounts shown as serving sizes, this is not a big problem. But if you eat a lot more, it can be misleading.

For example, a carton of cream might say it contains zero grams of carbohydrate, because the serving size (1 tablespoon) contains only 0.41 gram. But if you ate a whole cup (16 table-spoons), it would contain 6.6 grams of carbohydrate, which could be significant for someone on a low-carbohydrate diet.

When you see zero grams of something on a label and you're going to be using large amounts, the best way to check is to look at the amounts in standard nutrition tables (see For Further Reading).

○ Pay special attention to the listed portion size. The label on Food A says it has 10 grams of carbohydrate, and the label on Food B says it has 20 grams of carbohydrate. But the portion size on Food B is a half cup and the portion size on Food A is a whole cup. So both foods actually contain the same amount of carbo-hydrate when you use the same portion size.

○ When looking at the *DV (daily value)* percentages, note that they are based on a 2000-calorie diet. If you need more or fewer calo-ries than that, your needs may differ.

It's Time
to Get Moving

NEXT TO controlling your food intake, taking exercise is probably the best thing you can do to control your diabetes. Unlike medications, exercise is 'all natural' and has no side effects.

Exercise really works

Exercise will usually make your blood glucose (BG) levels go down and will continue to help control them for hours after you stop. Exercise will also help to build up your muscles, and muscles are the tissues that use the most glucose and hence are most important in keeping your BG levels from going too high.

If you've always loved exercise, you're in luck. Keep it up. If not, here's another reason to start moving. Studies have shown that after you've lost weight, no matter how, the best way to keep that weight off is to continue a regular exercise program.

Many people with type 2 diabetes don't want to hear this information. Especially if you're overweight, your idea of the ultimate pleasure in life is probably not to strap ice picks on your shoes and climb up the side of Canary Wharf instead of taking the lift, no matter how much electricity it saved.

However, exercise really does work, and if there is any way you can get more of it, you'll ultimately be glad that you did. My idea of the perfect exercise has always been strolling through the aisles of a bookstore or pulling open the door to a refrigerator. But since my diagnosis, I find that when I exercise regularly, my muscles *want* to be used. One day, I was watching a film in which a bunch of peasants were throwing huge mounds of hay onto an even bigger hayrick. 'That looks like fun,' I thought. I was astounded at my reaction. My muscles used to complain that turning the pages of a book was too much hard work. Now they wanted to sling pitchforks of hay.

The trick to getting into the habit of taking exercise without passing out from fulminating boredom is to find some way of moving more that is fun for you.

It doesn't have to be vigorous

Exercise doesn't need to be vigorous to benefit you in some way. You don't need to think that you'll have to spend the next 25 years running the London Marathon while carrying weights or leaping over gates with one bound. Just walking can help.

You may be middle-aged or elderly, maybe with painful arthritis, severe obesity or previous strokes that have left you unable even to walk. You still may be able to get some exercise. If you can't stand up, maybe you can swing your arms. Painful joint diseases make exercise more difficult; in that case a **physiotherapist** may be able to help you find some movement that doesn't hurt but works some of your muscles.

The important thing at the beginning is just to do a little more exercise than you're accustomed to doing. Then gradually increase it until you're getting in about 30 minutes to an hour of moving every day.

If you prefer organized exercise routines with lots of company, there are myriad aerobics classes at gyms, community centres and adult education programs. If you prefer to move your, er, sumptuous body in private, there are a multitude of books and videotapes on exercise that will give you specific exercise movements that you can do alone or with one or two close friends. But exercise doesn't need to be regimented. You don't need to say, 'Now I'm going to exercise,' and then run through a dull set of specific movements. You can often sneak exercise into your daily routine. Instead of parking as close to the shopping centre as possible, park as far away as you can. Instead of taking the lift to the second floor, walk up instead. When that becomes too easy, walk up two floors. You're saving energy and slowing down global warming as well as helping your own health. Instead of using the shopping trolley to carry your packages to the car, see if you can carry them in your arms instead.

Walking is especially good exercise because it doesn't require any special equipment and it doesn't cause damage to the joints as hard running can. The trick here is to turn the daily walk into something that is fun, something that you look forward to.

I live in a small town with many scenic back roads, and I've set a goal of walking every single road in town. I note where I left off, and the next day I drive to the place I stopped and start from there. In this way, I've found fascinating places I never knew existed and I've also put in a lot of exercise time.

If you work in a city, you could eat a quick lunch and then take the rest of your lunch hour to explore neighbourhoods near where you work, if that's safe. Or you could park a mile or so from your office and walk the rest of the way. Or you could park somewhere on your way home and explore those neighbourhoods.

Make your exercise interesting

Walking with friends usually makes the activity more enjoyable. Anything you can do to make your exercise seem like an interesting social occasion instead of a dreaded exercise routine will increase the probability that you'll do it. And actually doing a little bit of exercise is much more therapeutic than sitting in an armchair planning on doing a lot of exercise tomorrow.

Another trick for making the exercise interesting is to listen to recorded books. I don't usually do this when I'm walking the back roads in town, because just exploring the woods is interesting enough. But I also lift weights, and this is, let's face it, dull. That's when I put on the recorded books. I don't allow myself to listen to the books except when I'm lifting the weights, which means I sometimes actually (no really, I mean it) look forward to the time when I can get out the weights.

There are obviously days when it's too cold or too hot or too rainy or whatever to enjoy walking outside. Some people then walk in a shopping centre. You can also obviously work out in a gym. Or you can get your own exercise equipment for use on such days.

Some people find exercise bicycles a good solution, but a lot of the bicycles end up being used as coat racks. A treadmill might be a better choice. With either of these machines, you can watch TV or listen to recorded books, or music if you prefer, or even read a book or magazine as you exercise.

Laura R., who listens to books as she walks on a treadmill, said one book she chose was so interesting that she ended up walking for three hours because 'I didn't want to put the book down.'

Aerobic and anaerobic exercise are both good

There are two main types of exercise that will help your diabetes. The first is **aerobic exercise**, which is running or walking fast, the kind that gets your heart rate up. This type of exercise is good for your cardiovascular system. And because diabetes is associated with cardiovascular problems, this is a good thing.

The other type of exercise is **anaerobic exercise**, lifting weights, which is the kind of exercise that makes your muscles stronger. Men will see an increase in the size of their muscles with this type of exercise. Women will find that their muscles are stronger and slightly larger but needn't worry that they'll end up looking like a bodybuilder. Our physiology is different, and without all that bothersome testosterone, we don't bulk up like the men do.

Anaerobic exercise is especially good when you have diabetes because muscle tissue uses the most glucose. So the more muscles you have, the easier it will be for you to lower your BG levels when they get high. A nice side effect is that anaerobic exercise will turn some of your fat into muscle, so you will feel and look thinner as well, even at the same weight.

Here's how Edd A. described his results with weight lifting: 'I was very determined to be thin, so I dieted a great many years. And it got me nowhere. A few times, I actually got thin. But it always came back. I'm probably fatter now from all the dieting than I would have been if I'd never wasted my time. I can't say I enjoyed being fat, but I'd become reconciled to it. I decided I would waddle through life as proudly as I could.

'Well, the weight lifting has put a new spin on all this for me. In the several months since I began, I've lost over 12 centimetres around the waist. I've lost about 13.5 kilograms. That amount of fat should weigh more than 13.5 kilograms, so the difference seems to be more muscles on my frame.

'Since I stopped dieting, I've lost my obsession with food. When I dieted, I thought about food all the time. Now I don't struggle with food 24 hours a day. I don't have to muster my willpower.'

Weight lifting increases blood pressure

One caution: lifting weights can cause an increase in your blood pressure. So if you have high blood pressure, glaucoma, **retinopathy** (see Month 10), kidney disease or other medical conditions that can be aggravated by such pressure increases, you should not try lifting weights without checking with your doctor first. Such caution is also warranted for anyone who hasn't been off the couch for years and suddenly embarks on an exercise program of any kind, but it's especially important for potential lifters of weights.

For women thinking of trying the weights, I recommend the book *Strong Women Stay Young* by Miriam Nelson. One nice thing about this book is that it's aimed at middle-aged women trying to get stronger, not young things trying to bulk up, so the exercises seem realistic, something we could all really do.

Nelson has done research showing that even people in their 90s can increase their muscle mass with the regular lifting of weights. She recommends working with the weights only 30 minutes two or three times a week, which isn't a lot of time.

Even this small investment of time brings results. One thing I like about weight lifting is that you're not supposed to do it two days in a row. The idea is that the exercise causes small tears in the muscle tissue, and you need a day or so for those tears to repair and for the new muscle to grow. It's so nice to have a good excuse not to exercise every day.

Another thing I like is that as you get stronger, you increase the weight of what you are lifting, but you don't need to increase the time. That's not true of many other kinds of exercise. Once you can do 10 situps, you're supposed to do 15. When you can do 15, you do 25. It's as if you're always being punished for your success by having to spend even more time doing the dull routine.

Find something that is fun

Whether you do weights or walking or waving your arms to catchy music or swimming or dancing or skiing or roller skating or climbing mountains or even leaping vaulting horses at a single bound, the most important thing is to find something that you enjoy doing, so you'll do it.

When you start out being more active, you may think you won't be able to stick with it for long. Maybe you've failed in the past. But the combination of getting your BG levels under control and moving a lot more makes most people feel better than they've felt in many years. Try it, one day at a time. You may get addicted.

IN A SENTENCE:

> *Moving more is one of the most important things you can do to control your diabetes.*

learning

Understanding
Lab Tests for Diabetes

UNDERSTANDING YOUR diabetes means learning how
to interpret the results of the many lab tests you will have. Some
of these tests are specialized, and you may not have them done
right away, or at all. So don't feel you need to learn, or even read,
everything in this section right away. Later, if you have a new test,
you can come back and read about it here.

Blood glucose levels are basic tests

Some of you were diagnosed with diabetes because your blood
glucose (BG) levels had become quite high and you were exhibit-
ing typical diabetic symptoms: constant thirst, frequent urination,
recurrent yeast infections and even weight loss.

Others may have had mildly elevated BG levels that were
ignored for years, either because doctors saw the small elevations
but had the old-fashioned notion that **borderline diabetes** wasn't
important or because you just never had standard lab tests and
didn't know your BG levels were high.

No matter which category you fit into, the measurement of your BG level was undoubtedly critical in the diagnosis of your disease. The BG test is a straightforward lab test to understand. It's what you can do yourself using your own BG meter. It tells you what concentration of glucose is in your blood at the time the blood was drawn.

For diagnosis, your BG level is sometimes measured after a 6- to 14-hour fast (meaning no food or beverages except water for 6 to 14 hours before the blood is drawn) to give a level called (not surprisingly) the *fasting level*. The current cutoff point for a diagnosis of diabetes is a fasting level of 7 millimols per litre (mmol/L, sometimes written mM) in the European, Australian and Canadian system of units or 126 **mg/dL** (milligrams per decilitre) in the current American system. Many people feel that this cutoff point, which was only recently lowered from 7.8 mmol/L, should be lowered even further so that people could be diagnosed sooner, when it is easier to control the disease and before they have had a chance to develop any debilitating side effects. (Note that for reasons I will describe later, the values that you get when you use your BG meter *may* be lower than the lab values.) Don't try to learn all these units right now. I mention them only for reference. If you come across the American units in your reading and wonder what they mean, you can come back here and check. To convert from the American to the European system, divide the mg/dL by 18; to convert from the European system to the American, multiply by 18 (see conversion chart on pages 18 and 19).

Another test is a *random BG test*, which is a BG measurement taken under nonfasting conditions. In this case a reading of at least 11 mmol/L is considered a good indication of diabetes. Some doctors would then recommend a fasting test to confirm the diagnosis.

Glycohaemoglobin and haemoglobin A1c measure long-term control

Another test you may take is called the **glycohaemoglobin** test, sometimes the more specialized **haemoglobin A1c**, usually referred to simply as the **A1c**. The glycohaemoglobin test is based on the amount of glucose that is attached to the **haemoglobin** in your blood.

Everyone has glucose in the blood. You need it to produce the energy that runs your body. With time, some of this glucose becomes attached to the haemoglobin (the red pigment in your **red blood cells** that carries oxygen from the lungs to the tissues). The amount of glucose that becomes attached to the haemoglobin depends on how much glucose you have in your blood, so people with diabetes who have elevated BG levels also have higher levels of **glycated** (glucose-containing) **haemoglobin**, or *glycohaemo-globin* for short. Just to make things more complicated for you, some people use the term *glycosylated haemoglobin* instead. It means essentially the same thing, and you'll see both terms used when you read about diabetes. Different sources define *glycation* and *glycosylation* in different ways that would be of interest primarily to biochemists. For our purposes, they're the same, and I'll use *glycated* because it's easier to spell.

Chemists can separate the glycohaemoglobin from the rest of the haemoglobin and express it as a percentage of the total. There are several different ways to measure glycated haemoglobin. In the past, results were often reported simply as *glycohaemoglobin*. Normal values for this test are about 6 to 7.5 per cent. Someone with poorly controlled diabetes might have a glycohaemoglobin level of 16 per cent or even more. As the diabetes is brought under control, the glycohaemoglobin level should come down towards normal.

Once glucose gets attached to a haemoglobin molecule, it essentially stays there for the lifetime of the red blood cell that contains the haemoglobin molecule. Most red blood cells live for about 120 days, and then they are broken down by the body and replaced by new cells with new haemoglobin molecules that have no glucose attached. So the glycohaemoglobin level gives an esti-mate of the *average* glucose level since about three months ago, especially in the past few weeks, as I'll discuss in Month 4.

The A1c test tells you the same thing as the glycohaemoglobin test, but it is even more specialized. Chemists can separate haemoglobin into various fractions called haemoglobin A (for adult), haemoglobin F (for foetal), haemoglobin S (for sickle cell), and so forth. In addition to the major adult fraction haemoglobin A, there are minor fractions called haemoglobin A1 and A2, and the A1 fraction can be further separated into A1a, A1b and A1c. It turns out that the A1c fraction is the one that contains most of the glucose and hence most accurately represents the average level of BG for the past month or so.

When labs report results simply as *glycohaemoglobin*, they are usually reporting the level of haemoglobin A1 (A1a +A1b + A1c). But the word *glycohaemoglobin* means 'haemoglobin with a sugar attached', so some people use it to refer to both the A1 and the A1c tests. If your results don't specify A1c, try to find out which test you had.

Today, most labs report their results as an A1c level. For the A1c, results are usually about 1 percentage point lower than the results of the A1 test, with a normal range usually about 4 to 6 per cent. (Results are often expressed without the per cent sign: 6 means 6 per cent.) So if you had a glycohaemoglobin result of 7.6 and then had an A1c result of 6.6, it would probably mean your control was about the same, just that you'd had a different test.

With both the plain vanilla glycohaemoglobin test and the more specialized A1c, there are different methods to separate out the haemoglobin fractions, and they give slightly different results, so each result must be compared with the *normal range for that particular laboratory*, not the number viewed in isolation. In a lab that had a normal range of 4 to 6, an A1c of 7 would indicate good control but well above average. The same A1c of 7 would be considered normal in a lab with a normal range of 5.5 to 7.5.

Thus you should never simply accept a number as a result of a glycohaemoglobin or A1c test. **Always insist on knowing the normal range for your lab**. And don't be discouraged just because someone else has a lower test result than you do. Their laboratory might have a different normal range.

I discuss various factors that affect the glycohaemoglobin and

A1c tests in Month 4. For now, you should just understand that this test gives an estimate of the average BG level over the past few weeks or months. Although it is not usually considered diagnostic of diabetes by itself, it gives a good indication of how much your BG levels have been elevated and for how long. If your BG levels were elevated for months before you were diagnosed, your A1c will be high when you are diagnosed. People with type 1 diabetes, which can manifest quite quickly, may have normal A1c levels when they're diagnosed.

Fructosamine measures a shorter time period

Like the A1c, the **fructosamine** test measures the average level of glucose in your blood over an extended period of time, but the measured time period is shorter.

Instead of measuring the sugar attached to haemoglobin, the fructosamine test measures the amount of sugar attached to other proteins in the blood, primarily **albumin**. These proteins don't live as long as haemoglobin, so the test measures the average BG level over the past two weeks.

There are different tests for fructosamine, and different labs use different units in reporting the results, so again, make sure you find out what the normal range is at the lab you are using.

Glucose tolerance test is used for gestational diabetes

Occasionally, and especially when doctors are diagnosing **gestational diabetes**, the kind that is precipitated by the stress of pregnancy and then usually goes away after the baby is born, you may be given what is called a **glucose tolerance test (GTT)**.

In this test your fasting BG level is measured and then you are given a huge dose of glucose solution and your BG levels are measured every so often for several hours. This is because some people in early stages of diabetes are able to keep their fasting BG levels in the normal range, but they can't keep them normal after meals. This intermediate state between normal BG control and overt diabetes is called **impaired glucose tolerance**.

In most cases, however, by the time you or your doctor has begun to suspect that you might be diabetic, your disease has progressed beyond this point, and most doctors no longer do the GTT except in special circumstances, for example, testing for gestational diabetes.

Urine tests are also useful

Glucose in urine means diabetes. Sometimes your diabetes may be diagnosed on the basis of a routine urine test. This is because your kidneys are very clever, and when the BG level gets too high, usually about 10 mmol/L, the kidneys start extracting the extra glucose from the blood and excreting it in the urine, which becomes sweet. In ancient times, people noticed that the urine of some people attracted more flies than usual because of the extra sugar. And even in the recent past, dyers of indigo cloth who fermented the plant in a urine solution preferred the urine of diabetic people in their vats because the extra sugar resulted in a faster fermentation.

In fact, this is the reason for the name *diabetes mellitus* (sometimes abbreviated to *DM*). The *mellitus* means 'honey sweetened' and distinguishes it from a form of diabetes called *diabetes insipidus*, in which the urine is extremely dilute and not particularly sweet. This form of diabetes is much less common and has a different cause than diabetes mellitus. Even today some people refer to diabetes mellitus as 'sugar diabetes'.

Today there are **dipsticks** that measure the glucose level of your urine. You dip the stick into a little urine and it changes colour depending on the level of the glucose in the urine. If you enjoy messing around with chemistry sets, you can also buy tablets that you mix with a diluted sample of urine. The solution fizzes and then changes colour if there's sugar in the urine, and you match the colour of the solution with a chart provided with the kit.

In the bad old days, people with diabetes had no way of measuring their BG levels except for these tedious urine tests. But because it takes the kidneys a while to extract glucose from the blood, and because the bladder may then store the urine for several hours, urine tests can only measure how high your BG level was several hours before and are not useful in daily treatment now that we have ready access to BG meters.

Also, because the BG level has to exceed about 10 mmol/L before you begin to 'spill' glucose into the urine (and sometimes the threshold can even exceed 10 mmol/L), urine tests are not a good method for detecting the minor BG elevations that are seen in the early stages of the disease. Nevertheless, they are cheap and painless ways to screen large populations for diabetes.

Ketones in urine mean you're burning fat. Another urine test you may have had is the test for ketones. Normally, cells use glucose as their main fuel. However, when glucose is scarce, the cells burn fat instead. Such a glucose scarcity may occur in starvation, if you are on a low-carbohydrate diet, or in the absence of effective insulin, that is, too little insulin or too much insulin resistance (IR). In the latter case, there may be plenty of glucose in the blood, but it can't get into the cells because the insulin doesn't work (in the analogy in Day 1, the drinks machine is broken) so you don't have enough glucose transporters. Thus as far as the inside of the cell is concerned, there's a scarcity of glucose.

When the body is burning a lot of fat, it also produces products of fat breakdown called *ketones*. Some cells can use these ketones for energy, but there are usually more of them in the bloodstream than the cells can use, so the extra ketones – like the extra glucose in the blood when the BG level is high – are excreted in the urine. When the levels get extremely high, some of the ketones are converted to sweet-smelling substances that give the breath a fruity smell like banana.

Even small amounts of insulin can slow down the formation of ketones, and most people with type 2 diabetes still produce enough insulin to stop the production of a lot of ketones. So people with type 1 diabetes are more apt to spill ketones into the urine than people with type 2. Thus finding a lot of ketones on diagnosis might suggest to the doctor that you were type 1 and not type 2. However, because other factors such as eating very few carbohydrates or eating a lot of fat can also stimulate the metabolism of fat and the formation of ketones, finding ketones in the urine does not necessarily mean that you do not have type 2 diabetes.

Like the glucose dipsticks, ketone dipsticks can be used to test your urine for ketones at home. You can also get double-duty dipsticks that test for both sugar and ketones on one strip. There are also meters that will give a numerical value for ketone levels, just like a BG meter.

Protein in urine means your kidneys are damaged. Healthy kidneys keep protein out of the urine (see Month 10 for a more detailed discussion of kidney function). When your kidneys are damaged, they begin to let blood proteins leak into your urine.

The most accurate test for this is what is called a *24-hour microalbumin test*. In this test, you collect all your urine for 24 hours, and the urine is then tested for the presence of small amounts of the protein *albumin*. This test allows the doctor to quantify exactly how much albumin you are excreting every day.

There are also simpler, but less accurate, tests. A standard dipstick test will detect a lot of protein in the urine, but by the time this amount of protein is detected, the kidney damage has progressed to the point that it's not apt to be reversed. A special dipstick will detect microalbumin levels. A test for albumin in a random sample of urine (not a 24-hour collection) will detect smaller amounts of protein (earlier stage of kidney damage) than the standard dipstick but is not as accurate as the 24-hour test.

Strenuous exercise can increase the protein level in your urine, so one positive test is not conclusive for kidney disease.

Kidney function can also be estimated by testing for other substances. One of these is called *creatinine*. It is a normal waste product of your muscles, and thus its level in your blood is proportional to your total muscle mass. A muscular man has more creatinine than a small woman.

The creatinine is normally removed by the kidneys. When your kidneys are damaged, the creatinine isn't removed, the creatinine level in your blood increases and the level in your urine decreases. So sometimes you are tested for creatinine levels in both your blood and a 24-hour urine sample and your *creatinine clearance rate* is determined.

The creatinine clearance rate can be estimated using only the serum creatinine level and a formula that corrects for your weight (larger people produce more creatinine) and your age (even normal kidneys decline in function with age).

Another substance that can estimate kidney function is the level of urea in your blood, expressed as *blood urea nitrogen (BUN)*. Urea is a waste product from the normal turnover of protein in your body. Like creatinine, BUN is usually removed by the kidneys, and levels increase when your kidneys are damaged. However, BUN levels also increase when your liver is breaking down a lot of protein and can be elevated in dehydration; a high-protein diet; starvation or low insulin levels that cause your body to break down its muscle proteins for energy; fever; internal bleeding and some drugs. BUN levels can be low with liver disease, a low-protein diet or excessive urination.

Thus doctors often measure several different markers of kidney problems before concluding that your kidneys are damaged.

C-peptide test tells how much insulin you're making

A test that is not often ordered as a routine part of diabetes diagnosis is called the **C-peptide test**. This test can help determine whether you have type 1 or type 2 diabetes and approximately how much IR you have.

The simple explanation of this test is that it gives an idea of how much insulin you are producing. This is because when insulin is synthesized in your pancreas, it is produced as a large protein called *proinsulin*. Before it is secreted into the bloodstream, it is snipped into two smaller protein molecules called *insulin* and *C-peptide*. For every molecule of insulin that you produce, you also produce one molecule of C-peptide. Insulin doesn't last long in your blood. It's quickly taken up by the liver. The C-peptide hangs around longer. Also, insulin tests are not accurate in anyone who is injecting insulin. For these reasons, the C-peptide test is used as an indirect way of finding out how much insulin your pancreas is producing.

As with the A1c test, the normal C-peptide ranges differ slightly from laboratory to laboratory, and different labs may use different units to express the results. At one laboratory they range from 0.5 to 1.5 picomols per litre (pmol/L). If you tested 0.3 pmol/L at this lab, it would mean you weren't producing a lot of insulin and probably had type 1 diabetes. If you tested 4 pmol/L, it would mean you had a lot of IR (you needed to produce extra insulin to achieve the same effect as someone without IR could achieve with insulin levels in the normal range; in the analogy in Day 1, you would need to put extra money into the drinks machine to get out the same number of cans).

Most doctors don't order C-peptide tests because they would treat the disease the same regardless of the results. If your doctor doesn't mention the test, ask about it. I'll discuss the reasons for wanting to know your C-peptide results in Week 4. For now, you should just be aware that such a test exists.

Anti-islet cell antibodies tell if you have type 1 diabetes

If your doctor thinks there's a possibility that you might, in fact, have type 1 diabetes, there are a few specialized tests that you might have done. In most cases, type 1 diabetes is what is called an autoimmune disease. Normally, the immune system of the body attacks any foreign invaders but leaves its own cells alone. Sometimes, for example in rheumatoid arthritis, rheumatic fever and type 1 diabetes, something goes wrong and the immune system starts destroying the cells of its own body.

In the case of type 1 diabetes, the immune system attacks the beta cells in the pancreas that produce insulin, eventually destroying them almost completely. Scientists are beginning to learn which particular molecules in the pancreas are the targets for the immune system, and they can test for the **autoantibodies** (**antibodies** against an organism's own tissues) that produce this damage.

As a group, these antibodies are called *anti-islet cell antibodies*, because the beta cells are one type of cell found in structures called the *islets of Langerhans* in the pancreas, or islet cells for short. Many of the tests for these antibodies are done only in research centres. There are several antibodies that can be tested for. The most common one is called *anti-GAD* (glutamic acid decarboxylase). Don't worry about what the name means. The important thing is to understand what the test results mean. A person with type 2 diabetes almost never tests positive for anti-GAD antibodies. People with type 1 diabetes test positive for the anti-GAD antibodies about 80 per cent of the time. So a negative test means you *probably* don't have type 1 diabetes but doesn't prove it. A positive test means you *probably* have type 1 diabetes but again is not proof.

As type 1 diabetes progresses and most of the beta cells have been destroyed, the anti-GAD antibodies begin to disappear. So if it is done at all, an anti-GAD test should be done as soon as possible after diabetes is suspected.

Other tests may be important too

Your doctor may also order a battery of other tests, for example, tests for *cholesterol* and other *lipid* levels (see Month 6) or tests for thyroid function. These tests aren't specific for diabetes but they provide important information about your general health.

When you have any of the lab tests described here, refer back to this section to see what they mean. If you have questions, make sure your doctor explains. Worrying about a slightly abnormal lab test is stressful, and there may be a simple explanation for an out-of-range test.

IN A SENTENCE:

> *Learning how to interpret your lab tests is an important step towards taking charge of your diabetes.*

Will Diabetes Disable Me?

MOST PEOPLE have heard about some of the serious complications that can result from years of high blood glucose (BG) levels. The main complications are what I think of as the Three O'Pathy Sisters – **neuropathy** (damage to the nerves), **nephropathy** (damage to the kidneys) and *retinopathy* (damage to the retina of the eye) – and their backup band led by Arthur O. Sclerosis – **atherosclerosis**, which can lead to heart attacks, strokes and open wounds on the feet and legs.

The O'Pathy Sisters are often grouped together as **microvascular** complications, meaning they result from damage to small blood vessels. The results of atherosclerosis are usually referred to as **macrovascular** complications, meaning that they involve the larger blood vessels in the body.

Unfortunately, these complications are no joke; they are real and serious. You should be aware of their symptoms, make sure you are tested for their presence and, most important, *keep your BG levels as close to normal as possible so these complications never occur.*

Landmark study showed that good control matters

People used to think that complications of diabetes were inevitable, that it didn't make much difference whether you kept your BG levels near normal or not. In fact, some health care professionals preferred that their patients kept their BG levels elevated above normal, because doing so reduced the chances of low BG levels that can cause people to pass out.

Then in 1993, a 10-year study of 'normal' versus 'tight' BG control in 1441 relatively young people with type 1 diabetes was reported. Normal control was what health care professionals had been recommending for their patients: haemoglobin A1c values averaging 8.9, where normal was anything under 6. Tight control meant aiming for lower BG levels by injecting insulin more often; these patients had A1c values averaging 7.2, still above the normal limits.

This trial, called the **Diabetes Control and Complications Trial**, usually referred to as the **DCCT**, showed beyond a doubt that people with tight control of their BG levels had significantly fewer complications (decreases ranging from 35 to 76 per cent) than those on the normal treatment regimens that allowed their BG levels to go higher.

Later, in Japan, a similar effect was shown in 110 people with type 2 diabetes. And in 1998, the results of a 20-year study in the UK (the **UK Prospective Diabetes Study**, or **UKPDS**) showed that complication rates in more than 5000 people with type 2 diabetes decreased when BG levels were kept lower. Lowering blood pressure to 144/82 also reduced both micro- and macrovascular complication rates.

If those studies don't convince you, recent studies have shown that **even in people who don't have diabetes, the lower the average BG levels, the lower the rates of cardiovascular events** (heart attacks and strokes).

What all these studies mean is that yes, these complications exist. If you let your BG levels stay high for a long period of time, it is very likely you will develop some or all of them (Table 1). The good news is that these frightening complications are not inevitable. **Keeping your BG levels normal may mean that you will never develop any complications at all**.

TABLE 1

PERCENTAGE CUMULATIVE RISK OF FIRST-TIME THREE-STEP PROGRESSION OF RETINOPATHY

				A1c			
Yr	6	7	8	9	10	11	12
2	1	1	2	3	3	5	6
3	1	2	3	5	7	12	17
4	1	2	4	7	11	18	27
5	1	3	5	9	16	27	41
6	2	3	7	12	23	39	58
7	2	4	8	16	31	53	76
8	2	4	10	21	41	69	91
9	2	5	13	28	53	85.	100
10	2	5	16	36	67	97	
11	2	6	19	45	81	100	
12	2	7	23	55	93		
13	2	8	28	66	100		
14	2	9	34	78			
15	2	11	40	89			

Calculated by Ron Sebol on the basis of published graphs.

Fern H., who has been working incredibly hard to keep her BG levels in the normal range, has had diabetes for almost five years and has no signs of complications at all. She described her friend Dewitt, 'the Bowling Club guy who was diagnosed at the same time I was. He's in terrible shape. Neuropathy, retinopathy and now his hair is falling out. He's the one who wouldn't give up his pizza or desserts for anything. He'll have a piece of every dessert at the Christmas party even if he has to hobble to the dessert table.'

The sacrifices are worth it

Keeping your BG levels down will not be easy. I know. I've been there. But I think the sacrifices are worth it.

If you're tempted to eat a big slice of thick chocolate cake with supersweet icing, ask yourself, 'Which is more important to me? About 30 seconds of pleasure from this sweet dessert or having good enough vision in 10 years that I can see my first grandchild celebrate her first birthday?'

If your friends are going out for pizza and beer and you know pizza and beer make your BG levels go sky-high, ask yourself, 'Which would I rather do? Have pizza and beer with the guys or order grilled chicken so I won't have to spend the day in the dialysis centre when my son is graduating from university?'

As Sophie C. said, 'I still miss my old habits of eating massive quantities of whatever tasted good, but not as much as I would miss spending time with my husband instead of pushing up daisies!'

Could any piece of cheesecake taste so good that it's worth the risk of having a stroke in a few years? Well, OK, yes, there are times it probably might. No one is perfect. Being diabetic doesn't mean you have to totally give up all these treats forever. The trick is to **remember the stakes and limit the damage** from the occasional dietary indiscretions.

How many times have you been on a diet, blown the diet with a small lapse, and then figured, 'Oh what the heck. I had one taste of apple pie so I've blown the diet. Might as well eat the whole thing with whipped cream. Tomorrow I'll be really, really good.'

That logic doesn't work when you're diabetic. **Smaller indiscretions mean smaller increases in BG levels**. If the temptation is overwhelming, there's no need to eat a whole pie. Have a taste instead.

It's too bad to have to use a negative motivation – fear – to stick with your programme. But let's face it, fear is a powerful motivation. You have probably been trying other motivations for getting into better shape for years, and they haven't worked. Now you've got diabetes. This is different. This is serious. It's not a question of starting on a healthy diet next week, or maybe next month or three months from now when Christmas is over. We have the evidence now. The longer your BG stays high, the greater the chance that you will develop some complications.

You may have had diabetes without knowing it

One thing to remember is that it usually takes about 10 years of high BG levels before the complications begin to manifest themselves. 'Oh good,' you may think. 'No need to start on my new healthy lifestyle right away.'

Unfortunately, you may have had high BG levels, especially after meals, for many years before being diagnosed. One reason for this is that the blood tests that are usually done during regular checkups usually measure only fasting BG levels, not how high they go after meals. Many people who develop type 2 diabetes have years of normal fasting BG levels and high BG levels after carbohydrate-containing meals, or *impaired glucose tolerance*.

Another reason is that some doctors who were trained in the old days, when it was felt that slightly elevated BG levels were no big deal, may have noticed your fasting BG levels going up every year but didn't bother to tell you, because they thought your diabetes wasn't 'serious' enough to be treated, or that because of possible employer prejudices you wouldn't want to be labelled *diabetic* before such a label was absolutely necessary.

Some doctors used to tell their early type 2 patients that they had 'a touch of diabetes' or say, 'Your blood sugar is a little high; you should watch your sugar' and left it at that. Or they might have said, 'You have a little diabetes. Here, take this pill and that will fix it' so you went home and took your pill and kept on eating what you'd always eaten and exercising as much as you'd always exercised, meaning as little as possible.

Also, not everyone has regular physical exams with lab tests, either because they are not aware they have a medical problem or because they simply don't like going to see a doctor.

For whatever reason, because of this delay in treatment, you may have developed early diabetic complications even before you were officially diagnosed. This is even scarier than worrying about something that might happen to you in five or ten years.

Early complications can often be reversed

The good news is that bringing your BG levels close to normal can actually reverse some of the microvascular complications of diabetes such as tingling or pain in the feet or early signs of kidney disease. Obviously, if you've already had a heart attack or a stroke, controlling your BG levels can't reverse that fact. But it can lessen the chance that it will occur again.

If you can keep your BG levels as close to normal as possible, the chances that you will be disabled from the complications of diabetes are small. They are, however, real. There are no guarantees. There is no threshold BG level below which you can be assured of never getting complications. A tendency to having complications seems to be genetic, and some ethnic groups have higher complications rates than others (see Month 10). Even a 1 per cent risk is small but real. You should never forget the dangers of high BG levels, but you should also not be frightened.

You may remember a diabetic grandmother who was blind and in a wheelchair when she died, and this memory may frighten you so much that you can't focus on learning how to take charge of your own diabetes. Or maybe, remembering her, you think her fate is inevitable and it's so hopeless you might as well give up trying to control your BG levels and just enjoy life for the few years you've got left.

Keep in mind that things have changed a lot since your grandmother, or your father or your great-uncle had diabetes. They probably had their BG levels measured once a year, if that, and tried to 'watch their sugar' but otherwise ate pretty much as they always had.

Technology for people with diabetes has changed a lot in the past number of years, and it will change even more in the future. Treatment options have also expanded severalfold. Only 10 years ago, doctors had a choice of either insulin or one type of drug for their patients with type 2 diabetes. There are so many treatment options for type 2 diabetes available today that if you are willing to stick to whatever treatment works best for you, the probability that you will be disabled is very small.

It's not easy, but the results are worth the effort.

IN A SENTENCE:

Keeping your blood glucose levels as close to the normal range as possible reduces the chances that you will ever develop diabetic complications.

learning

Frequently Asked Questions

MOST PEOPLE have the same questions when starting out. These are the ones that are asked most frequently.

What are normal blood glucose levels?

Normal fasting blood glucose (BG) levels are usually considered to be between about 3.9 and 6 mmol/L (millimols per litre). After meals, nondiabetic people can peak as high as 7.8 mmol/L, although lower increases from about 4.4 to about 6 or 6.7 are more common. The amount of the increase depends on the type of food eaten and each person's physiological response. After a small meal that didn't contain a lot of **processed carbohydrate**, the BG level might stay below 5.6. After candyfloss on an empty stomach, it might go up to 7.8. BG levels in people without diabetes usually return to their starting levels within a few hours.

'I cannot get my BG over 6.7 mmol/L, no matter what I eat, or when I test,' said Jim D. 'And it is at that high for only a few minutes, before plunging. Even getting it over 5.6 is rare, and takes a LOT of sugar. Any slower carb, and I will not go above 5, no matter what the quantity.'

The peak BG level also depends on how low the BG level is when a person eats. A person who starts with a BG level of 3.9 mmol/L can increase several points and end up around 5.6. Someone who started at 6 (near the top of the normal fasting level) would obviously end up higher with the same increase.

Figure 1 shows how the BG level of a nondiabetic person might vary throughout the day. People who have tested their friends with their home meters say that some never go over 5 mmol/L, even after huge carbohydrate-containing meals. Children tend to have smaller BG excursions than older people.

FIGURE 1. Blood glucose (BG) levels in a nondiabetic person over a 24-hour period. Notice how the increase in BG levels and the time it takes to return to the starting point vary with different meals, larger meals having higher peaks that take longer to come down again. This nondiabetic person took almost five hours to come down to 5 mmol/L after lunch and supper.

I was told to test two hours after the meal. Does that mean two hours after I start eating or after I finish eating?

If you gulp your whole meal in five minutes, it doesn't make much difference. Most people take a little longer, and if you always spend the same amount of time on a meal, it doesn't matter much either, as long as you're consistent. What you're looking for here is some way of comparing your control from one day to the next, so you don't want to test two hours after starting a meal on Monday and two hours after finishing a meal on Tuesday.

Because most people spend different amounts of time eating from day to day, it's easier to calculate the time after you *started* to eat. If you're told to keep your BG level under a certain value 'after meals', this usually means two hours after the meal has started.

My vision is blurry. Does this mean I'm going to lose my sight?

Most people have heard that diabetes sometimes causes blindness, and it does. This blindness is called *retinopathy* and involves the retina of the eye. I'll discuss it in more detail in Month 10. It usually, although not always, occurs after many years of high BG levels.

There is another effect of BG levels on the eyes, however, and this effect is temporary. When the BG levels in your blood are high, the increased *osmotic pressure* causes the fluid levels in the lens of the eye to change. Changes in the fluid levels change the refractive index of the lens, and this causes visual changes, usually increased myopia (nearsightedness).

If your diabetes has been progressing very slowly for many years, your eyes may have been changing very slowly as well, and you may not have noticed the changes. Or it may have happened fairly quickly, causing you to complain of 'blurry' vision and having your glasses changed too frequently.

Once your diabetes is diagnosed and your BG levels start falling, the fluid levels in your eyes start to change again and you start becoming more farsighted (hypermetropic). Then if you can finally stabilize your BG levels at near-normal levels, the eyes will adjust to that level and your vision will revert to what it should have been in the first place.

If your BG levels continue to roller-coaster from high to low during the day, you may continue to see fluctuating vision during the course of the day. Some people find that their vision changes about 12 hours after an episode of high BG levels. This is another reason to try to normalize your BG levels as much as possible; it's no fun when you can't see well.

If you do have vision changes after you're diagnosed, don't rush to the optician for new glasses. There's no point in wasting money on a new pair of glasses that won't last.

When I was diagnosed with BG levels above 22 mmol/L, I had become quite myopic, meaning I could see quite well up close, but I needed glasses to distinguish a sheep in my pasture from a white rock. After I brought my BG levels down towards normal, I became farsighted. I could now see the mountains across the road quite well without glasses, but I couldn't see a person sitting at the other side of the kitchen table without wearing what used to be my reading glasses. This period of farsightedness seemed to peak at about two weeks, and then I started to revert to my 'normal' state of slight shortsightedness.

Just remember that these changes are usually temporary and are not damaging to your eyes. You are not going blind.

The real problem is how to see well enough to do things like driving and working for the month or so while these changes are going on. I bought a pair of cheap glasses that I took out of their frames and pasted over my distance glasses with Scotch tape, because I needed the astigmatism correction in my prescription glasses. It looked a bit odd, but I'm not vain about my appearance, and it worked for me.

In a work situation in which you need to look fashionable, maybe a pair of cheap glasses alone might work for you. If your vision changes are not great, you might be able to get along with your old glasses, or with no glasses at all.

Why is my blood sugar higher in the morning than when I went to bed?

This comes as a big surprise to almost everyone. I remember the first time it happened to me. I measured my BG level before going to bed. It had come down from a high number earlier in the day, and without eating all night I figured it would be even lower the next morning, just as one expects to weigh less in the morning if one hasn't eaten anything since dinner. It's logical, right?

The next morning, I eagerly got up, zapped my finger, put the blood on the strip and waited. The reading was more than 1 mmol/L higher than it had been the evening before. Huh? I was puzzled. Was my meter broken? It turns out this is a common phenomenon that is referred to formally by those who are not intimately acquainted with it as the **dawn phenomenon**. Those who know it only too well often call it the **dawn effect**.

Maintaining your BG level in a rather narrow range is a very complicated process that involves various different hormones that interact with various different organs in the body. The two big players are *insulin* and **glucagon**, and it's the ratio of these two important protein hormones that determines whether your BG levels will go up or down. Insulin makes the BG level go down so you don't go high (when everything is working perfectly, which it isn't when you have diabetes), and glucagon makes the BG level go up, so you don't go too low and pass out. When I say 'you don't go too high or low', what I mean, of course, is 'your BG level doesn't go too high or low'.

The rising BG levels after a meal make the pancreas produce insulin, which brings the BG level down again. As you sleep at night without eating, the falling BG levels make the pancreas produce glucagon, which brings the BG level back up again.

But sometime in the early morning hours, levels of other hormones such as **cortisol** and **growth hormone** begin to increase. Some of these hormones, called *insulin antagonists*, or **counterregulatory hormones**, seem to make the insulin less effective. Some people also think that the liver clears the blood of more insulin in the morning. For our purposes, the mechanism doesn't really matter. The important thing is the net result: a sort of temporary morning insulin resistance (IR).

In nondiabetic people, who also have a dawn effect, this might make the BG level increase slightly, which might help the person wake up and have enough energy to get started with the day's work. If the BG level went up too much, a nondiabetic person would quickly secrete a burst of insulin to bring it back down.

If you have diabetes, however, and produce less insulin than usual to begin with, you can't quickly secrete more insulin if the BG level goes too high, so the BG levels are often considerably higher in the morning, and eating carbohydrate for breakfast seems to increase the BG level even more than it does later in the day.

Some people find that they have a real 'dawn' effect, meaning that the BG level begins to rise around three or four in the morning and keeps going up all day until they have something to eat. (Yes, they *did* set the alarm for the wee hours to test for this.) But the continuing rise is not universal. Others find that if they don't eat anything at all, the BG level will increase in the morning for a few hours and then come back down again.

Some people find that the dawn effect is really more like a 'getting up effect'. In other words, if they measure at 5 or 6 a.m. and then go back to bed and measure again when they get up at 8 or 9 or even 11 a.m., the readings will be exactly the same. But once they get up and start moving around, no matter what the time, the BG level starts going up.

Some have wondered if 'morning people' who leap out of bed eager to get going have a real dawn effect that gives them the extra energy to wake up quickly and 'night people' who sit comatose for a long time before they are able to face the day have a 'waking up effect'. I don't know that anyone has ever studied this.

Remember the term *YMMV* (Your Mileage May Vary). We are all different and often react in different ways. If your dawn effect doesn't follow the textbook pattern, don't worry about it. Just understand that some kind of dawn effect is normal, and keep testing until you understand how yours usually works. Then you can design your menu choices around your particular dawn effect.

Many books on diabetes discuss another supposed cause of increased BG levels in the morning. This is the *Somogyi phenomenon*. The Somogyi phenomenon is a rebound from episodes of low BG levels; the body overcompensates, and if the lows occur during the night, the morning readings are too high. The way to distinguish this from the dawn effect is to measure your BG level at 3 a.m. If it's low and the morning BG reading is high, you might have the Somogyi phenomenon.

However, some people are now beginning to question the importance of the Somogyi phenomenon in causing high morning BG levels. If it does happen, it occurs mostly in people with type 1 diabetes, and even then, not very often. I mention it only because you'll come across the term if you read about diabetes, and you might wonder what it is.

Will exercise always make my blood glucose levels go down?

The effects of exercise on BG levels are confusing. In the long run, exercise is extremely important in helping you control your diabetes. But sometimes exercise makes your BG levels increase temporarily.

When you start to exercise, your body senses that you are going to need more energy than usual. So if your BG level is normal or slightly low, the liver will quickly pump more glucose into the blood to send to the muscles, and the BG level will temporarily rise.

In a nondiabetic person, the increased BG level will trigger a fast release of insulin, and the muscles will quickly take up the glucose, so the BG level won't go up very much. But if you're diabetic, you can't release a lot of insulin or the insulin won't be as effective, so your BG level may go up a lot when you start to exercise.

However, if your BG level is high when you start to exercise, your liver will sense that you probably won't need a lot more glucose than is already there, and it won't pump any more glucose into the blood. In addition, when you exercise, whatever insulin you have in your system becomes more effective. So if you start exercising with a high BG level, you'll also have a high insulin level, and you'll usually find that exercise brings your BG level down faster than usual.

If you start exercising when you have almost no insulin in your system, for example, first thing in the morning, that tiny bit of insulin can't do much even if it is more effective. Twice zero is still zero.

One trick that works with some people is to eat a little bit of carbohydrate before you exercise. About 30 or 45 minutes before your workout seems to be best. This has two effects. First, it makes your BG level go up so the liver doesn't worry about not having enough glucose to send to the muscles and doesn't pump more into the blood. Second, the increased BG level stimulates the production of at least some insulin. The exercise makes the insulin more effective, and this helps to bring the BG level down.

Even if this method doesn't work for you in the short run, the exercise will help you in the long run, as the muscles will continue to take up glucose for hours after you have done your exercise. In addition, exercise makes more muscle, and muscles are what burns a lot of the glucose in your blood.

I'll discuss exercise in more detail in Month 8. For now, just understand that it's not unusual to see your BG level increase after an exercise session.

IN A SENTENCE:

> *Most people have the same questions at first, so don't ever think your questions aren't worth asking.*

DAY 7

living

Breaking Bread

IN ALMOST every culture in the world, sharing food with other people is a way of bonding. Serving food to guests, even strangers, is sometimes considered an obligatory part of the social exchange. Not to accept it is considered rude.

Every celebration has special foods, often specially rich and sweet ones. They not only taste good, but eating them reminds us of similar celebrations in past years, connecting us with our youth and with those who are no longer here to share those special foods with us.

When you are on a strict diet that doesn't permit most of the special celebratory foods and even restricts the most common everyday fare, you face an immense challenge. How can you maintain your social connections without compromising your diabetes care?

As with so much of diabetic control, the answer is, it's not easy, but it's possible.

Eating at home is the first challenge

The first challenge is dealing with eating at home. You may live alone, in which case it's relatively simple to toss out all those tempting cream-filled pastries and sweets that you are no longer supposed to eat. Revising all your favourite recipes to use only the foods on your diet is not easy, but it is probably easier than it is for someone who has to eat a hunk of lettuce seasoned with lemon juice while the rest of the family enjoys an aromatic pizza or garlic bread, smacking their lips and commenting on how wonderful it all tastes.

Having to eat with nondiabetic family members is especially difficult at first. 'I have to leave the room every time Carl eats an orange,' said Barbara F., who had just started a low-carbohydrate diet that didn't include fruit. 'I want it so much, and the smell drives me crazy.'

If you're not the cook in your family, you'll have to educate the cook as well as yourself. Ideally, the whole family will help you stick to your diet plan by joining you in your new, healthier way of eating. But life is often not ideal, and family members may not be willing to make such changes in their diet for another family member. 'Why should I give up mashed potatoes and gravy just because Dad is sick?'

Cooking for others means constant temptation

If you *are* the cook, the temptations may be even greater. On one hand, you will have more control over what foods you serve to the family. You may be able to wean them gradually away from the least healthy foods, serving less and less of them and slowly substituting more and more of the healthier things that you can eat. They may not even notice the changes if they are gradual. Or they may discover that they actually prefer some of those nicely spiced high-fibre vegetable dishes you're learning to serve instead of mashed starch with thickened grease sauce. Maybe some nondiabetic family members will lose some weight without realizing what's going on. You may even help prevent them from developing diabetes in the future.

On the other hand, if your family simply refuses to eat 'rabbit food' and insists on macaroni cheese or sweet and sour pork balls fried in batter followed by chocolate brownies every night, you'll have to make all this forbidden stuff and smell it and feel it and lick the edges of the mixing bowl without realizing what you're doing because that's what you've always done. It means facing temptation, and being reminded of your deprivations, at least three times a day for 365 days a year. This is not an easy thing to do, and it's one reason networking with other people who are going through the same thing and sharing tips for overcoming these temptations is beneficial.

Take-away food is often not healthy

If everyone in the family works and you've always relied on take-away food, you've got another difficult problem. Most take-away food is high in processed carbohydrate and saturated fat, two things that are bad for diabetic control no matter what kind of a diet you're on. In this case, you'll have to either look for take-away places that serve at least one dish that works with your diet or else make up your own individual meals at weekends, freezing them for future use.

You may be tempted by supermarket low-fat frozen meals that are supposed to be 'heart healthy'. Read the ingredients carefully. Many of these meals do have less fat than other convenience foods, but they usually substitute those fat calories with highly processed carbohydrates that raise your BG levels quickly. Quite often the calorie and fat count are low because the portions are tiny, and they often leave you hungry. You're better off eating larger portions of dishes made with home-prepared fresh vegetables that are full of fibre and will fill you up.

Institutional food may not offer choices

If you live in a retirement home or a nursing home where a dietician decides what a 'diabetic diet' should be, you may not have much control over what you eat. It would still be good if you could learn as much as you can about how various foods affect *you*. If their diabetic menu isn't working for you, see if the dietician will work with you to come up with better choices.

Eating out means new challenges

Eating at home is difficult enough. Eating out is even more difficult, because you are surrounded by enticing sights and smells and specialties of the house and extra-rich party desserts. It will take a long time before you become accustomed to saying no to such alluring fare, but it really does become easier the longer you've lived with diabetes.

When you're invited out to dinner, one thing that helps is to eat something beforehand, not enough that you're stuffed, but enough to make it easier to say no. Then if the hosts have food that you can eat, you can enjoy a little. If there's nothing you can eat, you won't be ravenous.

Another thing that helps is to remember that the main point of a social gathering is to socialize, not to stuff oneself with free food, although the evidence at some parties seems to contradict that theory. If you're not distracted trying to figure out how you can dump Mrs Ennui and race to the buffet table for a second piece of chocolate cheesecake before it's all gone, you can enjoy the conversations a lot more.

When you join your friends at a dinner party or a restaurant meal or just eat in the cafeteria at work, you not only have to find foods you can eat, but you also have to avoid insulting your friends and colleagues by refusing their offerings when you shouldn't eat them.

One challenge facing anyone on any kind of diet is the inconsiderate 'friend' who keeps urging you to try some treat you know is not good for you: 'Oh come on. One bite won't hurt you.' It helps if you decide ahead of time how you're going to respond to this.

What works for me is simply to say, 'No thank you.' If they ask again, I say, 'No thank you' again. If several repetitions don't turn them off, I'll say, 'I'm diabetic, and I can't eat that food.' That usually stops the urging, but if I get the 'one little bite' plea again, I'll say, 'If I ate one bite, I'd eat the whole plate of biscuits. And if I eat the whole plate of biscuits, it would increase the chances that I would go blind someday.' Anyone who persists after a refusal like that doesn't deserve to be dealt with.

Jennifer L. has another approach: 'When it comes to diabetes, I discovered that I had to change *can't* to *don't* in my thinking and speaking. I *can't* eat pasta means "Poor me, someone or something is not allowing me to eat pasta." I have no choice. It's beyond my control (which also means that sometimes if I do eat pasta, then it's a "cheat" and there is the ensuing guilt and shame for being a bad diabetic).

'I *don't* eat pasta means that I have made a choice. I am in control (which also means that sometimes if I do eat pasta, I have just decided at that moment to make a different choice, no guilt; it's just my decision at that moment).

'A bonus to this way of thinking and talking is when you are out and about and someone offers you something you would rather not eat at the moment, *don't* works better than *can't* to get them to understand. If you tell them you can't have ice cream, they will tell you can, that just a little won't hurt. If you tell them you don't eat ice cream, what are they going to say? "Yes, you do"? And if they say, "Well you used to," you can always say "I don't any more." '

Eating at work can be tricky

If you don't want your colleagues at work to know you're diabetic, you've got a special challenge. What can you do when William, who loves cooking, brings in freshly baked cake for morning break every day? Or how about those Danish pastries they pass around at staff meetings? Or the leaving parties that always feature home-baked treats?

As mentioned in Day 3, if you're overweight you can always announce that you've decided to stick to a strict weight-loss diet, which is usually true. If you're not, you can say you've learned you are allergic to wheat or you've decided to give up white sugar, or white flour or your dentist told you to avoid sweets as much as possible.

Any of these strategies can backfire when thoughtful William brings in gluten-free pastries, or honey-sweetened Danish made with whole wheat. In that case, the only thing you can do is take one and break your diet or just eat a little bit, saying you're saving the rest for later and then give it to someone else.

Learning how to say no to those delicacies when you're so ravenous that even boiled cardboard would tempt you is more difficult. If possible, bring your own snack food so you can be absorbed in eating it when William wheels out the coffee break array. One trick is to bring something that takes a long time to chew. Then you'll still be chomping away when everyone else has gobbled down their pastries and you may not feel quite so deprived.

Eating at restaurants lets you choose

Eating at restaurants has the advantage that you can usually choose what you order. If you need to have a lot of business meals, you'll of course face the same challenges as you do with the office coffee breaks. If your best client wants to eat at the House of Fat, where everything is served in a bowl of melted butter, or insists that everyone try the breaded sweet and sour boar at the new Asian place where the cooks are all retired sumo wrestlers and the portion sizes are just as large, you may feel silly ordering grilled chicken with a salad instead. But 'I'm watching my cholesterol' is always a good explanation if you don't want your clients to know about your diabetes.

Sometimes starters have less carbohydrate and fat than the main courses, and by ordering two or even three starters instead of one main course, you can avoid the worst offenders to your diet. Just explain to the others that you enjoy trying different things and ask the waiter to bring the starters when bringing the main courses to the other diners. Depending on their personalities, your business associates may be impressed with your independence and ability to break the 'rules'.

When you don't need to disguise your diabetes, eating out is a bit easier, but it's still very difficult at first. When everyone else is trying some delectable new ethnic treat that isn't on your diet, or when they're all pigging out at the pizza restaurant, it's hard to sit there with your lean turkey on wholemeal bread and watch them eat as the delicious smells waft under your nose.

Take a Taste. One thing that helps when you're with family or good friends (probably not recommended when eating with business clients for the first time) is taking a taste of what the others are eating. The first bite of anything tastes the best. Taking little bites of various dishes that other people have ordered, even the desserts, may make your BG levels go a little higher than they usually do after a meal, but it probably won't make them go through the roof.

At least taking a taste will be better than what would have happened if you ordered a whole portion for yourself. Sometimes you'll discover that what they've ordered really isn't very good after all, and your 'diet food' may taste the best. I once went to an Italian restaurant with friends who all ordered huge plates of pasta covered with red stuff. I ordered a salad with flame-broiled chicken strips on top. When my meal arrived, everyone stopped talking, looked at it and asked what it was and how I'd managed to find it on the menu. They thought my meal looked better than theirs.

Some waiting staff are helpful. When a restaurant isn't overly busy, some waiters and waitresses are good at letting you know which dishes have a lot of added sugar or starch or fat. When you explain that you have diabetes, some of them will even check with the cook to make sure. But others can't be bothered, especially when the place is crowded and diners are lining up to get in. You can usually sense which ones can be trusted. If you're not sure, you can stick with grilled foods and salads.

Take your own dressing. Unless I'm being taken to a fine place that I know will have good-quality olive oil and vinegar, I even bring my own salad dressing, because sauces and dressings are often full of added substances of all kinds. It's easy to put into your handbag or pocket a small well-sealed plastic bottle of your kind of dressing, in a sealed plastic bag for insurance.

Take a doggie bag. I also sometimes carry my own 'doggie bag' so I won't have to ask for one. I use one of those plastic containers with several compartments and a well-sealed cover, so I can save portions of all the parts of the meal and have a multicourse lunch the next day or give the portions I can't eat to someone else. For a person raised to belong to the Clean Plates Club, it also reduces temptation if you remove half of the meal to the doggie bag before you even start to eat.

Check the diet drinks. One word of warning about 'diet drinks' in restaurants. Studies have shown that ordering a diet fizzy drink in a restaurant doesn't guarantee that you will get one. Especially when they're busy, or if they've run out of diet drinks, some places will serve you a regular drink instead, figuring it won't make any difference. One solution to this problem is to carry with you the test strips designed to detect glucose in the urine. These strips change colour in regular but not diet drinks. (Although the strips detect glucose, not table sugar, they seem to work in commercial drinks. If you can, check someone else's regular drink with the test strips before relying on them.) You can also use the strips to test for starch, but in this case you've got to put the food in your mouth for a minute or so to let the starch-digesting enzyme *amylase* break some of the carbohydrate down into glucose, which the test strip can detect.

What to order. I won't attempt to suggest what types of food you should order in restaurants. It depends on which type of diet you decide is best for you. You'll probably start out on some kind of diabetes exchange diet that limits fat, and it seems that every magazine or Sunday supplement or brochure you pick up wants to give you tips on cutting fat out of your diet. If there's anyone who hasn't been told at least 1025 times to 'Select a lean turkey sandwich on wholemeal bread for lunch instead of a cheese-burger and fries' or 'Choose a bran muffin with margarine for breakfast instead of bacon and eggs,' that person must have been living in a cave in the Arctic for the past 25 years.

In case you *have* just returned from 25 years in the Arctic, ask your doctor or dietician for a pamphlet suggesting good restaurant choices for your particular diet.

Plan ahead if you eat on the run

Eating on the run, when you have no time to seek out a suitable restaurant, or maybe just need to grab a bite from a street vendor to keep you going, is even more difficult than eating in a restaurant, because most fast food is both greasy (and so off-limits for a **low-fat diet**) and starchy (no good for a low-carbohydrate diet).

In this case, you just have to make the best of what's available. Be creative. If there's nothing in sight but a burger bar and you're on a low-carbohydrate diet, you could get the burger and throw away the bun. If you're on a low-fat diet, you could ask for a bun filled with onions and tomato, or whatever kinds of garnishings they offer. If you're on an exchange diet, the burger would probably be OK with the bun as long as you don't load it up with extra calories.

Another solution when you know you'll have a busy day is to prepare ahead of time and bring snacks or stop in a suitable place in the morning and get enough to last throughout the day. If this happens a lot, you might consider preparing several daylong food packages and putting them in the freezer. Then if you had to leave in a hurry one morning in anticipation of a busy day, you could just grab a package from the freezer and head out the door.

Sometimes if you don't bring some food along, there may not be anything at all you can eat. In this case, you have to choose between going hungry and eating something like doughnuts that may cause food cravings for the rest of the day.

Learn to avoid psychological games

As I said earlier, learning to enjoy socializing in the presence of scrumptious food when everyone but you is guzzling down ambrosial treats is one of the most difficult burdens of having diabetes. Add to that the burden that some people take it as a personal insult if you refuse their offerings of food, even when they know you're diabetic.

Some people feel, consciously or unconsciously, that feeding you is a way of expressing their love or friendship. 'You won't eat my food,' a woman once said to me in a peeved tone, even though I'd told her I was diabetic and she never offered me anything but cheesecakes and tarts. She obviously felt that by rejecting her food, I was rejecting her – on purpose.

Some people with diabetes give in to these psychological games and eat foods that aren't good for them because they don't want to hurt their friends' feelings. Don't worry about your friends. Right now you have to think of yourself.

Sharing with others helps

It takes time to learn to deal with all these difficult situations, and I'm afraid there are no miracle solutions. But you should know that it usually gets easier the longer you've lived with diabetes.

Sharing your frustrations and angers and solutions to eating problems with others in the same boat – local friends or support groups or fellow travellers you meet through the Internet – will speed up the process of learning to cope with this most difficult aspect of managing your diabetes. As always, remember, you are not alone.

IN A SENTENCE:

> *Maintaining your social connections without seriously breaking your diet is very difficult, but you can learn to do it.*

learning

Stress and Blood Sugar Levels

STRESS WILL increase your blood glucose (BG) levels. That's the condensed-book version of this chapter (very condensed). Maybe for now, that's all you want to know. If you're getting into the swing of things and want to understand how to fine-tune your BG level control, keep on reading.

There are many kinds of stress, and except possibly for some long-term emotional stress, they all increase BG levels, even in nondiabetic people. In order to understand how stress affects BG levels, you first have to understand how BG levels are controlled in nondiabetic people.

Normal control systems are like thermostats

In people without diabetes, BG levels are always fluctuating, going up a little and then down a little.

But the body has a complex control system that, like the thermostat to your furnace, keeps the BG levels in a very narrow range, usually considered to be about 3.5 to 7 mmol/L (millimols per litre) with normal meals. With a very large carbohydrate load, the BG levels might go up to 8 mmol/L and a person still wouldn't be considered diabetic. After a huge slug of glucose (usually 75 g) on an empty stomach – the *glucose tolerance test* – the BG level could go up to 11 mmol/L and still be considered in the normal range if it came down again quickly. Most people lose some control of their BG levels as they get older, so children usually keep their BG levels in a narrower range than adults.

You could think of the normal control system as analogous to a boiler that keeps the temperature of your house high enough when it gets too cold and an air conditioning system that keeps your house cold enough when it gets too hot. If you set the boiler to come on when it gets below 18°C and the air conditioner to come on when it gets above 21°C, you'll keep the temperature of your house in a narrow temperature range between 18 and 21°C.

When you have type 2 diabetes, it's as if you have the boiler, but the air conditioner is on the blink.

In the nondiabetic human body, when the BG level gets too high, the beta cells in the pancreas quickly secrete the hormone *insulin*, and the insulin brings the BG level down. When the BG level gets too low, the **alpha cells** in the pancreas quickly secrete the hormone *glucagon*, and the glucagon brings the BG level up. There are other controls, including nervous system signals, that fine-tune the system, but the glucagon/insulin ratio is the major player.

Glucagon is like the furnace in the analogy just described, and insulin is like the air conditioner. When your 'air conditioner' is broken, signals that normally might produce small beneficial increases in BG levels may make your BG levels soar.

Different types of stress increase blood glucose levels

Stress includes physical stress such as infections, trauma, surgery or intense heat or cold. In all these situations, insulin resistance (IR) increases and BG levels in nondiabetic people increase slightly. Another physical stressor is taking various drugs. Even pregnancy and adolescence normally increase IR.

Stress also includes emotional stress. For some people, chronic emotional stress seems to have relatively little physiological effect on BG levels. However, chronic emotional stress can affect how well you are able to maintain your diet and exercise programs. Depression might even make you stop taking your medications on time, or altogether. Thus chronic stress can have an *indirect* effect on BG levels.

Intense emotional stress that triggers the release of **adrenaline**, the **fight-or-flight response**, increases BG levels slightly in nondiabetic people and can make a diabetic person's BG levels soar.

Infections increase insulin resistance

Let's start with physical stress, such as infections. When your body is infected, it gears up to defend itself. One thing it does is to increase IR. This normally results in a small increase in the BG level, so the **white blood cells** that are sent out to fight the infection will have plenty of 'food' (energy) to keep them going. As long as this increase is small, it's a good thing.

In nondiabetic people, when the increased IR makes the BG level go too high, the body just produces more insulin, and this brings the BG level down. When you have diabetes, you can't secrete this extra insulin when the BG level gets too high, so the BG level may skyrocket. And when the BG level gets *too* high, instead of helping the white blood cells fight infection, it seems to slow them down. This is why people with uncontrolled diabetes sometimes have sores that take a long, long time to heal.

When you have an infection of any kind, you should keep a careful eye on your BG levels. If they go too high, your doctor may want to give you some insulin on a temporary basis to bring the BG levels down enough that you can fight the infection. When the infection is gone, you'll usually stop taking the insulin. The better controlled your BG levels are normally, the less they will increase under conditions of stress, and not everyone with type 2 diabetes needs insulin when under stress.

Quite often, the increase in BG levels actually *precedes* the diagnosis of the infection. Your body is more intelligent than your doctor; it can recognize an infection before there are any obvious signs, maybe one or two days before. So if you find that your BG levels have increased for no obvious reason, be on the alert for other signs of hidden infections, such as a bad tooth or a sore on a foot that you didn't notice, or even a cold that just hasn't shown its ugly face yet.

Trauma and other stresses also increase insulin resistance

Trauma and surgery affect people the same way that an infection does. Medical people call this *stress hyperglycaemia*, and it's a normal response. IR increases and BG levels go up a little in nondiabetic people and a lot in those with diabetes. In these cases, the doctors dealing with the trauma or surgery should be informed that you are diabetic and should know what to do to keep your BG levels under control.

Other stressors such as adolescence, pregnancy and even the fluctuations of the menstrual cycle can increase IR and affect your BG control. More and more young people are being diagnosed with type 2 diabetes and may have to deal with these additional stresses.

Drugs can make blood glucose levels go up or down

Steroids. Drugs can also raise BG levels. A major contributor to raising BG levels is **steroid** drugs, for example, **cortisone** and prednisone. In fact, these drugs can actually *cause* diabetes. There are obviously some conditions for which you really have to take such drugs, and in that case you should go ahead. You might have to take insulin on a temporary basis until the effects of the steroid wear off. The BG levels usually return to your normal levels when you stop taking the drugs. Long-term steroid therapy can cause enough damage that it can't be reversed.

Birth control pills and postmenopausal oestrogens and progestins can also affect BG control. Reports on the effects of these hormones differ. Some say oestrogens make BG levels go down and progestins make them go up, but others report just the opposite. It may depend on the specific oestrogen or progestin preparation used, the dose and the particular study group. The effect of combinations of the two hormones depends on what hormones are used and in what proportions. For example, in the past, birth control pills often made BG levels go up, but newer formulations often do not. In any case, if you are taking any of these drugs, you should keep careful watch on your BG levels to see if there are any significant changes.

Alcohol. Alcohol makes BG levels go down by reducing the amount of glucose made by the liver.

Glucosamine. Another popular drug, or 'dietary supplement', that may affect BG levels is glucosamine. This supplement is taken to treat arthritis, but there is evidence that it increases IR and makes BG levels go up in people with diabetes (YMMV, Your Mileage May Vary). Again, if you take this supplement, keep careful watch on your BG levels. It may take a month or even more before you see any change in either arthritic pain or BG levels, so don't conclude that it will have no effect on your diabetes control if you see no worsening after a few days or weeks.

Niacin and fish oils. Some people take niacin or fish oils to improve their lipid profiles. There have been contradictory reports on their effects on diabetic control. For some time, people have been told that fish oil supplements (not the fish oils you get from eating fish) and niacin would increase BG levels in people with diabetes. More recent studies have reported that there is no effect on diabetic control.

Remember, YMMV. Formal studies are done on populations of patients. If 100 patients are studied and 25 get better, 25 get worse and 50 stay the same, the study would seem to show no effect of a

TABLE 2
DRUGS THAT MAY AFFECT BLOOD GLUCOSE LEVELS

Increase
  Acetazolamide
  Alpha agonists
  Beta blockers
  Bumetanide
  Caffeine (large doses)
  Calcium-channel blockers
  Cimetidine (Tagamet)
  Counterregulatory hormones (glucagon, growth hormone, epinephrine [adrenaline], cortisol)
  Cyclophosphamide
  Cyclosporine
  Diazoxide
  Epinephrine-like drugs (decongestants and diet pills)
  Fish oils
  Furosemide
  Glucosamine
  Indapamide
  L-Asparaginase
  Lithium
  Minoxidil
  Niacin (nicotinic acid)
  Nicotine (large doses)
  Nonsteroidal anti-inflammatory drugs
  Older contraceptive formulations
  Pentamidine isethionate
  Phenobarbital sodium
  Phenytoin (Epanutin)
  Steroids (cortisone, prednisone, progestins)
  Thiazide diuretics
  Thyroid preparations
Decrease
  ACE (angiotensin-converting enzyme) inhibitors
  Alcohol
  Alpha blockers
  Fibric acid derivatives (Clofibrate)
  Oestrogen
  Salicylates and paracetamol (large doses)
  Warfarin

drug. But if you're in one of the groups that gets better or worse, the drug might help or hurt you. Some studies show effects and others do not. So as always, if you try niacin or fish oils, monitor your BG levels closely to make sure they don't increase when you take them.

Other drugs that may affect your BG control are listed in Table 2. Not everyone is affected by every drug on the list, and some people have reported effects from drugs not on the list. Some drugs affect BG levels indirectly, by increasing the effectiveness of sulphonylureas. Whenever you start a new medication, check to see if it has an effect on your BG levels.

Short-term stress can trigger adrenaline release

Long-term emotional stress, even major stress such as grieving for a departed spouse, parent or child, probably won't affect your diabetic control unless the natural depression that follows such events makes you careless about your treatment program. However, short-term stress that triggers the release of adrenaline can have a major effect on BG levels.

For example, I depend on my computer for my income, and I once had to replace a fan on my computer's Pentium processor. The technician talking me through the procedure didn't seem very sure of what he was telling me, so I was very nervous, so nervous I dropped the Pentium processor on the floor. By the time I hung up the phone, I was literally shaking. Out of curiosity I tested my BG level. It was up to 11 mmol/L. So I decided to take a walk to calm down, and after 30 minutes of walking it was back down to about 5.

Adrenaline causes insulin resistance

What happens in a stressful fight-or-flight response such as the one I've just described (I wanted to flee, but I didn't know where; I wanted to hit the technician, but he was at the other end of the phone line) is that the body secretes a lot of adrenaline. Like glucagon, adrenaline makes the BG level go up by stimulating the liver to produce more glucose and export it into the bloodstream to send to the muscles. This is because whether you decide to flee or fight, your muscles will need more than the usual amount of energy.

Another reason to increase the BG level is that some kinds of stress reduce the blood flow to the brain. It won't help to have strong muscles if your brain decides to take a nap, so increasing the BG level provides enough glucose to keep the brain working even when its blood flow is slowed.

The adrenaline also keeps the liver from breaking down glucose for its own energy needs. Instead, it ships the glucose out to the muscles, which are more important in a fight-or-flight situation. (The liver is 'motherlike' and does a lot of metabolic chores like this for other parts of the body.) At the same time, adrenaline speeds up the metabolism of glucose in the muscles so the muscles can extract as much energy as possible out of the glucose that was kindly sent to it by the altruistic liver.

The problem is when instead of fleeing or fighting and using up that extra glucose for those tasks, you just sit quaking behind a podium before giving a speech, or in the wings before going on stage for a play or a concert or in a waiting room for a job interview. All that glucose just hangs around in the blood and your BG levels go high, as mine did when I dropped the Pentium processor.

In a nondiabetic person under the same conditions, when the BG level increased just slightly, the pancreas would shoot out some extra insulin and bring it down. When you have diabetes, your pancreas can't do that. So the BG level goes sky-high.

Low blood sugar also triggers the release of adrenaline, and this causes some of the same symptoms as short-term stress, including shaking, nervousness, sweating and hunger (see Month 2). Interestingly, caffeine also triggers the release of adrenaline, and some people report that a 'caffeine high' feels a lot like a 'BG low'.

Some people also find that black coffee increases their BG levels. Others do not. Studies have shown that caffeine increases

BG levels, but these studies usually used large amounts. One or two cups probably won't matter. If in doubt, test your BG levels after consuming nothing but coffee and find how it affects you.

Some other hormones also increase insulin resistance

Adrenaline isn't the only **stress hormone**. Under stressful conditions, other hormones called *counterregulatory hormones* are also produced. These include *growth hormone* and *cortisol*. These hormones counteract the effects of insulin. In other words, they cause increased IR.

In fact, in certain disease states, levels of these counterregulatory hormones can be increased enough that the resulting IR actually *causes* a diabetic condition. Too much growth hormone in adults produces acromegaly, and too much cortisol produces Cushing's disease; both these diseases are associated with diabetes.

You don't need to remember the details at first, but you should understand that the orchestration of BG levels during stress, and even during nonstressful times, is very complex. Most of the hormones such as insulin, glucagon, adrenaline, cortisol and growth hormone have multiple effects, and I've mentioned only the primary ones.

Like a complicated engineering system with checks and balances and counterchecks and counterbalances, the body has many different controls that interact to produce reactions to the stimuli of everyday life. When one of the control systems in the body is defective, sometimes another one can step in and take over. This is one reason we see YMMV in diabetic control. Some of you may have controls that are 'rusty' in one point of this complex system, and others may have defects at some other point.

In general, stress will make your BG levels go up. It's important, especially at first, to test under different conditions of stress to see how stresses of various kinds affect *your* BG control. Then with experience you can anticipate these changes, or when you encounter unanticipated stress – for instance, if you encounter a sabre-toothed tiger in your garden or your dentist tells you that you need root canal treatment – you will know what action to take to prevent your BG levels from going too high.

IN A SENTENCE:

Stresses of many kinds will make your BG levels increase.

MILESTONE

By the end of your first week, you've come a long way in understanding and accepting your diabetes:

- ○ YOU KNOW THAT YOUR DIABETES IS NOT YOUR FAULT — YOU JUST HAVE GENES THAT ARE UNSUITED TO A MODERN LIFESTYLE.

- ○ YOU'VE LEARNED WHAT DIABETES IS AND HOW DIFFERENT FOODS, EXERCISE AND STRESS CAN MAKE YOUR BLOOD GLUCOSE LEVELS GO UP OR DOWN.

- ○ YOU'VE BEEN INTRODUCED TO DIFFERENT DIETARY PHILOSOPHIES.

- ○ YOU KNOW HOW TO TEST YOUR OWN BLOOD GLUCOSE LEVELS, AND THE IMPORTANCE OF KEEPING THOSE LEVELS CLOSE TO NORMAL.

- ○ YOU UNDERSTAND THAT SHARING YOUR EXPERIENCES WITH OTHERS CAN HELP YOU ACCEPT AND DEAL WITH YOUR DIABETES.

You're Chairman of the Board

AFTER A week with this blasted disease, I hope you're beginning to realize that you're going to have to mobilize your emotional resources and take charge of managing your diabetes at some point.

That doesn't mean you should fire all your doctors, enroll in medical school and get a PhD in pharmacology on the side. You need the knowledge and experience of a number of people to help you get a grip on this thing. But a large part of the treatment of diabetes involves daily choices of foods and exercises, so in the long run, like the chairman of the board, you are the one who is going to make a lot of the decisions.

Right now, it's up to you to make sure you are getting all the medical appointments and tests you should have.

Some have a health care team

When you read diabetes magazines and books written by diabetes groups such as Diabetes UK or the American Diabetes Association (ADA) they always talk about your *health care team*.

This conjures up images of five or ten medical professionals sitting around a table discussing your case and deciding on the optimal, coordinated treatment for you. Or maybe they're dressed up in colourful costumes standing outside your house chanting, 'Rah, rah, rah. Sis, boom, bit. Diet and exercise. You can do it!'

These publications suggest that your health care team may include a primary care provider (PCP), often a family doctor; an **endocrinologist**, a doctor who specializes in endocrine diseases including diabetes, or even a **diabetologist**, usually an endocrinologist who has decided to specialize even more; a *diabetes nurse specialist*, to train you in things like using your blood glucose (BG) meter; an **ophthalmologist**, an optician who specializes in eye diseases rather than in prescribing lenses; a *chiropodist*, a foot specialist to check your feet; a **registered dietician** to work out a diet for you; a *pharmacist*, to explain the effects of drugs to you; a *social worker* to make sure you have no situations at home that would interfere with your diabetes management and even a *psychologist* to help you cope with the psychological stresses of this disease. The theory is that even if they don't sit around the table all day discussing your fascinating case, these specialists at least all communicate with each other and coordinate their efforts to offer you the best care possible.

In reality, even if you have consulted all these medical specialists you will probably find that they don't communicate very well with each other, if they communicate at all. You may have to tell your GP what the ophthalmologist found, for example. Or an endocrinologist may tell you to do something that is different from what the GP said, which is different from the advice you got from the practice nurse or diabetes specialist nurse.

You may not even have a team working on your case. This may be your choice. You may not have the time or inclination to consult so many people. Some family doctors may believe that they can manage diabetic patients by themselves without help from specialists.

Having your eyes checked

It is essential that your eyes be checked regularly for signs of retinopathy. You may have had elevated BG levels, especially after meals, for five to ten years before you were formally diagnosed, and you could already have some damage to the retina of your eyes. Up to 20 per cent of people newly diagnosed with type 2 diabetes already have some signs of retinopathy at the time of diagnosis.

You should have your visual acuity checked and the retina at the back of your eye examined through dilated pupils. This means that you have drops put into your eyes. The drops paralyse your pupils so that they do not contract when the bright light from the ophthalmoscope is shone into them. Without this the examiner would be in the position of trying to see the whole of a room while looking through a keyhole.

The routine eye examination may be done by a diabetes specialist in the hospital, a GP or an optician. Whoever does it, it is free. Some areas of the UK have an organized screening service for diabetic retinopathy using retinal cameras.

Most specialist ophthalmologists in the UK are too busy to do routine screening for retinopathy. However, all district general hospitals will have at least one ophthalmologist who is a specialist in the assessment and treatment of diabetic retinopathy. They may sometimes use a special test called fluorescein angiography in which a special fluorescent dye is injected into the blood stream and photographs are taken. An unusual 'side effect' is that, for a few hours afterwards, your urine becomes fluorescent!

If you do have signs of retinopathy, it doesn't mean you'll go blind. These days, laser treatments to the eyes can stop the progression of this complication pretty well. And bringing your BG levels down close to normal should keep new lesions from occurring.

If your doctor looks at your eyes and finds no signs of damage, this will be a big weight off your mind, but don't feel you're out of the woods and never go back for an appointment. You should have your eyes examined for this complication at least once a year, maybe even every six months, just to make sure that if retinopathy does occur, you can stop it in the very earliest stages.

You may want other specialists

Whether or not you need to see the other specialists really depends on your own personal needs. If you've always wanted an excuse to take up mountain climbing and are able to buy proper equipment and join a mountain climbing class and get your exercise by yourself, you don't need to see an exercise specialist for help in that area. But if you've got severe arthritis and a little bit of heart failure and any kind of movement is difficult for you, then a visit to a *physiotherapist* should help you to design an exercise programme that would be appropriate for you.

If you love reading books about food and nutrition and are good at working with numbers, you can probably design your own diet plan that will work with your food preferences as well as the dietary philosophy you think is best for you (see Day 4). If that seems like too much trouble, then a visit to a *dietician* may be a great help. Like doctors, dieticians vary greatly in their ability to communicate with their clients. Some of them have great gifts in listening to your food preferences, lifestyle and budgetary constraints and coming up with a diet that will be wonderful for you. Others, alas, tend to give all their diabetic patients pretty much the same diet, which may not work for you.

In my case, which I'm afraid may be all too common, a nurse handed me an American Diabetic Association (ADA) exchange diet (see Day 4) pamphlet for a 1500-calorie diet and told me to follow it. That was the nutritional component of my health care team. If I'd followed that diet, I would have gained weight (I'm small) and would have had to eat less broccoli and spinach than I was accustomed to, and more small bread rolls. That didn't seem very sensible to me. So I pared down the total calories by eliminating some starch exchanges and substituted three vegetable exchanges for most of the other starch exchanges (three vegetable exchanges have about the same number of carbohydrate as one starch exchange) so I didn't have to rush out to the shops for a six-month supply of small bread rolls. I was hungry all the time, but I lost 13.5 kilograms.

It's important to find the right doctor

Whether or not you need to attend a hospital diabetic clinic depends on both the complexity of your disease and the personalities and expertise of the various doctors involved. The diabetologist should know a lot more about diabetes and the latest therapies than the average GP, who must keep up to date with not only diabetes but also hundreds of other diseases, both minor and serious.

You have to take charge

The most important thing, however, is to not sit back passively and stick with a particular health care person you don't feel is right for your diabetes control. For example, if you've been having A1cs of 9 and 10 and your doctor doesn't suggest making some major changes in your treatment, find another one. Having diabetes means spending a lot of time with health care providers, and you might as well get the best you can find.

Even if you have a wonderful doctor who listens and seems to be knowledgeable about diabetes treatment, you may eventually end up knowing more about diabetes than the doctor does. The doctor goes home at night and thinks about other things. You live with your diabetes 24 hours a day, 365 days a year. So you might as well start now and learn about things that should be asked and done when you see your doctor. If the doctor omits something you think is important, don't feel too shy to ask about it. For example, some people feel that every visit to a doctor should include careful examination of your feet, because people with uncontrolled diabetes are prone to foot infections that are hard to heal. Some people take off their shoes at every visit to remind the doctor to do the foot inspection. However, if your diabetes was discovered in the very early stages and you're still under excellent control, with no signs of neuropathy, you might get more from the doctor's limited time by discussing something else.

Your physical exam may include special tests

You may have had a thorough physical exam when you were diagnosed. You were probably still in shock and not paying much attention. If you were diagnosed after a routine blood test, you may be seeing your doctor for the first time after your diagnosis. By now, your shock should have abated a bit, and you may be able to pay more attention to what is involved in your examination.

A physical exam for a person with type 2 diabetes usually involves the same routine steps as any other physical exams. Because people with diabetes are more prone to heart problems than others of the same age, your doctor may also pay special attention to your cardiac health, including an electrocardiogram.

Haemochromatosis. Ask your doctor about the possibility of *haemochromatosis*, which can cause diabetes, especially if anyone in your family has had this hereditary disease. This is described in Month 2.

Pedal pulses. Make sure your doctor checks your *pedal pulses*, the pulses in your feet, and tells you if they are normal or not. This is because people with diabetes are more susceptible to **arteriosclerosis**, or hardening of the **arteries**, which can reduce circulation to the feet and eventually make you prone to slow-healing foot infections.

Tuning fork. Another test that should be done is the tuning-fork test. In this simple test, the doctor puts a tuning fork on an ankle bone and asks you to say when you no longer feel the vibration. This is testing for signs of neuropathy. A person with no neuropathy should be able to feel the tuning fork until the tester no longer sees it vibrate. Loss of this sense of vibration is one of the first signs of neuropathy, so if you have no loss in this area, there's a good chance you don't have other nerve damage.

If there's any sign of nerve damage or of poor circulation, make sure your doctor checks your feet at every visit, because small cuts or sores could turn into major problems.

Heart rate variability. When sensory nerves are damaged by high BG levels, you may feel tingling or pain. But when internal, **autonomic nerves** (see Month 10) such as the *vagus nerve* are affected, there are no clear symptoms. Such damage may lead to digestive problems or 'silent' heart attacks that lack the usual symptoms of pain or pressure. The latter can be deadly, because you won't know to seek help.

There is a noninvasive test for **autonomic neuropathy** called the *R-R interval* or *heart rate variability (HRV) test*. This test requires special equipment and can be expensive, and it's not likely to be offered except in a research setting. However, you should know that the test exists. If you think it's essential for you, talk with your GP and see if there's some way you could get this test.

Lab tests. Your doctor may order a lot of lab tests, including the haemoglobin A1c test and tests for kidney function. See Day 5 for an explanation of the most common tests.

Reducing worry. Not all doctors perform all these tests when you're diagnosed, because it usually takes ten or more years for diabetic complications to show up. However, you may have had high BG levels for a long time before you were diagnosed. In fact, sometimes it might have been early signs of complications that prodded you into seeing a doctor in the first place. Being checked for all the major diabetic complications soon after your diagnosis means that you know right away whether you have any early signs of them. Otherwise you may worry about the unknown. Worrying is stressful, and stress makes your blood pressure and BG levels go up.

Take charge and stay well

If you have no signs of protein in your urine, no loss of sensation on the tuning fork test, no loss of your pedal pulses and no signs of retinopathy in your eye examination, you are very lucky. You probably have no diabetic complications. Now your job is to make sure your BG levels stay as close as possible to normal so you will never develop any such complications.

Ask for copies of all your lab tests, even if you're not ready to try to understand them all. For one thing, if you decide to change doctors, you'll have your own record of what your lab tests were in the past. In addition, knowing your lab test results helps you understand where you are in your diabetes control.

One doctor told me my A1c results were 'normal', but I asked for a copy of the report. When I got it, I found my A1c results were above normal, in the 'well-controlled diabetic' range. I asked the doctor about it and he said, 'Well, that's normal for a diabetic.'

To control your diabetes, you need to have the correct facts. Unfortunately, you must sometimes insist and persist and demand. It's not always easy being chairman of the board, but it's worth the effort. It's your best way of ensuring that you stay complication-free for many a year.

IN A SENTENCE:

> *Taking charge of your diabetes is an important part of controlling the disease.*

learning

Guarding Your Beta Cells

THE CELLS in the pancreas that produce insulin are called *beta cells*, and to control your diabetes, you want to keep them as healthy as possible. High blood glucose (BG) levels are toxic to beta cells. This is called **glucotoxicity**, and the good news is that it's partially reversible if you can get your BG levels close to normal. The longer your beta cells are exposed to high BG levels, the more apt they are to suffer permanent damage.

There are vicious and virtuous circles

Although no one yet understands exactly how glucotoxicity works, high BG levels seem to increase insulin resistance (IR) or decrease the ability of the beta cells to produce insulin, or both. More IR and less insulin production make the BG levels go higher, and that causes more glucotoxicity, which further impairs the beta cells and increases IR. You get the picture. You're caught in a vicious circle.

On the other hand, if you can get your BG levels close to

normal, by whatever means it takes, the vicious circle reverses. Your beta cells become more responsive and your IR lessens. This causes lower BG levels, which causes even less glucotoxicity, which makes your beta cells work even better. Now you're in a positive circle, a sort of virtuous cycle.

Does this mean that bringing your BG levels back to normal will cure your diabetes? Unfortunately, no. While caught in the vicious circle of glucotoxicity, some of the beta cells may have stopped working, and scientists don't yet know how to revive them. This is why it's important to bring your BG levels back to normal as soon as you can, before too much damage has been done – and to keep them there.

Look out for a trap

This reversal of glucotoxicity sometimes can be a trap. Carmen W. was able to bring her BG levels back to normal just with diet and exercise. The glucotoxicity abated, and she found she could even eat a few desserts without having her blood sugar go above normal levels. 'I was thrilled. I thought I was cured. I'd planned to stick to my diet anyway, but I got into the habit of eating a nice dessert once a week as a treat. Then it was once a day. Then it was lots of bread, as well as dessert, at almost every meal. I sort of forgot about my diet (I was cured, right?) and went back to eating the big high-fat starchy meals the rest of the family enjoyed. I never tested anymore, because I assumed I was cured and I hated to prick my fingers.'

Then after some months, Carmen noticed she was thirsty a lot and she seemed to have to get up a lot at night. One day she tested and was aghast to see that her BG level had reached 22. Carmen knew what to do. She went back to her diet and started exercising again. Unfortunately, this time, the diet and exercise didn't do the trick. Months of high BG levels had knocked off a few more of her beta cells, just enough to make controlling her diabetes difficult, and she had to start taking tablets.

The same trap can occur in people with a lot of weight-associated

IR. If the diabetes is diagnosed at an early stage, and if you are able to lose a lot of weight, sometimes there are still enough beta cells left to cope with the smaller demand for insulin, and the BG levels return to normal without drugs. But you still have the diabetes genes, and if you regain the weight, the BG problems will return.

This achievement of normal BG levels with weight loss occurs more often in younger people who are diagnosed very early in the process, before many beta cells have conked out. There's no guarantee it will work. If you're overweight, some medical professionals may tell you that if you'd just lose a few pounds, your diabetes would 'go away'. Yes, your IR will go down and you'll find it a lot easier to control your diabetes. But having type 2 diabetes genes itself also causes IR, maybe about half the total IR found in someone who is very overweight. As with other things, YMMV (Your Mileage May Vary). It's definitely worth a lot of effort to try to shed the weight, but don't expect miracles. Even if you become sylphlike, you may still have some problems with your BG levels.

First you produce more insulin than normal

People have studied the way insulin-resistant people lose beta cells. You presumably start off like everyone else, producing just the right amount of insulin to keep your BG levels normal. Then, as your IR develops, you start producing even *more* insulin than other people. By doing this, you are able to keep your BG levels in the normal range.

Then when the beta cells become exhausted and start to fail, your insulin production falls, until it reaches the 'normal' level again. But remember, this would be the normal level if you had no IR. When you have IR, the 'normal level' is insufficient to let the muscle cells take up the glucose in the blood, and your BG levels will be high. Eventually your insulin levels may drop even below normal.

Figure 2 illustrates this process. It shows the amount of insulin people produce during a glucose tolerance test compared with the fasting BG level. Increased fasting levels suggest increased IR.

You can see that people with normal fasting levels (no IR) produce a certain amount of insulin. As the fasting levels increase, people produce *more* insulin than normal. In other words, they need more insulin to take care of the same amount of glucose. They are developing IR.

Studies have suggested that at a fasting BG level of about 6.5 mmol/L (millimols per litre), the beta cells are working as hard as they can to keep the BG levels in the normal range after meals, when the demand is the greatest. This represents the peak of the curve. When the fasting levels get higher than that, some beta cells begin to become 'exhausted' and expire. Now the insulin levels after meals begin to fall.

When the fasting BG level reaches about 7.5 mmol/L, the beta cells are working as hard as they can just to keep the *fasting* BG levels from increasing any more. When the fasting BG gets even higher than that, some beta cells give up the ghost even when you're not eating anything at all, and the fasting insulin levels begin to fall. By the time the fasting BG levels have reached about 11, the insulin levels are far *below* normal after a meal.

FIGURE 2. Variations in insulin secretion as the beta cells become 'exhausted'. The vertical axis shows how much insulin is produced during a glucose test (GTT). The horizontal axis shows the fasting blood glucose (BG)

levels, which increase as the diabetes gets progressively worse. Notice that at first the amount of insulin produced in the GTT *increases*. This is a sign that insulin resistance is increasing, so the beta cells have to produce *more* insulin to deal with the glucose in the test. Then, at a fasting BG level of approximately 6.5 mmol/L, the beta cells begin to deteriorate. At a fasting BG level of about 8.3 mmol/L, they produce 'normal' amounts of insulin in the test, that is, amounts that would be normal with no insulin resistance but are subnormal under conditions of insulin resistance. Eventually they aren't able to produce even normal amounts of insulin during the test. They are 'exhausted'.

The sooner you are diagnosed, the better

What this all means is that **the sooner you are diagnosed and work to keep the BG levels low, the more beta cell function will remain, and the easier it will be to control the diabetes**. Not taking your diabetes seriously because you were told you have 'borderline diabetes' just means you are creating more problems for yourself in the future. Doctors aren't apt to tell their patients, 'You have a borderline brain tumour. Watch your carcinogens.' The best time to treat a cancer is when it's small. Diabetes should be treated the same way, when the damage is small.

Unfortunately, current diagnostic criteria say that you don't diagnose anyone with diabetes until the fasting BG levels reach 7.0 mmol/L. This means that thousands of people have fasting BG levels high enough to cause some beta cell exhaustion but they're not being told that they have a problem. By the time they're diagnosed, it may be too late. They have enough beta cell damage that they won't be able to restore normal BG levels even if they reduce their IR by losing a lot of weight. Until several years ago, doctors didn't diagnose you as diabetic until the fasting levels were above 7.8, which meant even more beta cell damage had probably occurred.

Lipids are also toxic

High levels of fats in the blood seem to have an effect on the beta cells that is similar to glucotoxicity and is called **lipotoxicity**. Some say both effects work the same way and call it *glucolipotoxicity*. So controlling your BG levels but allowing your blood fat levels to skyrocket is not a good idea for the sake of your beta cells, as well as for your cardiovascular health.

People who are overweight tend to have more fatty acids (see Day 3) in their blood whether they consume a lot of fat or not. Thus losing weight may help reduce lipotoxicity as well as reduce IR and glucotoxicity and is therefore a good thing to do.

In Week 3 I'll discuss how all this affects decisions about what kind of treatment you should get for your diabetes. Now you know that by keeping your BG levels down, you can turn a vicious circle into a virtuous circle. **High BG levels promote high BG levels, but low BG levels promote low BG levels**.

If only chocolate cheesecake would promote low BG levels, most of us would have it made. Sticking to a strict diet and exercising a lot takes work, but it's worth it. Be good to your beta cells. Without glucotoxicity, they will be nicer to you.

IN A SENTENCE:

> *High BG levels are toxic to beta cells, and the sooner you can get them close to normal, the easier it will be to control your diabetes.*

living

Getting the most from the NHS

by Rhoda Martin

YOU ARE starting to recover from the shock of diagnosis. You're still learning how to deal with a chronic disease that can affect all parts of your life. Now you've got to learn how to get the best possible care from the National Health Service (NHS). Take a deep breath. It's not a breeze but it's straightforward – once you've become used to it. Do you remember how difficult it was to learn to ride a bicycle or drive a car? You wondered how you would remember everything. It's the same when you're diagnosed with Type 2 diabetes.

Rhoda Martin is a psychologist who has done clinical research on the ontology of pain perception, expression and development in premature babies and has taught on nursing, midwifery and psychology courses at university level. She has had Type 2 diabetes for 24 years and therefore has many and varied experiences of changing treatment regimes in the NHS.

Testing is vital to aid good blood glucose control and avoid complications

The most important thing to remember is that to maintain your quality of life and to prevent complications further down the line, you need to aim to reduce your blood glucose (BG) levels to non-diabetic or as near non-diabetic levels as possible, that is, 4 to 7 mmol/L. Diabetes UK advocates '4 as the floor and 10 as the ceiling'.

As you have already discovered, running all the time with BG levels at 10 mmol/L will put you in the 'damage zone'. Tighter control gives you more chance to avoid complications, so a little hard work can give you the best chance of a good pay-off for years to come.

The only way to get tight control is to know what your BG levels are. This means testing your own BG levels approximately 4 times a day. If need be, for example, when ill or trying new foods or on certain medicines, you may need to increase this. Your GP or diabetes clinic won't want to test your BG levels 4 times or more a day, even if you take up residence at their clinic. That means you've got to do it. Remember that if you want to find out how a certain food affects your BG levels, you need to test after a meal and not just before it as is so often advised.

You are the daily manager of your diabetes, not your doctor or diabetes specialist nurse (DSN), so you have to take responsibility for yourself and educate yourself as you are doing now.

Some diabetes clinics give out free BG meters, but they are not available on prescription. If you do not get a free one, definitely buy one. They generally cost around £15. At present there are 13 BG monitors available in the UK and all have their pros and cons. You need to check them out for yourself and decide what you want. Each manufacturer will send you details on request. Also, check with other people with diabetes to find out what they like and dislike about their meter.

A small but important concession from the Treasury is that because you have diabetes you do not pay Value Added Tax (VAT) on any item, for example, a BG meter. Thus when buying a meter you tell the sales assistant that you have diabetes and want to claim VAT exemption. Sometimes this causes them a bit of surprise, as many people with diabetes either do not know or forget about this tax benefit. You will usually be asked to sign a form (sometimes pre-printed within the meter box) to confirm that you have diabetes. Then you save yourself 17.5 per cent VAT on the purchase price. There has to be some benefit to having diabetes!

The same applies to which finger-pricking device you prefer. Since pain experience is an individual matter, it is impossible for someone else to advise you which one to have. All meters come with a finger-pricking device, and if you do not find it comfortable, then look for another one, preferably one that allows you to adjust the depth of the pricking. Finger-pricking devices are not available on prescription; however, some diabetes clinics may have a few available free of charge. If you are buying one, remember again to claim VAT exemption.

The lancets are the key factor here, and again you find the right one for you by trial and error and again checking with others. Most manufacturers will send you a free sample on request so you can find out before you ask your GP or diabetes clinic for a prescription for them.

Test strips too are available on prescription, and all meter manufacturers provide test solution to calibrate your machine, free of charge. Some, for example Roche, which manufactures the Glucotrend range of meters, also provide replacement batteries for life and record diaries free of charge. Record diaries are also usually available on request from diabetes clinics at hospital or your GP surgery.

Help is available with associated health costs

If you are treated by diet and exercise only, then you will be liable for prescription charges. Because each prescription item currently costs £6.20p, if you have 15 or more prescription items per year for any illness and not only diabetes, it is worth buying a Pre-Payment

Certificate. This comes for either 4 months or 12 months, costing £32.40 or £89.00, respectively. A Pre-Payment Certificate means you do not pay a prescription item charge for items related to any illness whether related to diabetes or not for the duration period of the certificate. Forms are available from your pharmacist. You complete the form and send off the appropriate fee to the address listed on the form, enclosing your cheque or postal order for either £32.40 (the cost of a 4-month certificate) or £89.00 (to cover 12 months). You do not need your GP to sign this form.

If, however, you are treated by any antidiabetic pill or insulin, you qualify for a Medical Exemption Certificate. A Medical Exemption Certificate means you do not pay a prescription item charge for items related to any illness whether related to diabetes or not for the duration period of the certificate. Again forms are available from your local pharmacy, but your GP, or diabetes consultant at the hospital diabetes clinic if you are treated there, has to sign one section to confirm that you meet the requirements. This certificate, when issued, is free of charge and valid for five years. You will receive a reminder letter from the Prescription Pricing Authority before your certificate expires. At this point you merely sign the form to say that you still suffer from diabetes and return it in the envelope provided and then wait for your new certificate to be sent to you. The certificate is a very valuable document, so do keep it safe.

If you are on Low Income and do not qualify for a Medical Exemption Certificate, you *may* qualify for help with health costs via the NHS Low Income Scheme: Telephone Number: 0191 203 5555. To check out what is classified as 'low income' in this instance, if in doubt call this number.

Exercise is for life and health

Exercise is an important element in maintaining good BG control and health. Most GP practices are subscribed to the Exercise Referral scheme. This goes under different names in different parts of the country. The essence is that to help give you a kick-start to exercise regularly the GP can prescribe you one course of exercise with a qualified sports therapist. You will discuss with the sports therapist what your needs, interests and goals are. The idea is to find an exercise activity that you enjoy and will be keen to maintain after the initial short-term course. If going to a gym is not something you would enjoy, then you can choose alternatives such as cycling, walking, swimming or other leisure physical activities available in your community. The range is vast. From hill walking to rambling to line dancing, whatever you enjoy and will continue to do for the long term is what matters.

Treatment will take place either at the GP surgery or a specialist Diabetes clinic at hospital

Initially, most of you newly diagnosed with Type 2 will be seen in your GP specialist clinic in the practice. Only if there is some difficulty in stabilizing your control will you be sent on to the diabetes clinic at your local hospital. However, if you are not happy with your care and have some unanswered questions, you can ask to be referred to the diabetes clinic at the hospital.

If your GP is reluctant to refer you to the hospital clinic, you can insist, as you have the right to request a second opinion on any medical matter. In this instance clearly state that you wish to discuss this with a specialist consultant in diabetes. If need be, reinforce this in writing, keeping a copy for your records. If this does not produce the result you want, you can consult the Community Health Council for your area that is listed in the telephone directory. If all else fails, find another GP practice that will refer you to the hospital.

To help you establish a good basis of control, you will have frequent checkups after initial diagnosis. When this happens you will be called back for checkups at 3-, 6- or 12-month intervals. At the review visits you will have various checks, for example, blood pressure, weight, eyesight (and this may involve eye drops that will dilate your pupils, so check on this beforehand as you will not be able to drive for several hours afterwards). A chiropodist will also check your feet, and you will have a blood test to check out your average BG levels over the past three months. The haemoglobin A1c test (see Day 5) is most common, although some doctors still use the fructosamine test, which covers only the last 14 to 21 days.

The important thing to remember is that either of these tests only gives an average of your BG levels and may mask a range of hypo- and hyperglycaemia episodes (low and high BG levels). This is why it is very important to keep a record of your BG readings and take them with you when you see your doctor about your diabetes.

Specialist advice is always available from the hospital

Wherever the checkups take place, the same tests are carried out, but at the diabetes clinic at hospital, you have a consultant doctor available who specializes in treating diabetes. There will also be a DSN who is available by telephone or appointment, or there may also be a drop-in arrangement. If you are unsure about anything to do with your diabetes, even if you are being treated at a GP specialist clinic, telephone the DSN. If a nurse is not available immediately, one will get back to you quickly.

Because poorly controlled diabetes can lead to foot complications, even gangrene and amputation, you are entitled to see an NHS chiropodist on a regular basis. The frequency of these consultations varies throughout the country depending on available resources and staff. You can arrange this either through the GP practice or the diabetes clinic at hospital. It is really worthwhile for you to make every effort to take advantage of this service.

Dietitians are your best friends!

Well, sometimes! Your GP or diabetes clinic can refer you to a dietitian. However, it is worth remembering that most give the standard line of the UK government's Healthy Eating Guidelines. This advocates a high-carbohydrate, low-fat, low-protein diet including five portions of fruit and vegetables every day. Diabetes UK also advocates this way of eating. If you have access to the Internet, you can see and read more of this on the government website at: www.wiredforhealth.gov.uk/teaching/nut/fact_bgh.html.

This suits some people and may well suit you, but if it doesn't, do not think you are a failure or noncompliant, or any other negative description that is freely bruited. Remember, diabetes varies very much with individuals and in individuals at different times, for example, when you are tired, are stressed, have done different exercise or are ill, then everything changes. And as for pregnancy! As one doctor described it to me, 'There is male, female and pregnant female!'

So whatever dietary plan suits you at one time may not suit you at another, and definitely 'one size or one dietary regime' does not suit everyone. This is what the professionals rarely mention to you. From experience, trial and error with careful testing, and analysing of the results of different ways of eating – for example, healthy eating guidelines, low carbohydrate, low glycaemic index (see Day 4) – you will find what works for you and your way of life to give you good BG control. Remember, this is not a diet. It is a way of eating for the rest of your life. As you try out new foods, test before, and one and a half to two hours after the meal, and if there is a high fat content, again around seven to eight hours after the meal to find out what that particular food choice is doing to your BG control. From the results you can decide whether this is a form of food you want to include regularly or only occasionally in your diet and make allowances for the effects it has on you.

Eye tests are free to people with diabetes

One of the most common problems you will find with diabetes is that your eyesight becomes blurred if your BG levels rise or drop suddenly (see Day 6). This soon settles down once good control is re-established, but eyesight problems that are not so easily resolved (see Month 10) may occur if you do not have good BG control. Therefore the NHS provides you with yearly eye tests free of charge at any optician. You just make an appointment at the optician of your choice and tell them you have diabetes and you will be asked to sign a form. This enables the optician to claim the fee for the eye test from the government. This is definitely something worth booking into your diary and doing on an annual basis.

Diabetes can affect your dental health

On your first visit to your dentist after diagnosis, tell the dentist that you now have diabetes. The office will enter this on your dental records to help them give you the best dental care. Again, if you have good BG control, this will help enormously in preventing dental problems that may occur.

Having diabetes affects driving and insurance

First of all the good news! If your diabetes is controlled by diet and exercise, you do not need to do anything other than inform your insurance company that you have diabetes controlled by diet and exercise, as a matter of courtesy. This should not affect your insurance premiums, but it safeguards you should you have to make a claim at some point.

However, if your diabetes is controlled with antidiabetic tablets or insulin, you are required by law to notify the Driver and Vehicle Licensing Authority (DVLA) in Swansea, Wales, soon after you have been diagnosed or your treatment has changed from diet and exercise to drugs or insulin. You will then be sent a form (Diabetic I) asking for more information, including the details from your GP or hospital doctor. You will be asked for your written consent so that the DVLA can approach your doctor directly if necessary. For some reason, not all people who treat their diabetes with tablets are sent this form.

The whole purpose of this is to ensure that it is safe for you to drive a car. For instance, if you drive while you are hypoglycaemic (have low BG levels) and cause an accident, you can be charged with various driving offences. So it is for *your* safety and that of other road users that these enquiries are made. If your diabetes is under control, there will be no problem with your being issued with a licence, although it will no longer be the 'until 70' version. You will have a license issued for one, two, or three years with an automatic review towards the end of this period. Renewals of restricted licenses are supplied free of charge.

If you have a motorcycle, the rules for informing the DVLA are the same as those for a car.

If you start insulin or antidiabetic drugs that may cause you to go hypoglycaemic, the DVLA may withdraw your license for anything up to six months until good BG control is established. It is definitely worth keeping copies of any correspondence with the DVLA on this topic and also keeping in close touch with your GP or hospital doctor while license enquiries are being made.

You must tell your insurance company that you have diabetes whether they have a question about it or not. If you don't do so, your insurance company may and often does invalidate any claim you make at a future date. So in this case 'honesty is definitely the best policy'.

If an insurance company refuses to insure you (whether for a motor or personal policy), or tries to 'load' (increase the premiums you are charged because of your diabetes), then look elsewhere. There are many reputable insurance companies that give good cover for people with diabetes without this extra charge. This is definitely a case of check it out for yourself!

You do not need to do this diabetes walk alone!

Diabetes support groups are often attached to diabetes clinics at hospitals or even locally. These are generally under the umbrella of Diabetes UK. These can be helpful to some, although often the groups lack input from patients themselves and tend to be driven by the professionals, whose needs, goals and interests may diverge from yours. If you are interested, Diabetes UK also produces several free or low-cost booklets on different aspects of living with diabetes (see Resources).

Others prefer online sources (see Day 4), and there are many diabetes support groups specific to the UK as well as internationally.

If you are technophobic, believe me you can readily learn how to use the Internet and e-mail for this purpose, and you do not need to buy a computer to do this. Every local public lending library has computers you can book to go online. Most libraries also offer free introductory courses, often on a one-to-one basis, to start you off. Other organizations, for example Age Concern, many local colleges, and even local BBC radio stations, offer free or very reasonable courses to introduce you to this invaluable resource. My determinedly technophobic sister went on one and now uses e-mail and the web. So miracles can and do happen!

The aim is to get the best out of the NHS and associated systems to help you achieve good control and a healthy life

In dealing with the NHS, you're not trying to get something for nothing. You're trying to get the services you need to help you achieve good control and a healthy life. In the long run, if the NHS gives you good services today, they'll probably avoid having to give you very expensive services to treat complications, so everyone will benefit. But remember that what is of importance to you as a patient may not be seen as important to your doctor, who usually thinks in terms of how something helps the diagnosis and treatment. Therefore, sometimes you may need to negotiate or be persistent in your approach.

If information you are requesting will help you manage your diabetes more effectively on a daily basis, you should make this very clear to your doctor.

You may be accused of 'being obsessive' in testing your BG more than twice a day. It happens! Once you have asked how else are you to know what is going on with your BG control and therefore how can you manage your diabetes, you could mention that several French studies published in 2003 showed that patients who monitored their BG levels regularly and had been taught what to do when they got high numbers, had better A1c results, even patients with type 2 diabetes not controlled by insulin.

An example of this difference in a patient's and a physician's viewpoints could be a request for a C-peptide test that would help you understand whether you are still producing ample amounts of insulin and therefore could act as a motivator for you to reduce your weight and so lower your insulin resistance. However, it would not help your doctor for diagnosis or treatment.

The resources are here. You may have to fight for them. Remember, if you write a letter to your GP or hospital consultant, they are legally bound to reply to you. When questions are over-looked in an appointment, it is worth using this route to explore them further.

If need be, you should submit letters to your local Primary Care Trust (PCT). In this you would cite the points you wish to make, backed up, preferably with research information gleaned from the library, medical resources, the Internet or patient support groups (for example, Input – this is the name of a support group – that helps patients seek funding for insulin pumps). The PCT is the finance issuing body for non-routine requests such as funding for an insulin pump. It is infinitely better if you can persuade your GP and/or hospital consultant to support you in such requests.

Finally, another source of support available to you is the Patient Advice and Liaison Service (PAL) based in each hospital. The staff are there to listen, advise and help you solve whatever problems you may be having at the hospital.

Remember, better control means fewer complications. Fewer complications means lower expenses for the NHS. So don't be shy about trying to get the best help available to you. Use the resources and have a healthy life with type 2 diabetes. Everyone will benefit.

learning

Oral Drugs

Sulphonylureas stimulate insulin secretion

TODAY THERE is a whole range of drugs avail-able for treating type 2 diabetes. *Sulphonylureas* were the first drugs developed for diabetes, starting shortly after World War II, when it was noticed that sulpha drugs used to fight infection often brought blood glucose (BG) levels down. They are still used, but there are now second-generation sulphonylureas that are more effective than the early drugs. Some examples are glibenclamide (*Daonil, Euglucon*), gliclazide (*Diamicron*), glipizide (*Glibenese*) and glimepiride (*Amaryl*).

These drugs work primarily by whipping your sluggish *beta cells* into producing insulin whether or not you eat. The sulphonylureas make the beta cells produce insulin all day, so if you miss a meal or don't eat enough carbohydrate with a meal, the insulin can make your BG level go too low. Thus if you take a sulphonylurea it is essential to maintain a regular meal schedule with a certain amount of carbohydrate with each meal or snack, whether or not you are hungry. Some people gain weight when they use sulphonylureas. If being overweight has contributed to your insulin resistance (IR), a sulphonylurea may not be the best drug for you.

Some people say that constantly flogging your pancreas to produce more insulin will make it even more 'exhausted' and wear it out faster. If simply producing a lot of insulin is what exhausts beta cells, this idea makes sense. However, there is no real evidence for this theory. Note that a lack of evidence doesn't mean that something isn't true; it may just mean that no one has done the right experiments yet. In the British UKPDS study I mentioned in Day 6, beta cell function in people treated with sulphonylureas didn't deteriorate any faster than in those on insulin, metformin (discussed later) or diet and exercise. Some people have concluded from this study that beta cell deterioration is inevitable, no matter what you do. However, people in all four groups studied kept their BG levels higher than normal, in some cases quite a bit higher.

Some new drugs work faster

Since 1997, a new type of drug has been available. Like the sulphonylureas, these drugs work by stimulating your pancreas into producing more insulin. However, unlike the sulphonylureas, these agents work for only a short period of time. You take them right before meals, and they do their work and then stop. As a result the risk of getting low blood sugar (**hypoglycaemia**) is much smaller. If you don't want to eat, you don't take the drug, which means you don't need to eat when you're not hungry. This may help prevent weight gains, although weight gain is listed as a possible side effect.

Repaglinide (*Novonorm*) and nateglinide (*Starlix*) are the two drugs of this type currently available. Repaglinide is considered in the *meglitinide* class. Nateglinide is classified as a *phenylalanine derivative* and is said to work faster. There is some confusion about the classification of these two drugs, and you may see nateglinide called a meglitinide. For our purposes, it doesn't matter what you call them. What matters is whether or not they work.

There is some evidence that when you use these drugs, the beta cells produce more insulin if you eat a lot of carbohydrate and less insulin if you eat less, which better matches the insulin output with the need and again reduces the probability of hypoglycaemia, although it still exists.

Repaglinide is excreted in the faeces, rather than the urine as many drugs are, and this would be beneficial if your kidney function is not good.

Biguanides work on the liver

Another type of drug is the *biguanide* metformin (*Glucophage*). This drug seems to have many different effects, but its main action seems to be to keep the liver from producing too much glucose when you don't need it. There is some evidence that it also improves *endothelial* (blood vessel lining) function.

You may remember the discussion of *insulin* and *glucagon* in Day 7. Insulin makes the BG level go down, glucagon makes it go up, and it's the ratio of the two that is important. When you have type 2 diabetes, you don't have enough effective insulin; you may have a lot of insulin, but it doesn't work very well. In addition, people with type 2 diabetes usually have more glucagon than normal, a sort of double whammy.

Glucagon is one of the hormones that tells the liver that the BG level is too low, so it should snap into action and produce some glucose to bring the BG level back up again. That's fine when the BG level really is low; it's what keeps you from passing out from hypoglycaemia. But when you have type 2 diabetes, the extra glucagon often tells the liver to keep spewing out glucose even when the glucose level is already high.

Insulin is glucagon's opposite. Insulin tells the liver to stop spitting out glucose. But when you have IR in your muscle cells, you usually have IR in your liver as well. So the extra glucagon is telling the liver to produce extra glucose, and, because of IR in the liver, the insulin is unable to turn it off. You can think of glucagon as the accelerator for glucose production by the liver, and insulin as the brakes. When you have diabetes, not only are your brakes rusty, but your accelerator is stuck on high. The net result is the production of a lot of glucose by the liver even when your BG level is already high enough.

Metformin is supposed to stop this process, although no one is yet certain exactly how it does this. Metformin also seems to help some people lose weight by reducing the appetite. It is thus often the drug of choice for overweight people with type 2 diabetes. Some doctors even prescribe it for weight loss in nondiabetic patients.

Metformin sometimes has side effects of nausea, gas and bad diarrhoea. Many people can control these side effects by taking the drug with meals and by starting with small doses and increasing the doses slowly. Others are never able to tolerate it.

Metformin can also have a very serious side effect called *lactic acidosis*, which can be fatal. An earlier-generation biguanide, phenformin, was removed from the market because of this side effect. Because poor kidney or liver function can contribute to lactic acidosis, anyone with evidence of either should not take metformin. Fortunately, lactic acidosis is very rare, but if you take this drug you should insist on getting the written instructions that come with the drug. Carefully read the symptoms of this rare occurrence, and stop taking the drug immediately and consult a doctor if you have any symptoms of lactic acidosis. Metformin should also not be used if you drink a lot of alcohol or have congestive heart failure.

Alpha-glucosidase inhibitors slow down starch digestion

Another class of drugs called *alpha-glucosidase inhibitors* keeps carbohydrates from breaking down into sugars in the intestines.

Acarbose (*Glucobay*) is the only one licensed in the UK.

You may remember that carbohydrates are composed of sugars. The long chains are called *polysaccharides* (many sugars). The intestines can't absorb polysaccharides, even when they are broken down into *disaccharides* (two-sugar units). They expect enzymes to break the polysaccharides down into *monosaccharides* (single sugars) like *glucose, fructose* or *galactose*, which can be taken up by the cells of the intestinal wall.

Drugs like acarbose keep the enzymes (called *alpha-glucosidases*) from doing their job, so much of the carbohydrate you eat just passes right through your intestine. The glucose it contains never reaches your bloodstream, and your BG level doesn't go up as much after a meal. Because they work on the enzymes that break down polysaccharides, however, they have no effect if you eat a monosaccharide like glucose or fructose. They are also less effective with milk sugar, lactose (only 10 per cent inhibition, compared with 90 per cent for starch). Furthermore, because they work on the carbohydrates that you eat, they must be taken with the first bite of any meal.

These drugs don't need to get into your bloodstream to be effective; they do their work in the digestive tract. For this reason they are thought to have fewer potential side effects on other organs, although they can cause reversible liver damage if used at high doses.

The glucosidase inhibitors do have one unfortunate side effect. Even though your own digestive enzymes can't break down the polysaccharides when you use them, the intestinal bacteria can. They munch happily away on the carbohydrate you didn't get to use and produce gas. Some people can tolerate the results, but some can't.

Thiazolidinediones reduce insulin resistance

Another class of drugs is the *thiazolidinediones* (TZDs), often called the *glitazones* by people like me who can't pronounce their formal name. These include pioglitazone (*Actos*) and rosiglitazone

(*Avandia*). Another glitazone, troglitazone (*Rezulin*) was withdrawn from the market after more than 60 people using the drug suffered fatal liver damage.

These drugs seem to work primarily on the underlying problem in most people with type 2 diabetes: insulin resistance. Many people who use insulin (see Week 4) find that their insulin needs are greatly reduced when they also take one of the glitazone drugs.

Unlike the other diabetes drugs, the glitazones somehow change the expression of certain genes. This process takes time, and it may take several weeks before you see any results from using these drugs and even more before they have their maximal effect.

Because of the fatal liver damage from the first-generation glitazone, if you have any kind of preexisting liver problems, these drugs should not be used. Even though the newer drugs are supposed to be kinder to the liver, it's essential to make sure your liver function is tested regularly when you use them. Some people find that when they take these drugs they retain fluid and thus gain weight. The weight gain usually reverses if you stop taking them.

Most other drugs have several effects

So far I've mentioned only what is considered to be the primary effect of each of the types of oral diabetes drugs. Most of them are reported to have other effects as well, and there is some overlap in their effects. For example, metformin and the sulphonylurea glimepiride may decrease IR, like the glitazones. The sulphonylurea glipizide may help with insulin secretion after eating, like the fast-acting insulin-releasing agents. The sulphonylurea glybenclamide appears to do both, although to a lesser degree. Metformin may inhibit the uptake of carbohydrate from the intestine, like the alpha-glucosidase inhibitors. The glitazones and metformin may also have a beneficial effect on lipid profiles.

Thus when choosing a drug for you, your doctor should take into account your need to lose weight, the amount of IR you have, your lipid profiles, your diet plan, your lifestyle and the health of your liver and kidney.

New drugs are being developed

Because type 2 diabetes is becoming epidemic throughout the world, selling new diabetic drugs is very lucrative. Drug companies are working overtime to develop new drugs to treat this disease, and you can expect to see many new drugs announced in the years ahead.

Some areas of investigation include inhaled insulin and insulin delivered through patches on the skin; oral *insulin mimetics*, compounds that mimic the action of insulin but might be able to be taken orally; *amylin*, a hormone secreted along with insulin that seems to delay gastric emptying; drugs to block the action of glucagon and other counterregulatory hormones that oppose the action of insulin; and drugs based on GLP-1, which is a gut hormone that stimulates the release of insulin from the beta cells. Research is also going on into drugs that reduce the complications caused by high BG levels.

Not long ago, doctors had a choice of only insulin or a first-generation sulphonylurea to treat patients with type 2 diabetes who couldn't control it with diet and exercise alone. Now there are six different classes of drugs, with several drugs in most of the classes. At the rate things are going, there will soon be a vast variety of drugs, each attacking type 2 diabetes at a different site.

IN A SENTENCE:

> *There are many different types of oral diabetes drugs, and they work at different places in the body.*

living

Depression

HAVING DIABETES can be depressing. In fact, there is a statistical association between diabetes and depression. More people with diabetes are diagnosed with depression than other members of the population.

Some people think this means that some kind of hormonal changes associated with diabetes cause depression. I think that anyone who *doesn't* get depressed when they are told they'll have to be on a strict, calorie-limited diet for the rest of their lives, not to mention spending a lot of their precious leisure time on an exercise bicycle, is probably a bit crazy.

Of course, there's a difference between just feeling sad, which is a natural reaction to learning that you have any kind of chronic, incurable disease, and clinical depression, which includes feelings of hopelessness that last for weeks or months. The latter condition is serious and requires some kind of outside help. Clinical depression is nothing to be ashamed of. Like diabetes, it is a medical condition that requires medical treatment. The sooner you are able to get help, the less you will suffer. Don't wait.

Just feeling blue is common

The other kind of depression, just feeling blue and tired and not interested in doing anything for a while, is more common with diabetes. This depression often occurs after diagnosis. One day you're just like everyone else, and suddenly you're different. You can't do the ordinary things that everyone else can do. A friend bakes bread and serves it slathered with fresh butter and home-made raspberry jam, but you can't have any. So you sit there and smell the freshly baked bread and watch the others eating as they comment on how delicious it is. Then they start discussing their favourite kinds of cakes, and their favourite bakery and their favourite kinds of pudding. And you know you can't have any, maybe forever. You're not like everyone else anymore; you're an outsider. Is it any wonder you might get a little blue?

Professionals want to cheer you up

Many of the authors of pamphlets and magazines written for people with diabetes realize that it's a bit depressing to get a diagnosis of diabetes, so they want to cheer you up and remind you of all the good things you can still do. One brochure for a diabetes drug is illustrated with photographs of people smiling happily as they take vigorous walks, grinning from ear to ear as they prepare salads with low-fat dressings, smiling adoringly at spouses as they stick needles into their fingers to draw blood for blood glucose (BG) tests and looking rapturous as dieticians point out the tiny serving sizes that will be allotted to them for the rest of their lives. I once went through a copy of *Diabetes Forecast*, the magazine of the American Diabetes Association, and couldn't find a single picture of anyone who wasn't smiling.

This outlook is understandable. If people published magazines showing people sobbing uncontrollably, or shrieking with pain when jabbing their fingers or sitting in the corner while everyone else ate cake and ice cream, no one would want to read them. A cheerful attitude and stories of people with diabetes who overcame their handicap and lead happy, fulfilling lives can sometimes be inspiring. It's especially important for children to see successful role models.

But sometimes the feeling that no one understands what you're going through can be more depressing than the disease itself. 'Don't think you'll never be able to eat delicious food again,' wrote one author in an article for the newly diagnosed. 'Diabetes diets can be both delicious and varied.' Yeah, right. Especially if you want to eat lettuce, low-fat dressing and lean turkey breast day after day while everyone else is tucking into pizza and Chinese food. Of course the foods you eat *can* be varied and delicious. If everyone were on the same diet, there wouldn't actually be much of a problem. People in some parts of the world eat rice and beans three times a day and don't get depressed because everyone else is eating rice and beans too. It's having to watch other people eat even more delicious foods three times a day, 365 days a year, that can get depressing.

Putting food in front of starving people and not letting them eat it is considered a form of torture. Yet people with type 2 diabetes, who are often hungry all the time because they are on low-calorie weight-loss diets, are expected to smile happily as they endure this day after day, year after year.

'I spent the holidays watching my family eat delicious foods,' said Victoria P. 'I felt like Tantalus.' Tantalus was the son of Zeus who was punished in Hades by constant hunger, surrounded by food. Whenever he reached for fruit from a heavily laden tree, it flew just out of his reach. The word *tantalize* comes from his ordeal.

Some professionals aren't sympathetic

Most medical people don't really understand what a person newly diagnosed with diabetes is going through. Some can be quite unsympathetic. 'I went into my doctor, literally breaking down into tears, saying how depressed I was and how unfair it was I developed diabetes,' said Dawn A. 'She just about shouted at me.

Just what I needed! But she told me that I should be thankful that all I was in there seeing her for was diabetes. She told me I was lucky that I wasn't being treated by her for cancer or some other incurable disease. I was LUCKY to have diabetes, because in the grand scheme of things, diabetes was controllable.'

Of course the doctor was correct. But that's like telling someone he has six months to live but he should leap with joy because someone else has only three weeks. We all expect to be the lucky ones, the healthy ones. Finding out we're not is depressing.

Family members may not understand either. 'When I phoned my sister-in-law,' said Ann G., 'and told her the reason I was declining her dinner invitations was because she never served anything I could eat, she said, "Well, you can't expect us to keep up with the ins and outs of your latest diet," as if my diabetic diet was some kind of self-imposed fad thing I changed from week to week. It's not. It's going to be medically necessary for the rest of my life.'

Being different and not being understood is often harder than the medical management of the disease. Think about it. Imagine that everyone else didn't have to worry about elimination, that their wastes just somehow evaporated from their skin, but you had a disease that required you to go to the bathroom instead. You would probably feel like a pariah. No one else would have to leave the classroom or stop during a trip or get up at night to do this disgusting thing that you had to do. 'Why me?' you might ask.

But when everyone in the world has to go to the bathroom, it never seems like a particularly odious chore. It takes a few minutes a day, but mostly we don't think about it.

Diabetes management can be the same. It means extra effort, extra work, extra planning and extra willpower. But it's doable, in most cases. Once you accept the reality of this disease and work its management into your normal lifestyle, the depression will tend to lift.

So you're different. So what. Lots of people are different; why should you be exempt? So you can't eat a lot of cake and pie. So what. Lots of people in the world go to bed hungry every night. Is giving up a little pie and cake really that bad?

There's also a positive side

I enjoy my food a lot more than I used to, when I often ate more than I needed because the food looked so good and I was raised to finish everything on my plate. After dinner I sometimes felt so stuffed I was uncomfortable. Now I concentrate on taste more than quantity. The first bite of everything usually tastes the best. By limiting the number of bites, I get a larger percentage of the best part of the food. I no longer eat anything I don't like just because it's there.

With time, most people also come to realize that increased activity makes them feel better, that in general their life has improved. I had been trying to lose a little weight for about 30 years, starting when I thought 52 kilograms was too much. In all those years I only managed to gain 18 kilograms. I'm sure you've been through it all. '*Tomorrow* I'll be really good.'

But when I got the diabetes diagnosis, I knew this was different. This was serious. I was hungry pretty much 24 hours a day, but I managed to lose about 13.5 kilograms. I slowly switched to a low-carbohydrate diet and stopped being hungry all the time. So far, I've managed to keep the lost weight off.

Having diabetes has had other benefits in my life. I've made a lot of friends all over the world by way of the Internet. The disease has rekindled my earlier interest in biochemistry, which I studied at college. Rather than seeing it as a handicap, I see diabetes as a fascinating, incredibly complex puzzle to be solved. Answers, no matter how trivial, have more potential benefits to other people than solving a crossword puzzle.

I've always enjoyed testing things. So of all the diseases I might have got, I'm lucky to have one that gives me an excuse to do a lot of tests. Of course not everyone has the same scientific approach to the disease, and some people do, in fact, suffer disabling consequences. But with good control, you will probably finally realize that you haven't gone blind, your kidneys are fine and you still have your feet. Your life may not be that much different from what it was before your diagnosis. In fact, with good control, you may even have more energy and feel healthier than you have in years.

Some people have met spouses as a result of being diagnosed with diabetes. Others have seen new careers open up. Some have discovered an interest in medical matters and have become specialist diabetic nurses, helping others deal with the disease. Some have even written books.

Letting off steam helps

The best way to overcome the initial depression is first of all to understand that it's a normal part of the mourning process and second to get in touch with other people who really *do* understand what you're going through, and this means other people with type 2 diabetes. As is true with other depressing situations like being widowed or losing a child, people who have never been in that situation can never really understand. Letting off steam, expressing your anger or your frustration or your depression to other people who understand, can be much more helpful than attending workshops run by well-intentioned health care people who usually don't have a clue about what it's actually like to live with diabetes.

Interestingly, some people who have had pancreas transplants so that they suddenly were no longer diabetic also go through a mourning process, in this case mourning the formerly diabetic person they were. Apparently, dealing with diabetes had become so much a part of who they were that even though they'd always wanted their diabetes to go away more than anything else in the world, when it actually did go away, they mourned their 'loss'.

Like any kind of mourning, mourning for your formerly non-diabetic self will eventually pass. In the meantime, remember that feeling blue after any major life change is normal. Don't worry that something is wrong. It's OK to be sad for a while. As is true after the death of a friend, it's better than pretending you don't care. Mourning helps with healing. You go through it, and then you come out the other side and get on with your life.

IN A SENTENCE:

Mourning the loss of your nondiabetic self is normal after you're diagnosed, but after you work through this stage, you may feel better than you have in years.

learning

What Treatment Should I Get?

YOU'VE PROBABLY started out trying diet and exercise, maybe with an oral drug, as the first treatment of your disease. Now you may begin to wonder if this is the best treatment for you.

The best treatment for type 2 diabetes is the one that gets *your* blood glucose (BG) levels as close to normal as possible. This will minimize glucotoxicity (see Week 2) and reduce the chances you'll ever develop diabetic complications. Today, there are many choices available, and what works best for someone else might not be the best choice for you.

The classic treatment of type 2 diabetes was to start with a trial of diet and exercise. Then you came back in a few weeks or months, and if your BG levels hadn't come down, you would be given a sulphony-lurea (see Week 3). If this didn't bring your BG levels down sufficiently, you would be given a big lecture about the importance of sticking to your diet and getting more exercise or you'd have to take insulin injections. Then you'd come back in a few months, and if your BG levels still hadn't come down, you'd be told you had to give yourself insulin.

Drugs may work for you

Just with the brief review in Week 3, you can see that there is a huge choice of treatments, with many different classes of drugs and different drugs within each class. Because of the multiple effects of the diabetes drugs and because people have different types of diabetes, the choice depends on your particular medical needs as well as your lifestyle and personality.

Quite often, you will be started out on one oral drug, and then if this doesn't bring the BG level down enough, another drug that works in a different way (see Week 3) will be *added*. For example, you might take metformin to keep your liver from producing too much glucose and a glitazone to try to reduce your insulin resistance (IR).

You can see now why something like the C-peptide test (see Day 5) might be useful. If you find you produce a lot of C-peptide, it means you're producing a lot of insulin, which means you've got a lot of IR. Thus starting off with a glitazone drug that reduces IR might make more sense for you than a sulphonylurea that would just make your insulin levels even higher.

But glitazones often cause weight gain. If weight loss is a major goal for you, metformin might be a better choice. If you're not seriously overweight and a C-peptide test shows that you're not producing a lot of insulin, then a drug that helps your sluggish beta cells out might be a better choice for you. If your C-peptide level is not high, you might want to start right off with insulin.

Insulin is another choice

Insulin? Some people think that insulin is used only for type 1 diabetes, and that if you take insulin you've converted from type 2 into type 1. This is not true. Many people with type 2 diabetes take insulin, either because none of the other options have worked for them or because they prefer using it.

Doesn't that mean painful injections? Why would anyone want to do that when all these drugs are available? Well, first let's try to understand the rationale for the classic diet-and-exercise, then oral drugs, then insulin approach to treatment.

Fear of needles. Most doctors assume that patients just diagnosed with diabetes aren't really champing at the bit for a chance to give themselves injections with hypodermic needles. There is some justification for this view. Some people are scared of shots of any kind, not to mention having to inject themselves. In the old days, needles were large and used over and over again until they got dull and hurt. And some type 2 patients do, in fact, burst into uncontrollable sobs when told their oral drugs aren't doing the job and they'll have to start injecting themselves with insulin. In many cases their sorrow comes not only from their fear of giving themselves shots but also from a sense that because they didn't succeed with the oral drugs, they are failures.

Unfortunately, because of the common fear of needles, some doctors use the idea of insulin injections as a threat. 'If you can't lose at least a couople of kilograms by next month, I'll have to put you on insulin.' This simply reinforces the idea that injecting insulin is a form of punishment, and a horrible fate.

But remember glucotoxicity and beta cell 'exhaustion'. They mean that **the longer your beta cells are exposed to a high-glucose environment, the greater the chance they will suffer irreversible damage**. Say you are started on a diet and exercise program for a couple of months and the BG levels are still too high, so you take oral drug A for another few months. If this doesn't work, you take a combination of drug A plus drug B. All this means your beta cells are going to be exposed to high BG levels for months until you find a treatment plan that works for you.

Starting on insulin. For this reason, some people feel that the best solution is to *start out on insulin* to bring the BG down to normal levels right away, and to maintain it there for a while. This reduces glucotoxicity and gives the beta cells time to rest and recover a bit from the stress they've been under for however long you've had diabetes without knowing it.

Then after the BG levels have been normal for a while, in many cases you can stop using the insulin and use only oral drugs or just diet and exercise. It may be scary to think about using insulin right from the start, but ironically, it might be the best way to ensure that you won't have to use it for long.

Injecting insulin isn't the painful and time-consuming procedure that it used to be. Syringes are disposable, and the needles are extremely thin. You can even get 'insulin pens' with the insulin already in a syringe so you can dial up the amount of insulin you need at a particular time.

There are some advantages to insulin therapy. Insulin is a natural substance, and there is less likelihood of unknown long-term side effects, as there always is with new drugs.

There are also some disadvantages. Like the sulphonylureas, insulin has the potential to produce *hypoglycaemia*. In addition, many people say their appetite increases when they take insulin, and they gain weight, just as they do when they take the sulpho-nylurea drugs, which make your own pancreas produce more insulin. If you're overweight to start with, and if this is contribut-ing to your IR, then insulin might not be the best way to start. However, this effect on appetite is not universal: 'It was certainly my experience that before I went on insulin I was *ravenously* hungry, and after I started, my appetite went *way* down, and 11 kilograms melted off like ice in a firestorm!' said Natalie S.

Hyperinsulinaemia. Another controversial aspect of insulin treatment is the question of **hyperinsulinaemia**, or high levels of insulin in the bloodstream. Some people think that high insulin levels cause heart disease. When you have type 2 diabetes, you are usually insulin resistant, and if you inject insulin you might have to use a lot more than the normal amounts that people with type 1 diabetes, and no IR, would use.

Other people think that high insulin levels do not *cause* heart disease. They say that it is the underlying problem, IR, that is associated with heart disease. People who are insulin resistant but have well-functioning beta cells produce more insulin than people without IR. Thus the high insulin levels that have been associated with heart disease may simply be a sign that these people have IR. This question has not yet been resolved.

Demanding insulin. Some people think the benefits outweigh the disadvantages. 'The idea of sticking needles into my body didn't thrill me, but I wanted to control the disease, and not have it control me!' said Carol M. 'Since going on insulin I feel so much better! I feel like I have "me" back again! I was in a fog all the time on the pills, and now I feel so much clearer and with more energy.' Some people actually *ask* to be allowed to use insulin, because they are not satisfied with their quality of life when using diet and exercise or some of the oral drugs. Sometimes they actually have to argue with their doctors, who still believe that insulin is a last resort, something to inflict on a patient who has failed to control the diabetes by any other way.

'I asked for insulin back in 1991 and it took me several months,' said Eleanor H. 'My doctor kept procrastinating, wanting me to "wait a little longer", try different drugs and so on. So I went to see another doctor. I found a young female doctor, who had only recently started work as a GP, and I looked her square in the eye and asked her to prescribe insulin for me. She said, "OK." It has been smooth sailing ever since. I love not having to take a bunch of pills and having direct control over my BG.'

Resting beta cells. You may not be as eager for insulin as Eleanor was, but even so, you should never look at insulin as a punishment for your sins. Insulin is just one of many kinds of treatment available for type 2 diabetes today. In some ways, it's easier to use. The many different kinds of insulin available today make its use very flexible, and once you learn how to count carbohydrates, it gives you a lot more choices of what to eat. Perhaps the best reason to think about using insulin right away is that insulin is kind to your beta cells. Even though there is now little concrete evidence that other types of treatment wear out the beta cells, we know that glucotoxicity is not good for them. If you can get your

BG levels down to normal with diet and exercise, or with one of the other drugs, that's good. But if this doesn't happen quickly for you, going right to insulin might be something you should consider.

If you *do* decide to try insulin, don't settle for one of the old once-a-day injection routines, in which you have to eat even when you're not hungry. This can make you gain weight. Like oral drugs, insulins now come in many varieties, and their usage can be customized for *you*.

Insulin may not be best for everyone with type 2 diabetes. For instance, if you have a tremendous amount of IR and need to lose a lot of weight, a glitazone that reduces IR, or metformin, which reduces appetite, might be better choices.

Just remember that insulin doesn't mean you are too weak to conquer your diabetes without it. Insulin means you are strong enough to take charge of your diabetes and take care of your beta cells. Someday you may be glad you did.

IN A SENTENCE:

> *No diabetes treatment is best for every patient, so you and your doctor have to figure out which one matches your own particular needs.*

MILESTONE

It's now a month after your diagnosis, and you're beginning to get a handle on controlling your diabetes:

○ YOU KNOW THAT YOU MUST BE IN CHARGE.

○ YOU UNDERSTAND MORE ABOUT WHY IT'S IMPORTANT TO KEEP YOUR BLOOD GLUCOSE LEVELS CLOSE TO NORMAL.

○ YOU HAVE BEEN INTRODUCED TO THE MAIN CLASSES OF DIABETES TREATMENT AND THEIR PROS AND CONS.

○ YOU UNDERSTAND THAT IT'S NORMAL TO BE A LITTLE DEPRESSED AT FIRST, BUT THIS PHASE SHOULD PASS.

Diabetes ABCs

YOU MAY wonder why I'm waiting until your second month with diabetes to give you the diabetes ABCs. Well, I'm assuming the basics summarized in this chapter were described to you by your doctor or a nurse, or in some of the many pamphlets they probably gave you right after your diagnosis. What I've tried to do so far is to discuss some of the things these people *didn't* talk about.

But now is a good time to take stock, go back and review some of the basics and make sure you understand what they are. You may have been in too much shock in those first days to take it all in, or maybe you were still in denial and thought it didn't apply to you. In any case, it never hurts to review the basic stuff in case something was left out in your initial training.

If you want more basic information, one good source is Diabetes UK (see Resources section for further details).

Keep your blood glucose levels as close to normal as possible

I may sound like a broken record, but this is just about the most important thing you can do to control your diabetes. Keeping your blood glucose (BG) levels in the normal range will almost ensure that you'll never develop diabetes complications. If you already had early complications when you were diagnosed, it can even reverse some complications like neuropathy.

Test regularly

Everyone is different. As described in the Learning section, there are many different kinds of diabetes. Furthermore, everyone has a different personality, lifestyle and budget. What works for someone else might not work for you. YMMV (Your Mileage May Vary). Don't take anyone's word for it. The best way for you to find out how your diabetes responds to various factors is to use your meter and test.

Keep records of your BG numbers (see Month 9 for a discussion of sophisticated record-keeping systems), along with brief descriptions of any unusual events in your life, so you'll learn how these events affect your BG levels.

Stick to your diet as closely as possible, but don't be afraid to modify it based on your test results

This is probably not something your doctor would have told you. The basic diabetes books usually say, 'Discuss this with your health care team, who will work out a plan that is right for you.' Many people don't really have a 'team', and doctors are often allowed to spend only a certain amount of time with a patient. Some of them don't really know much about nutrition.

I don't mean you should throw away your pills and suddenly adopt a crazy 'Lose 20 pounds in three days' weight-loss plan that involves eating only grapefruit and coffee grounds if the readings on your meter tell you that your initial diet is not controlling your BG levels.

But it never hurts to try small modifications, one at a time, to see if you can improve your BG readings. For example, if you find that the half a banana approved on your diet makes your BG readings go high but strawberries do not, substitute strawberries for bananas. Then if you make a lot of modifications and your BG levels improve significantly, make an appointment with your doctor and see if you can reduce or eliminate any drugs you may be taking.

Move as much as you can

Unfortunately for those of us who hate it, exercise is something that seems to benefit everyone. Not everyone is able to do strenuous exercise. But move as much as you can. It really will help you feel better and control your BG levels.

Be alert for low blood sugar incidents

If you aren't using insulin or taking sulphonylurea drugs that make you produce insulin all day, you probably don't need to worry about hypoglycaemia (low BG levels). Drugs like metformin or the glitazones (see Week 3) aren't supposed to cause hypoglycaemia. However, some people have reported incidents of hypoglycaemia when they were taking only metformin, and sometimes even when taking no diabetes drugs at all. So you should be aware of its existence, even if its likelihood is low.

If you sometimes go low, it's wise to wear a diabetic identification bracelet so people won't think you are drunk if it happens in public. Sources include MedicAlert (see Resources section).

Hypoglycaemia is usually defined as a BG level below about 3.5 mmol/L (millimols per litre). However, the symptoms depend more on the *rate* at which the BG level is falling than on the actual BG level itself. This makes sense. If you were several metres away from a child who was starting down a slide that would dump her into a pile of broken glass, you'd want to start running towards the slide to catch her *before* she reached the bottom. If you started when she was at the bottom of the slide, it would be too late. So too, the body is very intelligent, and if it senses that your BG level is falling rapidly, it wants to start correcting it *before* it's gone so low that you pass out. If the body waited until the BG level hit 3.5 mmol/L, you might have gone dangerously low before the corrective measures had taken effect.

Thus if you've just been diagnosed with BG levels in the 20s and you suddenly drop down to 10, you might feel symptoms of hypoglycaemia even though your BG level is still way above normal. As your body gets used to lower BG levels, you won't feel symptoms until you reach 3.5 or below.

Symptoms of hypoglycaemia vary slightly from person to person. Because some of the BG correction is a result of the production of adrenaline, many of the symptoms are similar to the 'fight-or-flight' reaction described in Day 7: shakiness, sweating, rapid heartbeat, anxiety and a feeling of nervousness or impending doom. Some people also feel hungry or irritable or act confused.

Because hypoglycaemia means the brain isn't getting enough glucose, when you go very low your thinking may be impaired. When Amal K. had hypoglycaemia, she saw an orange sweet wrapper on the kitchen table and concluded that the world was going to end in fire. When Karen G. had hypoglycaemia while travelling in France, she looked out the window and asked her husband why they were in Russia. He knew she was low and handed her a sweet.

Learn how much correction you need for hypoglycaemia

If you *do* get hypoglycaemia, you need to eat some fast-acting carbohydrate to bring your BG levels back to normal, and you should keep some with you at all times. Don't overdo it. Because of the feeling of panic that sometimes accompanies hypoglycaemia, some people eat and eat until their BG level is back to normal. And then it keeps going up and up and up. Remember, it takes a few minutes for anything you eat to get into your bloodstream.

One way to deal with this is to follow the 15-15 rule: eat about 15 grams of carbohydrate, wait 15 minutes and then retest. If you still need more correction, eat another 15 grams and test again. Glucose gets into the bloodstream the fastest, and you can buy glucose tablets or gels and know exactly how much glucose you're taking.

A better way is to test yourself *before* you have hypoglycaemia to find out how much correction you need. Sometime when your BG level is stable and not high, eat one glucose tablet and see how much your BG goes up. If it doesn't go up much, try two and then three, until you find out how many you'd need to take to raise your BG level by a certain amount.

When you have hypoglycaemia, don't eat something with a lot of fat or protein, like ice cream. The fat will slow down the emptying of the stomach and delay the effect of the carbohydrate. If you're taking an alpha-glucosidase inhibitor (see Week 3), starch or sucrose won't be able to help with hypoglycaemia (the inhibitor keeps the carbohydrate from being broken down into sugars) and you'll have to rely on glucose.

Liquids are usually digested faster than solids, and some people find that skimmed milk raises the BG level faster than anything else. The protein in the milk also adds some staying power.

If you have really serious problems with hypoglycaemia, you can get a prescription for glucagon, the hormone that counteracts the effects of insulin, and someone can inject it when you need it.

Learn the signs of high blood glucose levels

Different people react differently to **hyperglycaemia** (high BG levels). Some people get very sleepy, but others do not. Blurred vision is common, but it may come hours after a high-BG episode. Thirst and frequent urination are symptoms of sustained high BG levels.

Symptoms of high BG levels in one person might indicate low BG levels in another, so it's important to learn what your own symptoms are. Test, and even if you can't bring the BG level down right away, you'll know that whatever you did before the episode of hyperglycaemia is something you should try to avoid.

Be especially careful when you're sick

Illness is a stress that increases insulin resistance (IR) and may make your BG levels go up. In addition, if you're vomiting and have diarrhoea, you may get dehydrated, and dehydration also causes IR. Thus you shouldn't stop taking your medication when you're sick. In fact, if you're seriously ill, you may need to take insulin on a temporary basis to keep your BG levels from going too high.

But you also don't want to risk going too low from insulin or sulphonylureas if you're having trouble keeping any food in your stomach. In this case, work out ahead of time what kinds of foods you can usually tolerate when you're feeling sick and how much you'd need to keep you from going low. Make sure you keep them in the house, and instruct others in the family not to eat them because they're emergency rations for you. Maybe you can keep them in a special place.

If you don't live near a pharmacy, you should also stock sugar-free versions of any standard cough or cold remedies that you expect to take. Most cough syrups and drops contain a lot of sugar. One regular cough drop probably won't cause much harm, but many could.

Even if you're not being treated with insulin or sulphonylureas and don't need to worry about hypoglycaemia, vomiting and diarrhoea can also cause problems with dehydration, which can be serious if severe.

People with type 1 diabetes have to worry about something called **diabetic ketoacidosis (DKA)** which can be very serious. In the absence of insulin, the body burns fats and produces very high levels of *ketones*. Because the ketones are acidic, the blood becomes too acid, hence the name *ketoacidosis*.

When you have type 2 diabetes, you're not apt to get ketoacidosis, even though your body can produce some ketones when you don't eat at all, you eat a lot of fat or you go on a low-carbohydrate diet. The level of ketones that the body can produce depends on the amount of fatty acids in the blood. High levels of ketones stimulate the production of insulin, and it takes only tiny amounts of insulin to slow down the production of these fatty acids. Thus as long as you can produce any insulin at all, you can be in **ketosis** but your body has a fail-safe mechanism to protect against ketoacidosis. Many people, even some dieticians and doctors, confuse the two terms.

If you have type 2 diabetes, you can almost always produce enough insulin to stop ketoacidosis, even if you can't produce enough to deal with a lot of carbohydrate in your diet.

With type 2 diabetes, however, a related problem called *hyperosmolar hyperglycaemic nonketotic syndrome (HHNS)* can occur. It's rare, but when it does occur, the fatality rate is high, so you should know about it and become familiar with the symptoms.

HHNS can happen when you let your BG level go very high. Your body tries to get rid of the excess glucose by dumping it into the urine. This makes you lose a lot of fluid and you get dehydrated and thirsty. Thus the beginning of HHNS is very similar to what may have happened before you were diagnosed.

The problem with HHNS is when you are sick, especially with vomiting and diarrhoea, and may not be able to drink a lot of fluids to rehydrate your body. Maybe you're sleeping a lot or maybe you can't even keep liquids down. So your BG levels go even higher, you get more dehydrated, and as a result you may get confused or even go into a coma. If not treated, HHNS can be fatal.

Unlike DKA, HHNS usually has a slow onset, over several days, and occurs mostly in elderly people, especially when they're in nursing homes and not getting the attention they need. But if you're sick, make sure you keep track of your BG levels. If you're too sick to test, ask someone else to do it for you. If your BG levels go high (over 16.7 mmol/L) and don't come down, call a doctor for advice.

Have regular medical checks

Diabetes UK recommends that when you are newly diagnosed your diabetes care team should:

Give you a full medical examination.

Work with you to make a programme of care that suits you

and includes diabetes management goals – this may take the form of a record for you to keep.

Arrange for you to talk with a diabetes specialist nurse (or practice nurse) who will explain what diabetes is and discuss your individual treatment and the equipment you will need to use.

Arrange for you to talk with a state-registered dietitian who will give you advice about how to fit your usual diet in with diabetes – a follow-up meeting should be arranged for more detailed advice.

Tell you about your diabetes and the beneficial effects of a healthy diety, exercise and good diabetes control.

Discuss the effects of diabetes on your job, driving, insurance, prescription charges and, if you are a driver, whether you need to inform the DVLA (Driving and Vehicle Licensing Authority) and your insurance company.

Provide you with regular and appropriate information and education, on food and footcare for example.

Then Diabetes UK recommends that on a regular basis your diabetes care team should:

Provide continuity of care, ideally from the same doctors and nurses – if this is not possible, the doctors or nurses whom you are seeing should be fully aware of your medical history and background.

Work with you to continually review your care programme, including your diabetes management goals.

Let you share in decisions about your treatment or care.

Once a year you should have a formal annual review by a doctor experienced in diabetes. This should include the following:

You should have a haemoglobin A1c test.

You should have urine and blood tests of kidney function.

Cholesterol and triglycerides should be measured.

Blood pressure should be taken.

Legs and feet should be examined to check your skin, circulation and nerve supply. If necessary, you should be referred to a state-registered chiropodist/podiatrist.

Eyes should be examined regularly through a 'fundoscopy'

review, in which pupils are dilated to enable the optometrist/ophthal-mologist to detect any early changes at the back of the eye (retinopa-thy). Photographs may be taken to record the appearance at the back of your eyes.

The review should also leave enough time to discuss lifestyle issues.

In the first year, you should visit your doctor more often than six months until you have a treatment plan that works for you. Many people have an A1c test every three months.

Control your blood pressure and cholesterol

Having diabetes means you're at greater risk for heart disease. So make sure your blood pressure and cholesterol levels, as well as your BG levels, are tested, and take corrective action if necessary. This is known as the 'ABCs of diabetes' for A1c, Blood pressure, and Cholesterol.

Take care of your feet

When they hear about diabetes, some people think it means you're going to lose your feet. It can happen if you don't keep your BG levels under control. But it's not inevitable.

One problem with some books about diabetes is that they don't distinguish between different types of diabetes, different degrees of severity within the types or the length of time you have had diabetes. They just lump everyone together as 'diabetics'.

Thus some people will say diabetics should never go barefoot. Diabetics should use a mirror to examine their feet every day. Diabetics should wear special padded socks. Diabetics should call a doctor whenever they have a cut on their feet.

These admonitions *do* make sense if you have any signs of neuropathy or impaired circulation to the feet. If you have no feeling in your feet, you can easily let a small stone in a shoe, or even a callus, cause an abrasion that will turn into an ulcer and take forever to heal. Such ulcers can cause gangrene, and this is what may result in amputations.

If you think the feeling in your feet is impaired, make sure your doctor checks your feet for any problems at every visit. You can also get a small filament to check the feeling in your own feet at home. The filament is designed to produce an exact amount of pressure when it is pushed against the foot. As long as you can feel the filament, you should have enough sensation left to feel small cuts and bruises. So do be careful with your feet. If you get a sore, keep an eye on it and see a doctor if it doesn't heal quickly. Use a filament to see if you have any loss of sensation. But if the feeling in your feet is still normal, don't go overboard with the mirror routine every morning. Do something you enjoy instead.

Keep track of your total health

Remember, you're chairman of the board. **Keep track of all your health records yourself and know where you stand**. This makes it easier if you move or have to change doctors. It also gives you a better sense of where you are with your health and may let you know if it's time to change health care providers.

Stop smoking

If you smoke, you're already quite aware that you shouldn't. Everyone is already nagging you about it.

You may feel you've had to give up enough already. You're trying to eat less of your favourite sugary, starchy and fatty foods. You're trying to sacrifice precious free time so you can exercise more. If you have high blood pressure, you've probably been told to cut out the salt.

Now they want you to stop smoking too? It may seem like asking a lot, but it's really important. Smoking causes some of the very same problems that high BG levels do. If you've got diabetes, your chances of having a heart attack are already two to four times higher than normal. Add smoking to the diabetes and you're really asking for trouble.

It may be difficult. But if there's any way you can do it, dump the cigarettes. According to the American Diabetes Association, almost all diabetic people who need amputations are smokers.

IN A SENTENCE:

> *Basic diabetes care means learning how to keep your blood glucose levels as close to normal as possible using diet, exercise and medication if necessary; making sure you get regular medical checkups; taking care of your feet and being alert for high or low blood sugar levels, especially when you're sick.*

learning

Types of Diabetes

As you learned in Day 1, diabetes comes in many forms. The main distinction is, of course, between type 1 diabetes, the *autoimmune* kind that always requires insulin, and type 2 diabetes, which can sometimes be controlled with diet and exercise alone. Some types of diabetes, for example gestational diabetes, are now considered neither type 1 nor type 2. However, because such patients can often control with diet and exercise, in some ways they are more similar to type 2.

Overweight type 2 is the most common

The most common form of type 2 diabetes (almost 90 per cent have this form) involves insulin resistance (IR). (Some people refer to this as type 2R for *resistant*, but this term is not in general use. You may come across it when reading older books.)

When you have this kind of diabetes, you tend to be overweight when you are diagnosed, and losing weight may help you control your blood glucose (BG) levels, especially if you were diagnosed at the very early stages, while you still had a lot of beta cell function remaining.

In the early stages of this kind of diabetes, the body tries to compensate for the IR by producing more insulin than normal. Thus your C-peptide levels (meaning also your insulin levels; see Day 5;) are usually higher than normal. However, if you have had this kind of diabetes for a long time without knowing it, glucotoxicity and beta cell failure (see Week 2) may have destroyed enough beta cell function that your C-peptide level is normal, or even below normal, as I illustrated in Figure 2 in Week 2.

The important thing is to keep track of your BG levels, and if they don't come down pretty quickly with whatever treatment you start with, don't wait. Try something else. There are a lot of choices today.

Some thin type 2s don't produce enough insulin

Not everyone with type 2 diabetes is overweight when diagnosed. Some (a minority) are even quite thin, and the IR is normal. (Again, some people call this type of diabetes type 2S for *sensitive*, or 2D for *deficient*, but this terminology is uncommon.) If you have this kind of type 2 diabetes, it means that for some unknown reason, and probably for many different reasons in different people, your beta cells simply aren't producing enough insulin, especially after meals. In this case your C-peptide levels would be in the normal range.

Some people initially diagnosed with this kind of type 2 diabetes turn out to have LADA, a form of type 1 diabetes.

LADA is really type 1

LADA stands for *latent autoimmune diabetes of adults*. Like type 1 diabetes, it is an autoimmune disease in which your own immune system destroys your beta cells. So it is really a form of type 1 diabetes that occurs in older people. For some unknown reason, LADA usually proceeds much slower than typical type 1 diabetes in children, and because LADA occurs in adults, many people with LADA are initially diagnosed as having common garden-variety type 2 diabetes. Thus some people call it 'type 1.5'.

If you have LADA and your doctor thinks you have type 2 diabetes, you may be prescribed various oral medications and told to diet and exercise, but the medications won't work very well or very long. Don't feel bad. It's not your fault. It's just a different kind of diabetes.

One way to see if you have LADA is to test your C-peptide level. If the level is close to the bottom of the normal range, that's a good indication. Another way is to test for anti-GAD (see Day 5) antibodies. If you have the antibodies, you probably have LADA.

If you have LADA, eventually all the oral drugs will stop working entirely, and you will have to start using insulin. You're better off going right to insulin to give your pancreas a rest and help preserve the beta cells you have left. Type 1 diabetes is easier to control when you still have a little bit of beta cell function remaining, as many people with type 1 do.

Gestational diabetes may be an early warning sign

Gestational diabetes is not really type 2 diabetes but a form of diabetes that occurs in a pregnant woman and usually goes away after the baby is born. However, a woman who has had gestational diabetes is at much higher risk for developing type 2 diabetes later in life: between 40 and 70 per cent of such women eventually do.

In a sense, gestational diabetes is an early warning sign that tells you that you don't have much pancreatic reserve. What this means is that for genetic reasons, your pancreas is able to cope just fine as long as you don't make extra demands on it.

During pregnancy, IR normally increases because of increases in the levels of various counterregulatory hormones that are necessary for the growth of the baby. In a person with a strong pancreas, this is no problem. But if you don't have much pancreatic reserve, this extra stress may be just enough to push you over into diabetes. When the baby is born and the hormones abate, the IR becomes normal and the diabetes usually disappears.

However, if other stresses occur in the future, for example, surgery or a bad infection, or extra IR from being overweight, that may be enough to push you into a diabetic state again.

Thus if you've had gestational diabetes, it is important to work hard to keep active and keep your weight at a normal level to reduce the chances that you'll ever become diabetic again.

Because the effect of some of the oral diabetes drugs on the foetus is not known, if you have gestational diabetes you will be asked to control with diet and exercise or, if that doesn't work, with insulin.

Type 2 diabetes in children is increasing

Unfortunately, type 2 diabetes is being diagnosed more and more frequently in children. The most common form of type 2 diabetes in children is associated with obesity, often in ethnic groups that recently adopted a high-calorie, low-physical-labour lifestyle. Such children sometimes have signs of *acanthosis nigricans*, which is a soft, velvety darkening of the skin, especially on the neck and under the arms. Sometimes parents think it's dirt and try to scrub it off. Acanthosis nigricans is a sign of severe IR. Anyone with such signs should try hard to lose weight and get more exercise to avoid getting overt diabetes.

MODY stands for *maturity-onset diabetes of the young* and refers to a very specific type of diabetes that is inherited as a dominant gene. This means you only need to inherit a gene from one parent to get the disease.

There are a lot of subtypes of MODY, for example MODY1, MODY2 and so forth, and more is known about the genetics of some of these MODY subtypes than is known about common or garden variety type 2 diabetes. Different genes that cause MODY have been identified in different families with MODY.

MODY is fairly rare, and it is no longer considered type 2 diabetes. I mention it because you may run across the term in your reading. Some people have used it to refer to all children who don't have type 1, regardless of the cause.

Steroids can cause diabetes

Steroids like cortisone or prednisone cause IR and if taken for long periods of time can cause *steroid diabetes*. If you stop taking the steroid drugs, the diabetes usually goes away. But if you let your BG levels remain high for long enough, the resulting gluco-toxicity and beta cell failure may mean that your diabetes will be permanent.

Technically steroid diabetes is no longer considered type 2 diabetes, but because it's not type 1 and you may not need insulin, many people group it with type 2.

Haemochromatosis causes diabetes

Haemochromatosis is a genetic disorder that makes you accu-mulate iron. It's also called *iron overload disease* or *bronze diabetes*. The huge stores of iron that accumulate in the organs damage various organs, including the pancreas, and diabetes can be one result.

If untreated, this disease can be serious, even fatal. If detected, it can be controlled simply by giving blood periodically to get rid of the excess iron in your system. Lab tests for an iron-carrying protein called *ferritin* can diagnose the problem.

Polycystic ovary syndrome causes infertility

Polycystic ovary syndrome (or *disease*) (PCOS), also called *Stein-Leventhal syndrome*, is a disease of women characterized by IR and resulting in high insulin levels, irregular monthly periods and infertility, acne, excess body hair and thinning hair on the head and abdominal obesity, but as with type 2 diabetes, not everyone with the syndrome is overweight. It seems that in women with a genetic predisposition, high insulin levels stimulate the formation of too many male hormones (androgens), and these cause the symptoms.

More than a quarter of women with PCOS develop diabetes by the age of 30 years. The treatment is weight reduction (to reduce the extra weight-induced IR) and insulin-sensitizing drugs such as metformin or the glitazones (see Week 3). Some suggest low-carbohydrate diets to reduce insulin levels. Sometimes the drugs can restore fertility, which is listed as a side effect of these drugs, so if you have PCOS and take one of these drugs, be prepared.

Impaired glucose tolerance is the first step on the way to diabetes

Impaired glucose tolerance means that your fasting BG levels are within normal limits, and at the two-hour point in a glucose tolerance test your BG levels are not at diabetic levels (more than 11 mmol/L), but they don't fall below 7.8 by that time.

It's really the first step on the way to full-blown diabetes, and anyone who has impaired glucose tolerance should work like the dickens to do whatever is necessary to improve the BG levels. At this stage of the disease, you usually have a lot of beta cell function remaining, and sometimes just losing some weight and exercising more can keep you from ever developing diabetes. If you wait until your BG levels are quite high, it may be too late.

Impaired fasting glucose is a warning sign

Impaired fasting glucose means your fasting BG level is above the real normal limit (6 mmol/L) but not high enough for a formal definition of diabetes (7 mmol/L). As with impaired glucose tolerance, this is a warning sign that you'd better do something quickly to avoid progressing to diabetes.

Some health care organizations spend a lot of time defining limits for these various stages of disease. So if Toby has a fasting

BG level of 6.9 and Ben has a fasting BG level of 7.1, they'll say that Ben has diabetes but Toby doesn't. In fact, they probably have just about the same level of BG control and should take the same precautions to keep the condition under control.

This is the stage of diabetes that some used to call 'a touch of sugar' or 'borderline diabetes' so patients didn't take it seriously and usually progressed quickly into officially diagnosed diabetes.

There are many other kinds of diabetes

Many different diseases, especially those that cause abnormal levels of the various counterregulatory hormones like growth hormone (increased in acromegaly), cortisol (increased in Cushing's disease) and adrenaline (increased in pheochromocytoma), can cause forms of diabetes. Other diseases that disrupt the delicate balance between various hormones, or tumours that cause increased secretion of hormones like glucagon, can also cause diabetes. Most of these conditions are uncommon.

Damage to the pancreas from accidents or other diseases can also cause diabetes. In addition to steroids, some other drugs can also cause diabetes.

Defects in other BG-controlling substances, some of which are known and some of which have probably not yet been discovered, can also cause forms of diabetes.

Diabetes is really a symptom

As you can see from this brief discussion, diabetes is really not one disease, but many diseases. In fact, *diabetes is really not a disease as much as a symptom of many diseases*. And there are many people who don't fit neatly into any of the official categories, for example, a thin person with or an overweight person without IR. What diabetes really means is that your BG level is too high. Many different diseases can make your BG level go too high. So it's not really surprising that different people react differently to different diets and treatments. They may have different types of type 2 diabetes.

Most treatments of type 2 diabetes today are aimed at controlling the main symptom of this spectrum of diseases: high BG levels. This is, of course, extremely important. High BG levels are lethal.

The glitazone drugs (see Month 2) are the first type of drug aimed at controlling the cause of one type 2 subtype: insulin resistance. Researchers are studying other causes of type 2 diabetes, and many different genes have been suggested. Unlike MODY, which is caused by a mutation in a single gene, many kinds of type 2 diabetes are probably caused by more than one gene. As the research continues, more underlying causes of the other subtypes will undoubtedly be discovered and drugs will be developed to treat them more specifically.

Until then, don't despair if your particular type of diabetes doesn't react like someone else's. You're not mad. You may just have what Natalie S. calls 'type weird'. The cause of your diabetes may be slightly different from the cause of someone else's. Test your BG levels and find out how *your* diabetes reacts. No one can ask for more.

IN A SENTENCE:

> *There are many different types of diabetes, so you may react differently to a diet or a treatment than someone else does.*

MONTH **3**

living

Will Supplements Help My Diabetes?

SHORTLY AFTER you've been diagnosed with diabetes, you'll probably begin to notice all sorts of articles about vitamins and minerals and other supplements that are supposed to help control blood glucose (BG) levels. Do they work? Should you try them? Which ones?

Controlled trials provide evidence

As is true with most 'complementary' or 'alternative' medicine, opinions about some vitamins and minerals, as well as herbs, vary widely from people who swear they couldn't control their BG levels without them to people who say they're useless and maybe even harmful in excess. In many cases, the supporters are backed by anecdotal evidence, without controlled scientific trials.

When doctors prescribe any medication to a

patient, they need to be extremely careful. Hence mainstream doctors usually recommend only drugs that have been shown to be effective through randomized controlled clinical trials published in *peer-reviewed* journals. This is called *evidence-based medicine.*

A **controlled trial** means you don't just give a drug to a bunch of people and see if they get better. They might have got better anyway, or maybe they got better because of the *placebo effect*, the psychological effect that a fake (*placebo*) pill or 'sugar pill' can have on a patient who thinks it's really medicine. In a controlled trial, half of a group of randomly chosen patients are given a study drug and the other half (carefully matched by age, sex, health and so forth) a placebo. The patients aren't told if they are getting the drug. A **double-blind** controlled trial is even more rigorous. In this case, even the doctors and nurses don't know which patients actually got the real drug so they won't unconsciously communicate their hopes or fears to the patients.

When the trial is concluded, the researchers write up the results and submit the paper to a medical journal. The journal, in turn, sends it out to other doctors in the field (so-called peers) to ask whether they think the paper's methods were valid. If the reviewers say the research seems good, then the journal publishes the results.

Usually just one study, even if it's in a peer-reviewed journal, doesn't prove something works. Sometimes different research groups get different results or come to different conclusions, so several studies showing an effect or lack thereof is more trustworthy.

Doing controlled drug trials is expensive and time-consuming, and the trials are usually financed by drug companies. Drug companies don't want to spend money doing trials of drugs they can't patent. So the effect on diabetes of many of the supplements that some people say help has never been studied in such trials. There are usually more studies of vitamins and minerals than of obscure herbs from faraway places.

The other type of evidence for and against various alternative remedies is what's called *anecdotal evidence.* This means your aunt

Agnes told you that honey and vinegar make a good cough syrup and cinnamon helped your uncle Albert keep his BG levels down. Some people call such treatments *folk remedies*. Sometimes folk remedies turn out to have a basis in fact. For example, aspirin is closely related to a drug found in the bark of the white willow tree, which Native Americans used for pain and fever, and metformin is closely related to a drug found in goat's rue (also known as French lilac), which has been used as a folk remedy for diabetes since the Middle Ages.

Decisions about using supplements are complex

When supplements haven't been studied in controlled trials, most doctors won't recommend them. Does this mean they don't work? No. Does this mean they do work? No. In many cases we simply don't know.

You've got to decide for yourself how much risk you're willing to assume. If you're the supercautious type, you may want to wait until studies show that a remedy is safe and effective. If you enjoy experimenting and are willing to risk damage to your own body, you may want to try every alternative drug on the market and see what happens. As some people say, 'My body, my science experiment.' Most people fall somewhere between these extremes.

If you do decide you want to try a supplement to help control your BG levels, the best way is to try one thing at a time and carefully keep track of your BG levels as well as your general health while you do. If you suddenly start taking 27 different vitamins and minerals and find that your BG levels go up or down, you'll never know which ones were responsible for the change and you may be paying for a lot for stuff you don't need.

Read as much as you can about each one before you make up your mind. One way to get a somewhat balanced view is to read all the promotional material provided by the peddlers of vitamins, minerals and herbs and then read the diatribes against them by conservative medical people and make up your own mind. If you have access to the Internet, you can visit a site called Quackwatch that discusses alternative treatments they think are particularly bad.

Keep in mind that studies *in vitro* (in glass, meaning they are done outside the body) are not always applicable to situations *in vivo* (in the living body). Similarly, studies done with mice do not always translate into human cures. Remember leptin? Certain strains of mice were found to be deficient in the hormone leptin, and giving them the hormone made them slim down. Everyone hoped it would work with overweight people. A tiny number of leptin-deficient people were discovered, and leptin did work with them. But leptin deficiency turned out not to be the primary cause of obesity in humans. Leptin resistance may be involved.

Supplements can be like Dr Jekyll and Mr Hyde

When you're reading about the effects of supplements on the human body, remember that the body is a masterpiece of balance. Sometimes a substance that works miracles when given in small amounts can be toxic when given in large amounts. For example, you need iron to transport oxygen to your tissues, but too much iron can kill you.

Sometimes substances that help one condition harm another. For example, some anti-inflammatory drugs that help arthritis may harm the kidney or liver. It's a trade-off. Usually your doctor studies the published reports and decides if the benefits from a drug are worth the risks of harm in your particular case. If you supplement on your own, you'll have to make those decisions yourself.

An example of possible good and bad effects is the **antioxidants** that many people take to fight **free radicals**. There is some evidence that when you have type 2 diabetes, you have more free radicals and fewer antioxidants than other people. The process of producing energy from food produces free radicals, and many people with type 2 diabetes have huge appetites, so metabolizing all this food might cause some of the extra free radicals. High BG levels have also been associated with increased free-radical levels, even in people without diabetes.

What are free radicals? Free radicals are highly reactive compounds with unpaired electrons. If you don't remember the details from a chemistry course, it's not important. What is important is that the free radicals, and we're especially concerned with *oxygen free radicals*, are highly reactive and can be toxic.

You can think of free radicals as little bombs. When they hit other molecules they 'explode,' and, like molecular werewolves, not only damage the other molecules, but turn the other molecules into free radicals themselves, thus starting a chain reaction. Free radicals can cause **plaques** on arterial walls, contributing to atherosclerosis, or mutations to your genes, causing cancer.

The body contains a lot of antioxidants designed to keep the free radicals under control. Fruits and vegetables also contain antioxidants. Unfortunately, modern living, including polluted air, cigarette smoking and other toxins, seems to increase the number of free radicals we normally have. And if you're limiting your intake of calories, you may not be able to eat a lot of fruits and vegetables, especially fruits. Thus extra antioxidant vitamins seem like a good idea.

But here's one problem. The cell uses free radical bombs to get rid of some unhealthy invaders of the body, including bacteria and cancer cells. In fact, some anticancer drugs and radiation treatments work by producing free radicals that damage rapidly dividing cancer cells. Thus some researchers say people undergoing such cancer therapy should avoid taking antioxidants during the therapy. Others say the opposite, that the antioxidants actually help destroy the cancer cells and protect the healthy cells.

How about when you're not taking anticancer drugs and you don't have cancer? Are antioxidants good or bad? Some are probably good. At this point in our knowledge, no one really knows the exact amounts that are best. It undoubtedly depends on your own individual physiology, diet, lifestyle and so forth. Taking a supplement containing antioxidants doesn't guarantee that they'll reach the particular tissues or cells that need them. You'll just have to decide whether you're going to be conservative or go out on a limb and spend a lot of money on antioxidant pills.

Read as much as you can about each one before you decide to take a lot of it. You'll find that opinions not only differ but change from year to year, sometimes from week to week, it seems. Sometimes study A says a supplement is beneficial and study B says it has no effect. This can be because different studies used different populations, different methods, different time periods or different definitions of 'beneficial'. For example, a study of the effect of a supplement on cardiovascular events could measure its effect on deaths from heart attacks in a 20-year period, the incidence of nonfatal heart attacks during a five-year period in men 35 to 60 with no previous heart disease, the rate of second heart attacks in elderly women during a three-year period or many other 'end points'. News reports tend to oversimplify. Whenever possible, try to read the original reports of studies that interest you.

You can take too much

If you take several supplements that have the same effect, the total dosage may be too high. This can happen with some supplements that 'thin' the blood, a popular term meaning they make it less likely to clot.

Heart attacks are caused by clots that clog a blood vessel in the heart, and strokes can be caused by clots that plug up vessels in the brain (*ischaemic strokes*). In both these cases, **blood thinners** are helpful because they discourage the formation of clots.

But strokes can also be caused by ruptured vessels that let the blood leak out. In these strokes, called *haemorrhagic strokes* (or 'bleeds'), if the blood doesn't clot to plug the hole, you will bleed to death. In this type of stroke, blood thinners are harmful. Too many blood thinners can also increase the severity of preexisting diabetic retinopathy.

Popular nonprescription blood thinners include aspirin, vitamin E, fish oils, fenugreek, ginger, garlic, and *Ginkgo biloba*. Taking one of these supplements might seem like a good idea, because when you have type 2 diabetes, your **platelets** may be 'stickier' than normal, meaning they're more apt to form clots. But if you take them all, you may be getting too much of a good thing and increasing your chances of stroke and worsening retinopathy.

Supplements can interact with prescription medications

Another potential problem with supplements is that they could interact with prescription medications you're already taking. For this reason, if you do decide to take supplements, it's a good idea to tell your doctor exactly what you're taking. If your doctor isn't familiar with the supplements, ask your pharmacist. It's a good idea to get all your prescriptions from the same place, so the pharmacists there can keep track of all the medications you're taking and be alert for possible interactions. If you're also buying your supplements there, the pharmacist should be willing to take some time to discuss them with you. It's not easy to find a pharmacist who has time to explain things to customers. If you do find such a person, make that your regular pharmacy.

If you have access to the Internet, there are sites where you can plug in the names of the supplements and drugs you're taking to see if there are known interactions. Search on 'drug-supplement interaction' to find current sites (see Month 12 for tips on Internet searching).

There are no easy answers when deciding whether or not nonprescription supplements are for you. It's your body, your science experiment. But be cautious.

IN A SENTENCE:

> There is often less published evidence about the effectiveness of supplements than there is about prescription drugs, but learn as much as you can about a supplement before you decide to take it.

learning

Learning More about Testing: Blood Glucose Meters

BY NOW you should be comfortable using your first blood glucose (BG) meter, and it's time to go beyond the basics of BG monitoring.

Plasma readings are higher than whole-blood readings

The first thing to understand is the difference between plasma levels and whole-blood levels of glucose. *Whole blood* means the blood just as it comes out of your body, what you get when you prick your finger and get a drop of blood. Whole blood contains a liquid plus *red blood cells, white blood cells* and *platelets* (small disc-shaped structures in the blood that are required for clotting). When you remove the blood cells and platelets, the liquid that is left is called **plasma**. (When you let the blood clot and then remove both the blood cells and the clot, what's left is called *serum*, but we don't need to worry about that.)

The concentration of glucose in the red blood cells is a little lower than the concentration of glucose in the plasma. So when you remove the red blood cells, the resulting plasma gives a slightly higher BG reading than you get from whole blood, usually 10 to 15 per cent higher, depending on how many red blood cells were in your blood in the first place. People who are anaemic have fewer red blood cells.

When you read various books and pamphlets about diabetes, you'll probably find that they give different values for 'normal' BG levels. Some books may say normal BG levels are between 3 and 5.5 mmol/L (millimols per litre). Others might say between 4 and 7 mmol/L. Part of this is simply a matter of definition. Sometimes an official medical committee gets together and redefines things. As I noted earlier, in the 1990s the definition of diabetic fasting levels was changed from anything over 8 to anything over 7 mmol/L, thus giving a huge number of people diabetes with a stroke of the pen (and actually doing them a favour in the process, because the best treatment is early treatment). Some writers may be reporting the officially defined upper limit of normal and others may be referring to the most common levels. In addition, some may be using plasma levels (which are higher) and others referring to whole-blood (lower) values. They usually don't bother to say.

Most labs test the BG levels in your plasma. The home meters use whole blood. So when you test your blood on some BG meters, you may get a result that is about 12 per cent below the lab value. (See the instruction manual or call the manufacturer to see if you have a meter that gives whole-blood values. If so, find out what percentage below lab values it is supposed to read.) That's not a big problem. If you want to know the approximate lab value and your meter reads 12 per cent below the lab value, you just multiply your result by 1.12. If you want to convert the lab value into your home meter value, you divide the lab value by 1.12.

It used to be that all the home meters reported their results as whole-blood values. Then some people complained because their meters didn't give the same results as the labs. So some manufacturers started selling meters and strips that report the results as plasma values. This doesn't mean you have to separate your blood before you use the plasma meters. The meters simply measure the BG value of the whole blood and then do an additional calculation to convert it to an approximate plasma reading.

If you're interested in getting a new meter, decide if you prefer the whole-blood or the plasma readings, and make sure the meter you get reports the values you want it to report. Most of the newer meters give plasma readings, so in a few years this may not be an issue.

Some meters even give you a choice, with two types of strips, and you might inadvertently buy the wrong kind of strip without noticing. If your strips look different and your BG values seem higher or lower than before, check to make sure you don't have a different type of strip.

Venous blood can read lower than capillary blood

It gets more complicated. There is sometimes a difference in the BG level of blood from your veins and blood from your capillaries. Your blood flows out of your heart in blood vessels called **arteries**. This blood is bright red because it contains a lot of oxygen, and if you've just had a meal, the blood also contains a lot of glucose from the meal. This blood flows into smaller and smaller arteries and finally into tiny arteries that are called **capillaries**. The capillaries have thin, permeable walls and, like a combination of a grocery delivery and a waste collection, easily give oxygen and glucose to the cells that need them, picking up carbon dioxide and other waste products at the same time. Then the oxygen-depleted (bluish), glucose-depleted blood flows into larger and larger blood vessels called **veins**, goes through the liver to pick up more food, and goes back to the lungs to drop off the carbon dioxide and pick up more oxygen.

What this means is that *after a meal* the blood in the veins may have a lot less glucose in it than the blood in the capillaries, which dumped a lot of their glucose off to feed the cells. When you do home BG testing, you use blood from the capillaries. When you give blood at the doctor's surgery, they take blood from a vein. As long as you're testing fasting samples, there's not much difference in the BG concentration, so it won't make much difference where you get the blood. But if you were measuring after a meal, you might see a large difference, up to about 3.9 mmol/L, between capillary and venous blood.

Accuracy and precision mean different things

If you want to know how accurate your home meter is, the best way is to take it with you when you have your BG level measured by a lab. Do your testing right before they draw your blood. Don't be tempted to use a drop of the blood the technician takes from a vein. The chemical reaction used by many home meters depends on oxygenated blood, and sometimes the venous blood doesn't have enough oxygen for an accurate test. Do this testing several times and average the results. If you find your lab gives readings about 14 per cent higher than yours, then multiply your results by 1.14 to estimate the lab values.

Home meters are not guaranteed to be as accurate as lab tests. Most meters guarantee accuracy only plus or minus 20 per cent. This means that if you get a reading of 5.6 mmol/L, the true BG level could be between 4.4 and 6.7 mmol/L, and the manufacturer would consider the meter was just fine. In practice, most meters seem to be more accurate than the acceptable limits.

The term *accuracy* means how close to the true value your meter measures. There's another possible variation in results called *precision*. This refers to how close several readings taken one after the other will be. For example, a meter that gave readings of 5.4, 5.5 and 5.3 would be very precise. A meter that gave readings of 5.4, 6.7 and 4.4 would not be precise. Note that a meter can be very precise but not accurate. For example, if the blood being measured by the first meter had a true BG level of 6.7, the meter would be precise but inaccurate.

Don't try to measure the precision of your meter at a time when you think your BG level might be changing quickly. It takes a certain amount of time to do the test, and if the BG level is changing very fast, you might think it was imprecise when it was actually reflecting changing levels of glucose.

There are different types of meters

In addition to differences between whole-blood and plasma meters, meters have two slightly different methods of measuring your BG level. One type (which I'll call *colourimetric*; another name is colour *reflectance* meters) measures a colour change. The other type (which I'll call *electrochemical*; another term is *amperometric*) measures an electrical current. One way to tell which kind you have is to see if your meter has little flashing red lights when you turn it on. If it does, it's the colourimetric type of meter.

The strips in BG meters use **enzymes** to measure the glucose. Different brands of strips use slightly different measuring systems. In one of the most common ones, when you add blood to the strip, an enzyme called *glucose oxidase* oxidizes the glucose in the blood, producing peroxide. In the colourimetric meters, in the presence of a second enzyme, *peroxidase*, the peroxide oxidizes a dye to form a blue colour. The intensity of the colour is proportional to the amount of the glucose. In the 'old days', a similar procedure was used, but you had to compare the colour of the strip with a chart, which gave only an approximation of the glucose level. You can still buy such strips, which you use without a meter. But most people use meters that read the intensity of the colour and give you a numerical value.

The electrochemical meters start off oxidizing the glucose in a similar way. But then, instead of measuring a colour change, the small electrical current released in a couple of additional steps is measured, and you get a numerical reading from the meter.

The glucose oxidase method requires oxygen, and venous blood sometimes doesn't contain enough oxygen for an accurate test unless the sample is shaken before testing. If for some reason you need to test venous blood, check the written instructions that came with your strips to see if the method they use is accurate with venous blood.

With older meters, some people found the electrochemical meters more sensitive to temperature variations. When they used their meters in cold places, for example on ski trips, they said they found the colourimetric meters to be more accurate. Even so, it's important not to let the meters freeze, but to keep them underneath some clothing, although not right next to the skin, where they could get too hot and damp. BG meters have been used successfully even on expeditions up Mount Everest, so don't let problems with temperature control keep you from skiing or hiking or mountain climbing if that's something you enjoy.

Because they depend on measuring the intensity of the colour formed on the strips, the colourimetric meters can be sensitive to variations in light intensity. So you shouldn't move your meter or drastically change the amount of light falling on the strip during the test. Some colourimetric meters don't work well in bright light and may have warning signals if you try to measure in sunshine or under a bright lamp. The electrochemical meters aren't affected by light, so if you need to measure under a tropical sun, you might prefer that type of meter.

Many factors can affect test results

Humidity. All test strips are sensitive to light and humidity. Some brands come in individual foil packages that you unwrap just before you do a test. Others come in special dark vials that contain a desiccant (a substance that removes moisture from the air) to keep the strips dry. It's important to take out a strip quickly and then reclose the vial to avoid getting moisture on the strips. For the same reason, it's not a good idea to do a lot of testing in a humid room such as the bathroom.

Temperature. Most of the meters are guaranteed accurate only within a certain temperature range, and some of them have warning signals if you're out of range. Although the lower end may seem low (around 13°C; slightly different for each meter), if you're testing outside or live in a drafty old house heated with wood as I do, the temperature in the morning can sometimes be below the minimum given for the meter. So too, the high limit (around 35°C; this also varies with the brand of meter) can be a problem during heat waves when you have no air-conditioning. The humidity during a heat wave can also be greater than the maximum recommended for testing (about 85 per cent). You can still test under these conditions and get an estimate of your BG level. But don't expect super-accurate results.

Technology is constantly changing, and some of the newer meters are less temperature sensitive than the older ones. If you're apt to use your meter under extreme conditions, look for one with the largest temperature range.

Strips can also degrade at high temperatures. This means it's not a good idea to leave your strips in a closed-up car on a hot summer day. Sitting in direct sunlight isn't good for the meters either. If you need to travel with your meter and strips in hot weather, put them in an insulated box. Don't add ice. When you take something from a cold place and put it in a hot place, you get condensation, and the condensation could dampen the strips and make them ineffective. If you're in such a hot place that some kind of cooling is needed, the trick is to make sure the vial of strips is warmed up to ambient temperature before you open the lid. A few minutes at 38°C won't cause the same damage as several hours or days.

Even if you're very careful to keep your strips in temperature-controlled rooms, you have no control over what happened to the strips while they were in transit between the factory and the store where you bought them. They might have sat in the hot sun or in subzero temperatures while they were being shipped. So if you get a reading that really doesn't seem right, first retest using another strip from the same vial. If it still seems odd, try using a strip from a new lot. If you're still getting readings that don't seem right, use some control solution if you have it. If not, call the technical support number that should be in your instruction booklet. It might be that your meter is out of order. Most companies are very good at helping you find out what is wrong and sending free replacement strips or a new meter if there's any possibility that could be the problem. They want you to keep on using their strips.

Common problems. With all the meters, common problems causing incorrect results include not using enough blood, using old strips (check the expiry dates), using strips that have been exposed to high or low temperatures, not matching the code on the strips with the code on the meter, using a meter with a weak battery (some warn you when this happens), or adding a second drop of blood after the test has begun. It's also not a good idea to use a mobile phone or similar device in the area while you're testing.

Sometimes if your blood is very thick, it won't flow into the strips at a fast enough rate, and this can cause bad readings. Thus severe dehydration may give falsely low results. At high altitudes, the amount of oxygen in the blood is lower, and this can cause low readings. One study found that at altitudes above 10,000 feet, one electrochemical meter read high but a colourimetric meter read low. Check your meter instructions to find the limits for your meter. Other potential problems include extremely poor circulation, so your capillary blood doesn't reflect the BG levels in the rest of your blood vessels; and a low or high *haematocrit*, meaning too few red blood cells (anaemia) or too many red blood cells (polycythaemia), respectively. Readings can vary from 4 to 40 per cent for each 10 per cent change in haematocrit. In general, a low haematocrit will result in a reading that is too high, and a high haematocrit will result in a reading that is too low.

Various other factors, for example, extremely high levels of lipids or vitamin C, can affect the readings on your meter. Read the slips that come with each batch of strips carefully to find out which ones affect your meter's tests. If they don't say, call the manufacturer.

Know your meter. Because of all these variables, it's a good idea to stick with one kind of meter most of the time. Even if the results don't match lab values exactly, you'll learn to feel comfortable with the readings on your meter, and you'll know what they represent for you. My main meter reads low, but I know it reads low. And it's easier for me to compare my readings now with my readings two years ago without having to correct for a different meter. On the other hand, if you find a meter you like better, then switch. But unless you've done tests to show that two meters read the same all the time, don't go back and forth a lot.

From all this, you can see that the results you get from home BG meters can vary considerably depending on the type of meter, the freshness of the testing strips, the particular physiology of the person doing the testing and testing technique. So don't ever accept anyone else's BG levels as absolute numbers. If someone tells you they keep their postprandial readings under 7.8 and yours always go up to 10, don't feel they're necessarily doing better than you are. It could be they have a meter that reads lower than yours.

The important thing is to use your meter to tell whether you're doing better or worse than you were last week or last month, whether potatoes make your BG level go higher than lentils, whether starting or stopping a new drug helps or hinders your control. If you use your meter and modify your lifestyle as a result of what you find, you can control your diabetes instead of letting your diabetes – and complications – control you.

IN A SENTENCE:

> *Blood glucose numbers depend on the type of blood you are testing (plasma or whole blood), and the readings you get on your meter depend on the type of meter, the strips and your technique.*

Should I Take Vitamins and Minerals?

Dieters may need extra vitamins

SOME PEOPLE think extra **vitamins** are not necessary for anyone who eats a lot of fruit and vegetables, but almost no one will tell you that it's harmful to take vitamin pills that provide only the RDA (recommended daily allowance) amounts, or slightly more. A lot of research has been done to determine the amounts of vitamins and minerals needed in both humans and animals in order to avoid deficiency diseases. What is sometimes controversial is taking vitamins or minerals in much larger amounts, sometimes 10 or even 100 times the RDA, or the role of vitamins and minerals in controlling blood glucose (BG) levels in people with diabetes.

For people without diabetes, eating a lot of fruit and vegetables is probably the best way to get enough vitamins and minerals, because the produce may contain nutrients that haven't been added to vitamin pills yet, and the fibre is good for you. But if you have type 2 diabetes, you are probably trying to limit your total intake of food. Furthermore, fruit and even starchy vegetables can raise BG levels when you have diabetes, so you may not be able to eat a lot of them without sacrificing good BG control. Thus you should consider taking at least a multivitamin pill.

If you prefer to get your vitamins and minerals from foods, any standard book on nutrition will tell you which vitamins and minerals are found in which foods. Or ask your dietician for help with this.

There is also some evidence that people with type 2 diabetes have more free radicals than other people, so some people take a lot of extra antioxidants, including vitamins A, C and E, and alpha-lipoic acid. Be careful with vitamin A. Too much can be toxic. The precursor to vitamin A, beta-carotene, is much safer and has the same effects.

Vitamins C and E. People with type 2 diabetes tend to be low in *vitamin C*, which also protects against damage caused by the sugar alcohol **sorbitol** (see the box in Day 3). High levels of sorbitol are thought to contribute to the formation of diabetic cataracts. *Vitamin E* has also been reported to be beneficial in people with diabetes. Both vitamins C and E are antioxidants. Vitamin C is water soluble and works in the liquid portions of the body. Vitamin E is fat soluble and works in the membranes.

Folic acid. Another vitamin often recommended for people with diabetes is *folic acid*. This vitamin, which is found in green leafy vegetables, seems to reduce the concentration of a compound called *homocysteine* that is associated with higher levels of heart attacks, for which people with diabetes are at higher risk. If you eat a lot of green vegetables – as you should unless you are taking **anti-coagulants** – you should have plenty of folic acid, but it's not expensive and might be worth adding to your list of vitamins.

Vitamin B$_{12}$. If you've been taking metformin (see Week 3) for several years, you should consider taking *vitamin B$_{12}$* supplements. In some people, metformin inhibits the uptake of vitamin B$_{12}$ from food. You can get vitamin B$_{12}$ injections, to make sure it actually gets into your system. There are also sublingual pills that are supposed to be taken up more efficiently than the regular oral pills. There is one report that taking more calcium increases vitamin B$_{12}$ levels in people taking metformin.

Unless you're a vegetarian, this is not an immediate problem, as most people who eat meat have enough vitamin B$_{12}$ stored in the liver to last several years.

B vitamins. Some people with type 2 diabetes say the vitamin *biotin* helps control their BG levels. Others say it has no effect. Some say extra B vitamins help with their control, although again, this effect is not universal. Biotin is usually produced by bacteria in the gut, so most people are not deficient in this vitamin.

Alpha-lipoic acid. *Alpha-lipoic acid* has been used for decades in Germany to treat diabetic neuropathy. It's also a powerful antioxidant that is both fat and water soluble, and it recycles vitamins C and E after they have reacted with free radicals. When infused into the veins, alpha-lipoic acid can also reduce IR. Unfortunately, oral preparations seem to lack the latter effect to any great degree, and the lifetime of the lipoic acid in the bloodstream is very short. However, some people report that their fasting BG levels decrease when they take the supplement. The relatively low amounts in some vitamin pills probably won't have that effect.

Minerals can be both good and bad

With some minerals the body is in a delicate balance between too much and too little. I'll illustrate this with the situation in sheep, which I raise.

Sheep, as well as people, need the mineral *selenium*, which like vitamins A, C and E is also an antioxidant. Without selenium, their lambs may get something called white muscle disease, in which the heart muscle is defective. In the Northeast of America, where I live, soils tend to be selenium deficient, and many farmers supplement their sheep with selenium to make sure they get enough.

In the West, however, soils tend to be high in selenium. During periods of drought, the plants in the West sometimes concentrate the selenium in their leaves. The famished sheep eat the high-selenium plants and die from selenium toxicity. Thus both too little and too much selenium can be fatal in sheep. The same is true with copper. If you give your sheep grain formulated to have the proper amount of copper for cows, the sheep may drop dead from copper poisoning. Without copper they'll also die. It's a delicate balance.

Humans are likely similar with respect to a lot of minerals. We need them to live, but too much can be toxic. We get our food from all over the country, even all over the world, so it's hard to know whether it's from soil that was high in a particular mineral or mineral deficient.

Iron is a good example of a mineral that we need but which can be toxic in excess. Haemoglobin, the molecule that carries oxygen in the blood, needs iron to function. Older people used to be told to take extra iron for 'tired blood'. More recently, it has been suggested that too much iron actually *increases* the risk of cardio-vascular problems by producing free radicals, and older people seem to have more difficulty getting rid of excess iron, so geriatric vitamins usually contain less iron than the others. As noted in Month 2, the inherited iron-overload disease *haemochromatosis* can be deadly.

Chromium and vanadium. Two minerals you'll most likely hear about after you're diagnosed with diabetes are *chromium* and *vanadium*, both of which are heavy metals reported to help with BG control. There is no doubt that a deficiency of these minerals can cause problems with BG control. The real debate is whether most people are deficient in them and whether larger-than-RDA amounts can be toxic. Some people say that many Westerners, especially the older ones who tend to get type 2 diabetes, tend to be deficient in chromium because of marginal diets with too few fruits and vegetables. They say soils all over the world are becoming depleted of minerals so even when you eat plenty of fruits and vegetables, you may be deficient in some nutrients. Others say that is rubbish and worry that large amounts of heavy metals can harm the kidneys.

One study in China showed that chromium supplements improved BG control in people with type 2 diabetes. Critics say the Chinese who were studied were chromium deficient to start with. Some other studies have shown benefits and others have shown none. One possibility is the ever-present YMMV (Your Mileage May Vary). People who are chromium deficient may benefit from chromium supplements. Others may not. Eating a lot of sugar and other carbohydrate may deplete the chromium from your system. If you think chromium may help you, try it for a while and see if it has any effect on your BG levels. If it doesn't, stop taking it.

Note that the *trivalent* (meaning it has three positive charges) *chromium* used in dietary supplements is different from the *hexavalent* (meaning it has six positive charges) *chromium* you can get from industrial exposure to chromium metal dust. The latter is toxic, another example of how a mineral can be beneficial in certain areas and lethal in others. So don't think you can help your diabetes by gnawing on the chrome bumpers of old cars.

The situation with vanadium is slightly different. There are controlled studies that show that vanadium can reduce BG levels. The problem is that you have to use huge amounts to see an effect, and such large amounts cause side effects. The tiny amounts found in vitamin pills shouldn't be any problem. Taking a lot of vanadium can hinder your absorption of chromium, yet another example of the delicate balance your body must maintain for optimal health.

Magnesium and zinc. Two other minerals that some people say are deficient in people with diabetes are *magnesium* and *zinc*. As with the other minerals, without actually measuring the levels in your blood, it's difficult to know if you need extra magnesium or zinc or not. If you decide to supplement, be sensible; don't overdo it. Too much magnesium causes diarrhoea, and too much zinc can be toxic.

Note that some summaries of studies showing mineral deficiencies simply refer to 'people with diabetes'. This includes many people who are not well controlled, whose bodies are producing extra urine in an attempt to get rid of the extra glucose in their blood. Along with the glucose, they are losing minerals. The same applies to people taking **diuretics**. So, for example, high BG levels could cause low magnesium levels by increasing its loss in the urine, instead of low magnesium levels causing high BG levels. If your BG levels are well controlled and you're not taking diuretics or drinking huge amounts of beer or coffee, you're less likely to be deficient in minerals.

Calcium. Finally, *calcium* is a good idea for most people, especially if your diet requires you to limit your intake of dairy foods.

Reasonable amounts. In reasonable amounts, most vitamins and minerals shouldn't harm you. The problem is deciding what is reasonable. Water-soluble vitamins can usually be taken in much-larger-than-normal amounts without any side effects because they are simply eliminated from the body in the urine. One group reported that in very high doses, vitamin C might be a pro-oxidant (producing free radicals) instead of an antioxidant, but others say that study was flawed. In spring 2001, vitamin E was reported to be a pro-oxidant in smokers. All the fat-soluble vitamins, which means vitamins A, D, E and K, can be toxic if you take large amounts.

People with healthy metabolisms who don't smoke and live with clean air and water and eat diets rich in organic fruits and vegetables grown in healthy soil probably don't need any vitamin or mineral supplements. But having type 2 diabetes means your metabolism is out of whack. In addition, you may be on a diet that restricts your consumption of some healthy foods. Thus some supplementation with vitamins and minerals may be a good thing for you. Just don't go overboard. More is not always better.

IN A SENTENCE:

> *Because you're probably limiting your total food intake, you might want to take reasonable amounts of common vitamins, minerals and antioxidants.*

learning

Learning More about Testing: Haemoglobin A1c and Fructosamine

Haemoglobin A1c

AT THIS time you may be preparing to get a second haemoglobin A1c test to see how you're doing with your average blood glucose (BG) control. If you don't enjoy reading about technical stuff, you may not want to know all the details of this test yet. That's OK. Just read the subheads in this chapter to get a general idea of the things that affect this test. Later you may want to come back and read the details.

The A1c test measures only averages

The haemoglobin A1c (or the related *glycohaemo-globin* test, the A1 test [see Day 5]), measures your average BG levels over the past few months. Red blood cells live an *average* of 120 days; then the elderly ones are broken down, primarily in the spleen, and their parts are recycled. How much glucose gets attached to the haemoglobin in the red blood cells during their 120-day lifetime depends on how high your BG was on *average* during those 120 days.

Note the use of the word *average*. Not everyone's red blood cells live exactly 120 days. Some differences are because of differences in people's physiological makeup. Others are because of temporary illnesses, drugs or other factors.

Anything that reduces the lifetime of a red blood cell decreases the measured A1c. Such factors include *haemolytic anaemia* (anaemia caused by breakdown of the red blood cells), losing a lot of blood either through an accident or by donating blood, *haemochromatosis* (see Month 2), prolonged fever or genetic variations.

Conversely, anything that increases the lifetime of the red blood cell increases the measured A1c. One such factor is removal of the spleen, because the spleen is the primary site where the old, tired red blood cells get taken apart. Genetic variations could also increase the lifetime of the red blood cells. So if your A1c results don't seem to agree with your daily BG measurements, see if you and your doctor can figure out if there's any reason your red blood cells might live longer (your A1c is higher than you'd expect) or shorter (your A1c is lower than you'd expect) than average.

But wait! There's more involved with this average stuff. Remember that the A1c measures the average BG level during the past several months. An average says nothing about the highs and lows that you might have had. If you've had BG levels of 11 mmol/L for half the time and 2.8 half the time you will have an *average* BG level of 6.9 – ([11 + 2.8]÷2) – and you'll have the same A1c result as someone who has kept the BG level at 6.9 most of the time (an unlikely situation, as BG levels fluctuate even in nondiabetic people, but it's an easy example to understand). But the consequences of roller-coaster BG levels, going high one hour and very low the next, are very different from the consequences of smaller fluctuations. Fluctuating BG levels can cause symptoms of hyperglycaemia one hour and hypoglycaemia (see Month 2) the next. They can cause the osmotic pressure in your lens to keep changing, resulting in changing vision. And some people find that fluctuating BG levels make them hungry.

Remember that your A1c results indicate only what your average BG levels have been for the past month or more. You still need to do daily BG checks to learn how your BG levels fluctuate with food and exercise.

There are different ways to measure A1c

There are many different ways to measure glycated haemoglobin. As I mentioned in Day 5, some laboratories measure all the glycated adult haemoglobin, which means the haemoglobin A1, usually called just *glycohaemoglobin* on the lab report. Others use methods that separate the glycohaemoglobin into its haemoglobin A1a, A1b and A1c components and report only the results of the A1c, which is the fraction that contains the glucose. The other fractions contain different sugars.

Even when they're measuring the A1c, different technologies are used to do the tests. Some methods separate the A1c by its more negative charge, some by its structure. The different methods give slightly different results and are affected in different ways by various factors.

Most adults have primarily a form of haemoglobin called haemoglobin A (for adult). But some people have inherited variations of the haemoglobin molecule. One of the most common is *haemoglobin S*, which causes *sickle cell anaemia*. Several different mutations can cause different haemoglobins that cause *thalassaemia*, another type of anaemia found in people of Mediterranean descent. Many people with thalassaemia retain a lot of haemoglobin F (for foetal), which normally is not produced by adults.

Some of these variations (and there are many different rare types) separate along with the A1c fraction in certain types of tests for A1c. For example, if you have thalassaemia, your A1c results may be higher than they should be, because haemoglobin F moves along with the A1c in some of the tests. If you have sickle cell anaemia, your A1c results may be lower than expected, because the glycated haemoglobin S doesn't show up where the A1c is expected in some kinds of tests.

A newer test called the *total glycohaemoglobin test* measures *all* the haemoglobin types (haemoglobin A, S, F and other variants) that have glucose attached and may be able to give an idea of your control even if you have one of these unusual haemoglobin types. However, some of the unusual haemoglobins live for a shorter time than haemoglobin A, and this would also affect the results. If you're reading older books, note that in the past, some people used the term *total glycohaemoglobin* to refer to haemoglobin A1 (A1a, A1b and A1c), which can be confusing.

Some labs now measure the total glycohaemoglobin, then use a formula to convert the results to an A1c, and report it as haemoglobin A1c. In this case, the A1c results would usually reflect your average BG levels even if you had one of the haemoglobin variants.

If your A1c results don't seem to be what they should be, ask your doctor about the possibility that you may have an unusual type of haemoglobin. Then try to find out what kind of test the lab used to measure the A1c, and see if it's one of the ones that is affected by haemoglobin variants. If it is, you might want to have a fructosamine test (see later in this part), which isn't affected by variations in haemoglobin types.

Several other factors that have been reported to cause falsely elevated A1cs include kidney failure, chronic alcohol intake and high triglyceride (fat) levels. When the glycohaemoglobin test for all the haemoglobin A1 fractions is being used, factors that have been reported to cause false results include opiate addiction, lead poisoning, kidney failure and alcoholism.

Because of all the different methods and ways of reporting results, people are trying to standardize the results so you could compare your results from one lab with the results from another lab without worrying about different methods and normal ranges.

Glycation occurs in several steps

Nothing is ever simple when it comes to diabetes. This includes the process of glycation, or the addition of glucose to the haemoglobin molecule. This process occurs in several steps, and the first two are reversible.

What happens is this: When the BG level in the blood is high, the glucose first fairly quickly (over a period of several hours) attaches itself to the haemoglobin by a very labile bond (for scientists: it's a Schiff base). Some people call this temporary compound *pre-A1c*. You may also see it referred to as the *aldimine* form. This reaction occurs fairly rapidly, but if the BG level then goes down again, the glucose can come off. It's like suddenly having a high level of cash and quickly putting it into a bank. It's not a permanent situation. When your cash level goes down, you take the money out of the bank again.

But if your BG levels stay high, the glucose doesn't come off the haemoglobin molecule. In fact, it is slowly, over a period of several weeks, converted (for scientists: by an Amadori rearrangement) to a second compound, the haemoglobin A1c (you'll sometimes see this referred to as the *ketoamine* form) that is measured in the tests. This reaction is also reversible. It can revert to the pre-A1c again. But it takes a long time, several weeks, to go from A1c back to pre-A1c, so for the purposes of the testing, the A1c is pretty stable.

However, because the first step in this process happens fairly quickly and is a function of the current level of glucose in the blood, if your BG levels had been very good for several months but for the past two days you'd let them get very high, you could have very high levels of pre-A1c, the stuff that has 'temporary glucose' that can come off again if your BG levels go low. If the lab uses a test that measures both the temporary pre-A1c and the permanent A1c, your results might reflect your control in the previous days instead of over the past month or so.

This is also a good reason to be fasting when you have the A1c test done, even though the instructions for the test say that's not necessary. An extremely high BG level could cause an increase in this temporary pre-A1c, especially if the blood sat around for a long time before it was tested.

Some labs control for this by doing a first step that removes the pre-A1c. Others don't. In most cases it probably won't make much difference. But if your results don't seem to reflect your home testing, this is yet another factor that you might want to consider.

The A1c is a weighted average

Older books about diabetes may say that the A1c measures your average BG level over the past two to four months. In a sense it does. A few of your red blood cells are always close to 120 days old. But not many. In fact, mathematical analyses of the A1c can show that it is heavily *weighted* to the past two or three weeks. Some experts estimate that if your daily control suddenly got better or worse, 50 per cent of the change in A1c would occur in one month. Another person estimates 50 per cent of the change would occur in only seven days, about 75 per cent after two weeks, and 94 per cent after four weeks. These analyses depend on assumptions about the speed with which glucose goes on and comes off haemoglobin, and different people using different assumptions have calculated different values for this weighting.

Because you'll always have some red blood cells that are older than others, if you've had terrible control and suddenly decide to get your act together and your BG levels fall to close to normal levels, your A1c may begin to go down a little in a few days, but it will take a few weeks before you see a significant change and at least a month before the A1c reflects your current control. The same is true if you've had good control and suddenly let it slip. So if your daily control has changed significantly shortly before you get an A1c, don't be surprised if the result isn't what you'd expect from your BG readings in the past week or so.

Check the normal range

Everyone has glucose in the blood, so everyone has some glycation of proteins like haemoglobin, even people who are not diabetic. Hence no one will have an A1c of zero. What you want to know when you have the test done is how you compare with people who are not diabetic.

In order to do this, the laboratory will tell you what the range of nondiabetic A1cs is. There's one problem with this. A lot of people who have diabetes don't know it, and their labs don't know it either. For example, someone with a fasting BG level in the normal range might go very high after meals, which would increase the A1c, but no one would know about it because they wouldn't think to measure. This person's blood would be classified as nondiabetic and would affect the so-called normal range in that area.

Many labs use local blood samples to determine their normal ranges. If you live in an area where the incidence of diabetes is unusually high, there are also probably a lot more undiagnosed diabetic people than in other parts of the country where diabetes is less common, and hence the normal ranges in that area might not really be normal.

For all these reasons, some people feel that the low end of the 'normal range' is really the normal value. In most cases, people with diabetes are not apt to achieve A1cs that low, and if you can't you certainly shouldn't feel bad about it. Just keeping your BG levels close to the normal range is an achievement in itself.

Don't blame yourself

Many books on diabetes tell doctors in training that when the patient's A1c doesn't agree with the home BG tests, the patient probably doesn't know how to use a meter properly or is fudging the data. Another suggestion is that perhaps the patient measures only before meals, and not after meals, when the readings could be high.

All these factors are, of course, possible. Teenagers especially, who think no harm will ever come to them, have been known to make up good BG readings to gain the approval of their doctors. However, it is also possible that either the home meter readings or the A1c tests are being affected by some other unknown factors.

I once had an A1c test done at my local hospital and got a result of 5.6, which was well below the top of the normal range for that lab (4.4 to 6.4). The very same morning, I sent off a fasting sample to a research lab that was supposed to do very accurate testing. That lab gave a result of 7.1, which was clearly above the top of their normal range (4.2 to 6.1).

Remember, the A1c is simply one *estimate* we have of average BG levels. Because it's a pretty complicated test, small variations in the numbers don't mean very much. If your A1c was 7.1 last time and it's 7.3 this time, that doesn't necessarily mean that you're doing worse even if the test was done at the same lab. Maybe a few red blood cells lived longer this time. Or maybe something else interfered with the tests. Sometimes labs even make errors. Remember, the tests are usually run by human beings. It's only a major or consistent increase that is something to worry about, say 7.1, then 7.3, then 7.5 and 7.8.

Also, the A1c is not an absolute number. It's especially important to remember this when someone tries to tell you that a particular level of the A1c means your BG levels have averaged some number, or it means you won't have or will have complications. An A1c of 6 at one lab could be an A1c of 7 at another. The important thing is to use the A1c to see if your control is better or worse than it was three months ago, or last year. The best way to do this is to stick with one method done by the same lab. Then if you have some unusual condition that might affect one testing method but not another, you won't think your control has changed when in fact it's just a result of a different method. Unfortunately, you're not likely to have control over the methods used. Your doctor may start using a different lab, and this could result in a different A1c when your control was exactly the same.

Advanced glycation end products may cause aging

Glucose adds to many different proteins in the body by a mechanism similar to that described for the haemoglobin A1c. First comes a fast reaction and then a slow reaction, both reversible if the conditions are right, that is, if the BG levels approach normal. However, the second form, the ketoamine form, can form permanent compounds called **AGEs (advanced glycation end products)**. In other words, glucose attaches to a protein molecule, and then a lot of other, often unidentified, chemical reactions change the protein from its normal form into an abnormal form that is harmful to your body. These changes are irreversible. In the analogy used when discussing the several steps of glycation, this is as if instead of putting your money in the bank, where you could get it out again, you gave it to the bank, and they wouldn't give it back.

These AGEs may form cross-links between protein molecules. When glucose reacts with the protein *collagen*, which is an important component of your connective tissue, the cross-linked AGEs that result may contribute to the loss of elasticity that comes with age, including aging of the arteries. Letting your BG levels stay higher than normal would thus accelerate this aging process. Glycation of red blood cell membranes may make them stiffer and less able to pass through tiny capillaries. When glucose reacts with various enzymes in the body, it could also modify their effectiveness and cause numerous problems.

AGEs are thought to be responsible for some of the complications from diabetes. Because the AGEs are permanent, sometimes the complications continue to progress even when the BG level is brought back to normal. This is another reason to get your BG levels under control as quickly as possible. Early complications, like the aldimine and ketoamine forms, can sometimes be reversed. At this time, AGEs cannot.

Fructose can also attach to proteins, and it is estimated that it does so about seven times faster than glucose. Thus, although fructose (and the fructose in sucrose, table sugar) won't raise your

BG levels as fast as glucose, it is not completely benign.

A compound called *aminoguanidine* has shown some promise in breaking the cross-links of the AGEs, and eventually drugs may be developed that *can* reverse some of the later complications of diabetes. But don't count on it. Keep your BG levels down now and don't let the complications happen.

Fructosamine

If your A1c results don't agree with your home BG testing, it's always possible you have some unusual kind of haemoglobin. If you know you do or think you might, it would make sense to have a *fructosamine* test done.

Glucose can react with many of the proteins in the fluid part of your blood. The fructosamine test measures the glycation of these proteins, primarily *albumin*, which is present in high concentrations.

Because these proteins turn over (the body breaks them down, recycles the components and makes new proteins) faster than the haemoglobin in red blood cells, the fructosamine test is designed to measure your average BG level over the past two to three weeks. Like the A1c test, the fructosamine test is not perfect. A lot of things can change the levels of proteins in your blood, including individual variation. The A1c test measures the *percentage* of glycated haemoglobin in your blood, so if you had more or less total haemoglobin, it wouldn't matter for the test. The fructosamine test measures only the *amount* of glycated serum proteins. So a low result can mean either your BG control has been good or your serum protein levels are down. Also, fructosamine results may vary inversely with body weight; the higher your weight, the lower the fructosamine level. High levels of vitamin C also interfere with the test, and people are sometimes told to abstain from vitamin C for 24 hours before a fructosamine test.

However, like the A1c, the fructosamine test is a good approximation of your control.

With time, accurate and affordable home A1c and fructosamine meters may become commonplace. Until then, you must rely on labs to test your overall control. In general, they do a great job. Your job is to understand their limitations.

IN A SENTENCE:

> The haemoglobin A1c and the fructosamine test can be affected by numerous factors, so if your results don't seem to match your daily blood glucose readings, see if any of these factors could explain the discrepancy.

How about Herbs and Stuff?

HERBAL REMEDIES are usually more of an unknown than vitamins and minerals, because even less research has usually been done on them. In some cases, especially with exotic herbs, there's been almost none.

That doesn't mean they don't work and aren't safe. That just means no one has conducted controlled trials to show that they do work. Sometimes a study was done that showed that the herb helped people with diabetes, but the study was done in a foreign country and published in an obscure journal almost no one has ever heard of. Some people reject that evidence as something you shouldn't trust. If the journal in question is a legitimate one in some foreign country, that attitude is elitist. On the other hand, if the journal is one published by a group affiliated with the people who sell the supplements, then that attitude is valid. When the country is far away, it may be difficult to know the difference.

When deciding whether or not to try various herbal supplements, read as much as you can about them first and consider the following points.

Learn what is in the supplement

Most dietary supplements tell you what they are supposed to contain. The problem is that some of the supplements contain plants that many of us are not familiar with. Unless you're a herbalist, you probably won't even be familiar with the names of common European herbs, much less obscure plants found only in Siberia or Sri Lanka.

There are a few sources that will tell you more (see For Further Reading). Herbs are used frequently by doctors in Europe, especially Germany, and the German European Commission's report on herbal medicines is one of the most complete. Unfortunately, the entire report is quite expensive; see if you can find a copy at your local library or health food store. If you have access to the Internet, you can find information there. However, be aware that most articles found through standard Internet searches are written by people who sell these supplements and naturally tout their safety and effectiveness and ignore any indications they might cause harm.

Ask how many ingredients it contains

Many herbal preparations sold to help with blood glucose (BG) control contain many ingredients. When they do, it's difficult to know which particular one is helping with your BG control, if the preparation does work. There might be one useful ingredient and others that are doing nothing at all or maybe even doing harm. Of course the people who sell the supplements will say you need the exact balance found in their preparation to see any results. Maybe they're right. But probably not. Sometimes they're just trying to make their own particular brand of a supplement seem better. I remember the old advertisement for the painkiller that said, 'Contains not one, but a combination of ingredients', as if that were somehow a good reason to buy it.

It's better to try things one at a time, so you can find out which ones really work.

Try to find out how it works

Just because you don't know how a drug works is no reason it shouldn't be used. People used aspirin for years before scientists discovered at the end of the 20th century how it works.

Nevertheless, if you can find out as much as possible how an alternative supplement is supposed to work, you'll have a better idea of whether it might be a good idea for you. For example, some people don't want to take sulphonylurea drugs because they're worried that they might burn out the pancreas. Let's say you decide instead to take an obscure 'miracle supplement' from Asia that contains a plant you've never heard of. How do you know the plant isn't simply a natural form of one of the sulphonylureas you didn't want to take in the first place?

Again, do as much research as you can before making a decision. A good place to start is an article in the American diabetes magazine, *Diabetes Care,* called 'Traditional Plant Medicines as Treatments for Diabetes' (see For Further Reading). This article lists dozens of plants that are supposed to have BG-lowering qualities with summaries of their proposed mechanisms of action and references to any research that had been done on them by that time (1989).

Consider the purity

One problem with supplements is that they are not regulated as drugs are, so the active ingredients in the supplements can vary greatly from brand to brand and from the amounts stated on the labels. The composition of active ingredients in plants can also vary greatly depending on the soil conditions, growing conditions and time of harvest. So if someone grows a plant, dries and pulverizes the leaves and sells it as a supplement, its active ingredient might vary a lot from batch to batch. If the active ingredient is not very potent, this might not make much difference. In other cases it could. This is also a problem with studies of herbal remedies. The activities of the herbs used in different studies may not have been the same.

A perhaps greater concern is the inadvertent or even purposeful addition of contaminants. There have been reports of poisoning from lead and other heavy metals in herbal preparations from India and China. Even worse, some from China were found to contain manufactured sulphonylureas; phenformin, which was banned in the United States, or steroids. No wonder they worked. The companies just advertised their miracle herbs and added a cheap drug. Because supplements aren't controlled, there's no way to be sure this won't happen.

Consider the cost

Some herbal diabetes treatments are extremely expensive and are not available on prescription. If you're convinced the supplement helps you, maybe it's worth the cost. Otherwise, you might be better off spending the money on some very good food that would help you stick to your diet, or enrolling in some kind of exercise club, or joining a golf club or buying a brand-new mountain bike.

Make sure it's not snake oil

Some herbal remedies are sold by well-meaning people who really think they work. And some of them do. Unfortunately, others are sold by get-rich-quick snake oil salespeople who are out to get a quick profit from desperate people. How can you tell the difference?

One difference is in what they're charging. If a friend says he's found that cinnamon really helped him with his BG control, I'll probably try it. He's not selling me anything, cinnamon is cheap, I like the taste and it's not likely to hurt me. But if Sleeze E. Bague sends me a brochure advertising a Diabetes Miracle Cure and says he's willing to let me have a month's supply for only £75, my rubbish-detecting antennae will go up.

Another tip-off that you're dealing with snake oil is if the product contains a lot of 'mystery ingredients' and you can't find them listed in any references you consult. Another is if the product was discovered by some exotic means. Maybe the ingredients were dictated from another world while the maker was in a trance. Or maybe a mysterious manuscript with a formula for a lost diabetes cure was discovered in an ancient monastery in Tibet. Diabetes has been with us for a long time, and you can be sure that if anyone had ever found a cure, it wouldn't have been lost.

The decision is yours

You might think from all these concerns that one should never, ever even consider taking any kind of herbal supplement. But remember that some of the same concerns I've mentioned may apply to approved prescription and over-the-counter drugs as well.

We often don't know exactly how prescription drugs work. They're supposed to be pure, but everyone makes mistakes, and sometimes they have to be recalled because of errors. Manufacturers in France sold blood products without testing for the AIDS virus, and children with haemophilia died as a result.

Even carefully controlled, officially approved medications can be lethal. More than 60 people died from taking the drug troglitazone (Rezulin). People die from allergic reactions to prescription drugs. People die from taking prescription drugs during official trials. Many drugs cause kidney or liver damage. Even painkillers like paracetamol can be harmful, even fatal in combination with a lot of alcohol.

On the other hand, one must remember that just because a supplement is 'natural' doesn't mean that it is safe. Strychnine is all natural. So is poison hemlock.

So how do you decide? The first question you should ask before taking either a prescription drug or an herbal supplement is 'Can this drug harm me?' Try to find out the likely cost-benefit ratio of taking the drug. With a prescription drug, the leaflet that should come with the drug (if you don't get one, ask the pharmacist for it) should tell you what percentage of people during clinical trials showed what side effects. Every drug has some side effects. Most people are happy to live with the side effects of drugs like caffeine or alcohol or nicotine or too much chocolate cake. What you have to decide with a prescription drug is whether a 2 per cent risk of headache is a reasonable risk to take. Probably yes. A 5 per cent risk of fatal liver damage would be another matter indeed.

With herbal remedies you don't usually have such statistics, so you have to make the judgments yourself. If you're interested in trying herbal remedies, probably the best place to start is with common herbs and spices.

Some common foods are supposed to help

Many common foods have been reported to help with BG control. A lot of them contain a lot of soluble fibre, so it's possible that the fibre is what is doing the job. Fibre-rich remedies include prickly pear cactus (nopal), fenugreek, guar gum, barley, oat bran and flaxseed. Note that eating a lot of fibre can inhibit the uptake of some drugs, so try to take your medications when you are not eating huge amounts of soluble fibre. Other common foods and herbs that have been reported to help are cinnamon, onion, garlic, mushrooms, bay leaves, sage, allspice and thyme.

It's unlikely that any of these foods will cause you any harm in reasonable amounts. Don't go overboard, as huge amounts of common spices can be dangerous (for example, large doses of sage oil can cause convulsions; infusions are less toxic). If you want to test the effect of foods and spices, try them one at a time. Measure your BG levels before and after eating them (along with a meal whose effect on your BG level you've already determined if you don't want to eat bowls of garlic or tablespoons of cinnamon alone) to see if they have any effect on your BG levels, or add a spice to all your meals for a week and see if your average BG levels change. If not, don't bother with it unless you like the taste.

Many other herbal remedies have been reported

Diabetes has been known around the world for centuries, and many countries have folk remedies. The following are some of the ones you'll hear mentioned most often.

Gymnema sylvestre. This is an Ayurvedic remedy used in India, where it is called *gurmar*. When the leaves of the plant are chewed, the sweetness of food is blocked, so people stop eating sweets because they have no taste. There is also some evidence that it may reduce the uptake of sugar in the intestine.

However, the most controversial aspect of *Gymnema* is its reported ability to cause the regeneration of beta cells. Research showing this was published in the *Journal of Ethnopharmacology* in 1990. Critics say if there were any truth to it, the research would have been repeated elsewhere by now. Supporters say drug companies don't want to do the research because they can't patent it. Many 'miracle cures' you'll see advertised contain *Gymnema*.

Momordica charantia. This is a cucumber-shaped melon called *bitter melon* or *karela*, used in Asian cooking. It is (surprise) bitter, and it is used in Asia to lower BG levels. Many preparations that contain *Gymnema* also contain *Momordica*. You can buy the vegetable at Asian grocery stores. Extracts are usually used to control BG levels.

Ginseng. Ginseng has been reported to lower BG levels. The problem is that there are many different varieties of ginseng, and the active ingredients can vary a lot even within the same variety and depending on whether the product contains extracts of roots or leaves. Some types of ginseng have been reported to *increase* BG levels. If you decide to try ginseng, make sure the kind you read about is the same kind you try, and test your BG levels when you take it. Some preparations of ginseng have been reported to interfere with warfarin and diuretics.

Bilberry. Bilberry (*Vaccinium myrtillus*, not the same as blueberry, with which it is often confused) leaves have been reported to help with BG levels. Bilberry is also supposed to aid with night vision. But be careful as too much is toxic.

Fenugreek. In addition to its soluble fibre, fenugreek (*Trigonella foenum-graecum*) may contain compounds that help to lower BG levels. Unfortunately, taking a lot of fenugreek can give you a rather odd odour. It may also 'thin' the blood and should be used with caution by anyone taking other anticoagulants ('blood thinners') including aspirin.

Ginkgo biloba. Ginkgo has been shown to increase the circulation and is used primarily to increase circulation to the brain. It may also help with circulation to the extremities, which is often poor in people with type 2 diabetes. Because it is also a blood thinner, it should be used cautiously if you're also taking other blood thinners.

Evening primrose oil. Some people with diabetes find that *gamma-linolenic acid (GLA)* helps reduce the pain of neuropathy. It is also supposed to be synergistic with alpha-lipoic acid. Evening primrose is high in GLA. Another source of GLA is borage oil; there are reports that borage leaves can damage the liver, but borage oil is probably OK. GLA forms prostaglandin E_1, which is a blood thinner. Both GLA and alpha-lipoic acid are relatively expensive.

It's your body, your science experiment

Because herbal remedies are often unknowns, many doctors won't be thrilled if you say you want to use them. Some don't know much about herbs, and others may be sceptical if you mention them, especially if you say you got the information on the Internet. So if you have a personality that needs a pat on the back from your doctor, herbal remedies are probably not the way to go.

But if you're the adventurous sort who likes taking risks, you might want to try some of the herbal remedies. If you do, just be cautious. Read all you can about them before you try them. Try one at a time. Keep records to help you decide whether or not they work. If they don't, save your money.

Be on the lookout for possible drug interactions. As I mentioned before, sometimes too many supplements that might help individually can cause problems when taken together. Your pharmacist will probably know more about possible interactions than your doctor, but it's also a good idea to tell your doctor which supplements you're taking.

Herbal and other folk remedies sometimes are the starting point for so-called miracle medications. Some of the herbs may turn out to be beneficial, and some may work only by the power of suggestion. Until well-controlled studies of herbal medications are done and published, we won't know for sure. If they can't hurt you, the only thing you have to lose is your cash.

If they don't have much effect on your control and your budget is tight, it would make sense to spend your money on something that would help you stick with your diet or exercise instead.

IN A SENTENCE:

Many different herbs are used to treat diabetes in different parts of the world, and some of them may turn out to be good treatments, but there have not yet been controlled studies of most of them.

learning

How Does
Insulin Work?

INSULIN IS a *hormone* that helps the body take up glucose from the blood to either burn for energy or store for future use. This is a lot like what we usually do with money. We either spend it immediately or put it into the bank for later.

In order to understand what insulin does, first you need to understand a little about how glucose is stored in the body.

When glucose in the bloodstream is abundant, the body takes steps to store the extra glucose. The body can store energy in two main ways, either as **glycogen** in the liver and muscles or as *fat* (triglycerides) in the fat cells. Glucose is the source of quick energy. Glycogen is used for short-term storage. Fat is used for long-term storage.

Exercise depletes your glycogen stores

Glycogen is a *polysaccharide*, or a string of many glucose molecules linked together. If you want, think of glucose as tins of food and glycogen as tins of glucose taped together with duct tape so they won't fall apart and then set on a shelf in the larder for future use. This is analogous to the long chains of glucose molecules stored in the 'larder' of the liver and muscle as glycogen.

In a well-fed person who eats carbohydrates, up to 10 per cent of the liver may consist of glycogen granules. (This is why you'll see in nutritional tables that animal liver contains some carbohydrate.) Only 1 to 2 per cent of the muscle is glycogen. However, because our muscle mass is so much greater than our liver mass, the average person has more than twice as much glycogen in muscles than in liver.

This is one reason exercise is so important for people with diabetes. When you eat and then lounge around in front of the computer, as I'm doing now, the glycogen larder fills up. Just as you stop putting tins of food in the larder when the larder is full (and store your food somewhere else), the body stops making more glycogen when the glycogen stores are full. The extra goes into fat, where it's stored for future use. If you want, you could think of this as bottles of oil that you store in the basement. The basement is larger than the larder, and you can store more food there. But it's quicker to get food from the larder.

Because twice as much glycogen is stored in the muscle, and because the only way the muscle can deplete those stores is by exercise, exercising is (alas!) very, very important in type 2 diabetes control.

This also explains why the effects of exercise last beyond the period of exercise itself. Let's say you start with a full larder of glycogen in the muscles. As you exercise, some of the glycogen gets broken down to produce the required energy. This breaking down of glycogen is called **glycogenolysis.** But then when you stop and collapse on the sofa wishing you had another disease instead, the muscles start rebuilding their glycogen supplies. The way they do this is to extract glucose from the blood and 'tape it' together to make more glycogen. So until the larder is full again, the muscles, which have twice the storage capacity of the liver, help keep the blood glucose (BG) levels down. This also explains why muscle-building exercises are good. The larger your muscle mass is, the larger your larder and thus your capacity for taking up BG and storing it as glycogen.

The liver is altruistic

Although most of the glycogen in the body is stored in two places, liver and muscle, the liver is more 'altruistic'. When the BG level starts getting low (*hypoglycaemia*), the liver goes into its pantry to get glycogen, breaks it down, and ships it off into the bloodstream so it can be used by other organs that need it, for example muscles and brain. The muscles are more selfish. They use their glycogen larder stores only for themselves. This is because they lack an enzyme that is needed to export glucose from cells.

The liver can make new glucose

Just to complicate things, the liver (and the kidney) can produce glucose from protein when glucose needs are high. This involves breaking proteins down into their parts (*amino acids; see* Day 3) and converting the amino acids into glucose. This process is called **gluconeogenesis**, or making new glucose. This is analogous to finding that your larder was low on tins of glucose and putting more glucose into tins.

Remember I said that the muscle cells are 'selfish' and can't export glucose to other tissues when the BG levels are low. Well, maybe they're not completely self-centred. When the rest of the body needs glucose badly, the muscle cells break down their protein into amino acids and export them and other substances to the liver, where they are converted to glucose by gluconeogenesis. This is one reason that undiagnosed or uncontrolled type 1 diabetes was originally described as 'melting of the flesh'. In the total absence of insulin, the muscles 'melt' down to provide glucose for the brain (which doesn't need insulin to use glucose).

The end product of both glycogenolysis and gluconeogenesis is the same: they both produce glucose. The words also look alike, and some people get them confused (see the box *Confusing Terms*). In general, you don't need to know when your body uses glycogenolysis and when it uses gluconeogenesis. You really just need to know that a particular activity will increase or decrease the glucose levels in your blood. However, there is one instance in which the distinction is important. Alcohol inhibits the process of gluconeogenesis. It doesn't affect glycogenolysis. Also, if you're on a low-carbohydrate diet or you've just done a lot of strenuous exercise, your glycogen reserves may be depleted and glycogenolysis rates would be low. But gluconeogenesis could still occur.

The main players are insulin and glucagon

The two main hormones that control the storage and breakdown of glucose are *insulin* and *glucagon*. Insulin tells the body that food supplies are abundant and it's time to store the energy from food as glycogen or fat. In general, glucagon does the exact opposite of insulin. Glucagon tells the body that food supplies are scarce, so it's time to break down glycogen in the liver and fat in the fat cells and use them to produce energy. Levels of both insulin and glucagon fluctuate, depending on how recently you've eaten, and it's the ratio of the two that determines whether energy is produced or stored.

When you've eaten a meal containing carbohydrate, insulin levels rise. This tells the body that glucose and energy are abundant and it should shift from a mode of energy production to one of energy storage. Thus insulin inhibits reactions that produce glucose and those that produce fatty acids (see Day 3) from stored fat, both sources of energy, and stimulates reactions that store them (storage of glycogen in the liver and dietary fatty acids in fat cells).

When there's nowhere else to store glucose (the glycogen larder is full), insulin also tells the liver cells to convert glucose into fatty acids and ship them off to the fat cells, where they're slurped up and stored as fat. As usual, glucagon has opposite effects.

This is one reason that high insulin levels can stimulate weight gain (stimulating the storage of fat and inhibiting its breakdown). This fact is emphasized by authors of low-carbohydrate diet books. However, other factors also affect the gain or loss of weight, including how hungry you are, how many calories you consume in relation to your own particular caloric needs (which can vary a lot depending on your genetic makeup), how active you are and other factors discussed in Month 8.

Between meals, insulin levels fall and glucagon levels rise. This tells the body that it needs to get its energy from storage sites. Reactions that produce glucose and fatty acids are stimulated, and reactions that store them are inhibited.

Most diet books that discuss insulin focus on carbohydrates. But fats are important too. Many tissues in the body can burn fat as well as glucose for energy. In fact some tissues, for example resting muscle, actually prefer fatty acids to glucose. (Unfortunately, this doesn't mean you can lose a lot of fat by resting more often; it's the amount of energy you burn, not its source, that is important.) Other types of cells burn fat when their preferred food, glucose, is in short supply.

The fat stored away in the fat cells is broken down into its parts: mostly fatty acids with a little bit (about 10 per cent) of glycerol (see Day 3). The glycerol is shipped off to the liver to be turned into glucose. Thus fat can raise your BG levels a little, but only a small amount of the glucose actually comes from the fat. When fat raises your BG levels a lot, it may actually be raising your insulin resistance (IR). In this case, your insulin is less effective, so any carbohydrate you eat along with the fat will raise your BG levels more than it would have without the fat. The fatty acids from the fat are taken up by the muscle cells and any other cells that need them and burned for energy.

Insulin is also needed for cells to take up the amino acids that come from the breakdown of proteins, and protein as well as carbo-hydrate stimulates the formation of insulin. However, protein stim-ulates the formation of glucagon as well as insulin, and because it's the ratio of the two that controls the BG level, the insulin stimulated by eating protein doesn't affect your BG levels very much, if at all.

Confusing Terms

ONE problem when you're learning about diabetes is all those words that look alike, for instance *gluconeogenesis* and *glycogenolysis.* The best way to decipher these terms is to understand the etymology.

Both *gluc* and *glyc* come from a Greek root meaning 'sweet', but different people coining new words transliterated the Greek differently. Some of them used *glu* and others used *gly*. Very confusing.

> *gen* or *gon* means 'generates'
> *lysis* means 'breaks down'
> *neo* means 'new'

So now we can decipher the words.

Glucose: You should be familiar with this by now. Glucose is the sugar that the body breaks down for energy.

Glycogen: Glycogen means 'sweet generating'. It's a polysaccharide composed of many molecules of glucose (or tins of glucose taped together with duct tape if you prefer a picture). When it breaks down, you get glucose.

Glycogenolysis: Glycogenolysis means 'breaking down glycogen' to produce glucose. Taking a knife and cutting the duct tape that holds the tins of glucose together.

Glycolysis: Glycolysis means 'breaking down glucose' to produce energy. (Getting a tin opener to open those tins of glucose to get the energy out. Why didn't they call it glucolysis?)

Gluconeogenesis: Gluconeogenesis means 'generating new glucose'. In other words, you're building glucose out of building blocks from other types of food, like proteins. (A factory packing the glucose into the tins.)

Glucagon: Here's the tricky one. Unlike glycogen and glucose, glucagon isn't a carbohydrate. It's a protein and a hormone. Like glycogen, glucagon means 'sweet generating', but it does it indirectly by stimulating both glycogenolysis and gluconeogenesis in the liver. In general, whatever insulin does, glucagon does the opposite.

Once you get these words unconfused, understanding all the literature gets a little easier.

As the protein is slowly converted into glucose, it can cause a rise in BG levels in people with very little insulin production of their own. When you have type 2 diabetes and are able to produce some insulin, quite often your pancreas is able to deal with the slow release of glucose from the protein you eat, and you won't see much of a rise in BG levels as a result.

No one knows yet exactly how insulin works

Insulin works primarily on three main types of tissue: muscle, liver and fat. It used to be thought these were the only places that insulin had any important roles. But work done in the past few years has revolutionized the way people look at insulin. Researchers found evidence that insulin also plays important roles in the brain and beta cells as well.

There is evidence that IR in the brain keeps your appetite from being turned off by rising insulin levels, which normally seem to turn the appetite off. Injecting insulin into the brains of animals makes them eat less. This means that if you have IR, you would continue to be hungry after eating, when a person without IR would feel full. IR in the brain could keep your appetite turned on all the time, contributing to obesity. If you've always thought you were hungrier than other people, you were probably right.

So far, I've told you *where* insulin works, but not *how* it works. One reason is that no one really knows how insulin works. What is known is that insulin binds to receptors on cells called **insulin receptors** that are partly outside the cell (where they bind the insulin) and partly inside the cell. The insulin binding somehow changes the shape of the receptors so that the parts inside the cell activate enzymes that activate other molecules that activate other molecules and so forth in an incredibly complex chain of reactions that is not yet fully understood.

The end result of this chain is that *glucose transporters*, the little 'ferries' I mentioned in Day 1, are moved to the cell membrane, where they carry glucose molecules across the cell membrane into the cell. The formal name of the ferries in muscle and fat cells is GLUT4. Other types of cells have slightly different transporters named GLUT1, GLUT2 and so forth. Some types of transporters, for example the GLUT2 found in liver cells, are present whether or not insulin levels are high, which means those tissues can take up glucose even when insulin levels are low.

At the moment, this information has very little practical use to you. I discuss it because if you later read books or articles that mention GLUT4 or GLUT2, you'll have a better idea of what they're talking about.

Your mileage may vary

You can see from this brief discussion why type 2 diabetes is such a complicated disease. Different people might have deficiencies in one molecule involved in this complicated chain of events and others might have flaws somewhere else. This situation has already been shown in people with the relatively rare form of diabetes called *MODY* (see Month 2). Mutations in several specific genes have been shown, with different families having mutations in a single different gene.

So far, such genes haven't been found for common or garden-variety type 2 diabetes, which may be caused by variant forms of not just one but many genes. Depending on which molecule or molecules are involved and how much they are changed from normal, people might react differently to different situations and treatments.

Eventually, scientists will know how to tell where the defects are in the different subtypes of type 2 diabetes. Then they'll be able to develop treatments aimed at these specific defects. That time has not arrived. In general, certain approaches such as limiting calories and increasing physical activity, as well as BG-lowering and insulin-sensitizing drugs, seem to help the majority of people with type 2 diabetes, so until more is known, we'll have to stick with that. Diet and exercise aren't fun, but they work.

IN A SENTENCE:

> The relative amounts of insulin and glucagon in your blood-stream tell the body whether it should store energy as glycogen and fat (high insulin levels) or break down glycogen and fat to produce energy (low insulin levels).

Eating Out and Travelling

IF YOU need to eat out or travel for business, you've already had to deal with how to handle the difficulties that can arise when you're trying to stick to your diet plan in restaurants or even foreign countries where you may not be familiar with the food. If not, you may have put off facing the extra challenges of travel, or even just dining out at a local restaurant.

I've always loved to try new foods at interesting ethnic restaurants that serve dishes I've never heard of. In fact, one of my main social outlets had always been meeting friends at interesting new restaurants and sampling their fare. With my restricted diet, however, I couldn't eat most of the food at these interesting places, and because I loved it so much, I didn't want to be tempted. Easier to stay home. It was almost three years after my diagnosis before I trusted myself enough to go on a simple weekend trip.

Once you get over this initial hurdle of dealing with temptations, whether it's the week after you're diagnosed or several years, you'll find that travelling isn't that difficult if you do a little planning ahead.

Eating well when eating out takes practice

Unless you're just planning a trip to visit Auntie Em, travelling involves a lot of eating in restaurants, a sort of crash course in all the problems you face when eating out at home. I discussed some of these in Day 7. When you're travelling, however, you'll have to depend on others for *all* your meals. In foreign countries, choosing suitable meals can be even more daunting.

Thus it's probably not a good idea to take a five-week, 21-city European bus tour before you've mastered the art of dining out at home. Start small and work up. Get used to finding things you can eat at restaurants in your own city, learning to ask about ingredients and asking for substitutions. Then try a weekend trip somewhere nearby. Then maybe you're ready to try going further afield.

Don't be afraid to call ahead and ask if the hotel or bed and breakfast can accommodate your diet, whatever it is. If not, you might want to try another. When I did this on my latest trip, it turned out the hotel owner's father had type 2 diabetes, so she was very sympathetic and cooked me eggs for breakfast instead of the pancakes and maple syrup she served to everyone else.

If you're travelling with other people, don't be afraid to be assertive. You don't want to deprive your travelling companions of the pleasures of trying interesting restaurants just because they're not ideal for you. But you also shouldn't have to go to bed hungry. If you're not on a tour but are travelling with another person, you could try alternating restaurant choices. 'You pick the place for lunch, and I'll pick the place for dinner.' Then at least you should get one meal a day that will fill you up. Or buy food you can eat and bring it with you to restaurants that are going to be totally unsuitable for your diet.

If you're on a tour that includes all your meals, you'll have to check with the tour organizers before you sign up to see whether they'll be able to accommodate your diet. If you're taking a sulphonylurea or insulin and need to eat at certain times to avoid going low, ask the tour organizers before you sign up if meals will be regular. But try not to ruin things for everyone else by insisting that you all leave an interesting site before the others are ready just so you can reach the restaurant at the dot of noon. **Carry snacks with you at all times to deal with situations like that.**

Cruises usually have such a vast array of food that you should be able to find something you can eat no matter what kind of diet you're on. The problem will more likely be temptation from too much delicious food being offered too often than a lack of anything you can eat.

Planning ahead is important

Travelling with diabetes, like travelling without diabetes, is best done with a little advance planning. You need to plan for your health care as well as your itinerary. If you're going abroad, you need to do a little more.

The amount of extra planning you'll need depends on how you're controlling your diabetes. If you're controlling well with diet and exercise and you never have problems with low blood sugar, then you won't need to make quite as many extra plans as you would if you were using insulin and also might need to have other medications changed sometime during the trip.

If you're going abroad, one of the first things you should do is make an appointment with your doctor. The doctor may know if you need any special immunizations for the trip and if there are any special conditions in the countries you're planning to visit that would affect your diabetes. Otherwise, you can contact the International Association for Medical Assistance to Travellers (IAMAT) (www.iamat.org). You have to join to use their services, but membership is free, and they can provide a lot of useful information.

If you'll be crossing borders, it's important to ask your doctor for a letter, preferably in duplicate, explaining that you are diabetic and noting the medications you need, listed by their generic names. Also get prescriptions for the drugs. Guard the prescriptions as closely as you guard your passport. The letter is just in case a customs official asks about the drugs or syringes you are carrying. The list of drugs and prescriptions is in case you need hospitalization or run out of a drug, or lose it. The trade names in foreign countries may be different, so it's important that the generic names be used.

If you don't already have one, this would be a good time to get a diabetic identification bracelet just in case you need medical care and can't communicate your condition because of language problems, or if you're unconscious.

You may also want to get from IAMAT a list of doctors in the countries you're visiting who speak English. If you didn't do this ahead of time and you're in Europe, you can call the International Diabetes Federation in Brussels (32-2/538 55 11) or ask at a British embassy.

Find out from your travel insurance company whether or not hospitalizations are covered in the countries you're going to. If not, make plans for some kind of temporary coverage just in case.

If you're going to a non-English-speaking country, it's a good idea to memorize a few phrases before you leave, for example, 'I have diabetes,' and 'Please give me some sugar,' and 'I need a doctor.' Write the phrases down and keep them in your wallet in case you go low and forget how to pronounce them.

Take extra supplies

Make a list of all the medications and blood glucose (BG) testing supplies you would normally use during the period of the trip. Take twice as many as you expect to use. Pack half in your hand luggage with one copy of the prescriptions and letters from the doctor and put the other half in a bag or a baggy jacket. The duplication is so you'll have a backup if one of the items is lost, stolen or damaged. Don't put your meters or any drugs in your checked-in luggage. The temperature of the baggage compartment can get extremely low; insulin could freeze and meters and strips might get damaged. However, none of the meters are supposed to be affected by the X-rays used to check your luggage at the airport.

At the other extreme, if you're going to a tropical country and will be staying in places that have no air-conditioning, you should make some kind of plans for how you're going to ensure your meter is accurate (call the manufacturer for advice) and keep your strips or insulin from degrading. There are insulated packs designed to protect insulin from high temperatures. Remember not to keep meters or medications in a hot car.

If you have problems with hypoglycaemia, make sure you have a good supply of glucose tablets and keep them with you at all times. Don't pack them in your luggage where you can't get them if the plane is delayed or your baggage is sent to Sierra Leone by mistake.

Take a supply of sugar-free medications for nausea and diarrhoea in case they're not readily available where you're going. Both conditions are common when you're travelling, eating different foods and drinking water with different mineral contents. If such illness does strike, remember to check your BG levels frequently, as dehydration can cause serious problems, as described in Month 2.

Remember to take extra batteries for your meter. Some people take BG strips that are read visually as a backup in case the meter breaks. If you use urine-testing strips, of course you'll need to take those as well.

Take snacks to use en route

If you're travelling by air, you can usually get diabetic meals if you order them a couple of days in advance. But be aware that the airline's definition of a 'diabetic meal' might be quite different from yours. Some people with diabetes are following a high-carbohydrate and others a low-carbohydrate diet. You can't expect the airlines to know what you want. You can try calling ahead and asking what kinds of special meals will be available and choosing one that sounds as if it would match your diet. One traveller finds that special Asian vegetarian meals tend to have the low-glycaemic index foods that are on his diet. Another recommends low-sodium meals, which tend to include fresh fruit and vegetables. Some people find they're better off just getting the regular meal and picking out the things they can eat.

No matter what kind of diet you're on, it's safer if you carry a lot of snacks as well. Meals may be delayed, or you may find there's almost nothing you can eat. On shorter flights these days, you'll probably be offered only snack food that you may or may not be able to eat. Airport food tends to be fast food – greasy, starchy and relatively expensive.

The same problems apply to train or bus travel. When possible, carry picnic meals and snacks with you, as the offerings on the train or at the bus terminals will probably be limited. Remember to use glucose test strips to check the sugar content of fizzy drinks unless they are served in the bottle.

Changing time zones may be a problem for people taking insulin. When you're flying from London to New York, you gain five hours. When you go from New York to London, you lose five hours. With longer distances, the gains and losses are obviously greater. With oral drugs, this shouldn't be a big problem. Just take your next dose at the usual time. With insulin, check with your doctor before you leave to see how to adjust your doses.

Check your blood glucose levels often

Remember that your activity level affects your BG levels. If you normally walk for two hours after lunch but you've chosen to travel by rail, or a 12-city bus tour, your BG levels may be higher than usual. On the other hand, if you usually spend all day at an office job and you're walking from one museum to another, your BG levels may be lower than they normally are, and you can probably add a few treats to your menu.

Remember that stress makes BG levels go up, and happy stress such as excitement about a trip might affect your BG levels. So test more often than usual to see how the holiday is affecting you.

Take care of your feet

If you *do* plan to do a lot of walking during the trip, take along two pairs of well-worn-in shoes, and alternate them to make sure you don't get blisters on the trip. This would be a good time to try some padded socks, or the special nonblister kind, even if you don't have any signs of neuropathy. You don't want to ruin a nice holiday with blisters.

Eating abroad may be challenging

Eating in restaurants abroad will have the extra challenge that you may not know the ingredients of various dishes. As when you're at home, don't be afraid to ask. And if you can't eat part of the meal, ask if they can make substitutions.

If in doubt, go ahead and try a new food if you like adventurous eating, especially if you're normally in pretty good control. *Just control your portion sizes.* Part of the fun of travelling is trying new foods, and going a little high after a meal won't kill you as long as it's not your regular way of life. If you're embarrassed about asking for a doggie bag in a foreign country, where it might not be the custom, you can carry sealable plastic bags in your pocket or handbag and squirrel away part of the meal inconspicuously. If you find you *are* too high after a mystery dish, do some extra walking to get your BG levels down.

If you're controlling with a low-carbohydrate diet and planning a trip to a country like China, where rice and noodles and sugared sauces will probably play a large part in most of the meals, you might think about learning how to use insulin, or one of the fast-acting insulin-releasing drugs that you take before meals, so you can enjoy some of these delicious high-carbohydrate meals.

Of course you don't want to just get a prescription for insulin and set off for foreign climes. Practice before you go on the trip. That practice might come in handy at other times, for example if you ever get a bad illness or need steroid drugs that make your BG levels go up so much that insulin is the best temporary remedy.

If you're controlling with a low-fat diet and going somewhere like the Mediterranean, where everything is likely to be drizzled with olive oil, you'll just have to ask if they could hold the oil, or you'll have to pick and choose. But remember that unlike saturated fat, the monounsaturated fat in olive oil isn't detrimental to insulin resistance and lipid levels (see Learning section).

Have fun

Diabetes can be draining, because there is no such thing as a holiday from the disease. But you deserve a holiday for yourself. So take care of your diabetes when you're travelling, but don't let it be the focus of your trip. If you plan ahead, you're less likely to find yourself stranded in Rome while your suitcase containing your snacks and medications heads for Tierra del Fuego.

Plan ahead so you can enjoy yourself. Focus on seeing new sights, meeting new people, tasting new foods. Above all, have fun.

Note: Since the September 11 2001 tragedy, airline security regulations have changed and undoubtedly will continue to change. Hence, some of the travel recommendations may no longer apply. For example, many airlines no longer accept letters from your doctor certifying that you need syringes on an airplane. Before any such travel, call the airlines to determine current regulations.

IN A SENTENCE:

> *Eating out and travelling require a little more planning when you have diabetes, but there's no reason to limit such activities.*

learning

Syndrome X

HERE'S SOME good news. Being diagnosed with diabetes may have saved your life. What's that? How can getting a potentially lethal disease be good for your health?

The fact is, type 2 diabetes is strongly associated with cardiovascular problems. By now, you've probably heard a lot about the microvascular (small blood vessel) complications of diabetes such as neuropathy, retinopathy and nephropathy – the 'Three O'Pathy Sisters' I introduced in Day 6. These complications are, in fact, possible if you let your blood glucose (BG) levels stay high for many years.

The main problem is cardiovascular events

In type 2 diabetes, although you should never forget that these microvascular complications could occur if you let your BG levels stay high, they are actually less of a concern than the macrovascular (large blood vessel) complications of heart attack and stroke, which can be lumped together as *cardiovascular events*. Most people with type 2 diabetes eventually die from cardiovascular events. If you have type 2 diabetes, your risk for these problems is two to four times that of a nondiabetic person. Add smoking into the equation, and it's even higher.

What causes the cardiovascular problems? No one is sure, but there is some evidence that these macrovascular complications are caused not by the high BG levels themselves but by the underlying insulin resistance (IR) that contributes to the high levels of glucose in the blood, and the majority of people with type 2 diabetes have some or a lot of IR.

There seems to be a constellation of symptoms that go along with IR. These include high insulin levels; excess visceral fat (fat around your internal abdominal organs; the 'apple shape'); high blood pressure; high levels of triglycerides; low levels of **HDL (high-density lipoprotein)**; normal or only slightly elevated levels of **LDL (low-density lipoprotein)**; high levels of **small, dense LDL** and impaired glucose tolerance. This has been called **Syndrome X**, *insulin-resistance syndrome* or *metabolic syndrome*. Many of these same symptoms are found in women with *polycystic ovary syndrome* (see Month 2), which is also associated with IR.

All these symptoms are *associated with* increased risks of cardiovascular events. This doesn't necessarily mean that all or any of them actually *cause* the cardiovascular problems. It just means that having the symptoms of Syndrome X greatly increases your risk of having cardiovascular problems.

The effect of hyperinsulinaemia is controversial

One of the most controversial aspects of Syndrome X, and type 2 diabetes, is the role of *hyperinsulinaemia* (high insulin levels in the blood) as a factor in causing heart disease. Some people say that the high insulin levels themselves are the *cause* of the cardiovascular problems. Some studies have shown that the only factor able to predict heart attacks in a group of people was their insulin levels. These studies are often cited by people promoting insulin-lowering dietary approaches.

However, it's also possible that it's not the high insulin levels themselves but the underlying IR that is in fact the cause of the cardiovascular problems. After all, if you have a lot of IR and your beta cells are able to increase their output, your insulin levels will rise to overcome the IR.

Another possibility is that another, as yet unknown problem is causing both the IR (with its accompanying high insulin levels) and the cardiovascular problems. In this case they would simply be found together, but neither one would cause the other.

These questions have not yet been answered. What we do know is that Syndrome X is associated with a high risk of heart disease.

Diabetes is an early warning sign

Syndrome X sounds a lot like diabetes without the high BG levels. The difference is how much insulin your pancreas is able to produce. Imagine a bunch of people with Syndrome X, all at high risk for heart disease. A few of them will have diabetes genes that won't let their pancreas keep churning out insulin to overcome the IR that is part of the syndrome. Those people's BG levels will continue to rise until they're diagnosed with diabetes.

The rest of the group are 'blessed' with strong pancreases that can keep cranking out more and more insulin. They can get quite obese, will never develop high BG levels no matter how much candyfloss they eat and won't become diabetic. But they'll be just as much at risk for cardiovascular problems. Because they're not diabetic, they may not realize there's any problem until it's too late.

Having IR without getting diabetes can lead to heart attacks and strokes without the early warning sign of high BG levels. Being diagnosed with type 2 diabetes is thus in some ways a blessing. In most cases it warns you that you've probably got IR and gives you a chance to modify your diet and lifestyle before it's too late.

Heart Health Acronyms and Other Terms

WHEN you read about heart health, you'll usually come across a number of acronyms labelling all the different kinds of fats that are important for maintaining the health of your heart. The following are some of the most important acronyms and other terms that you need to know to understand heart disease and how to prevent it.

Cardiovascular. This is a general term referring to all kinds of issues involving your heart (*cardio*) or your blood vessels (*vascular*). Cardiovascular problems could include clogged arteries in your heart (leading to *heart attacks*), clogged or weakened arteries in your brain (leading to *strokes*), and clogged arteries in your legs and arms (**peripheral vascular disease**).

Cardiovascular event. This means an 'incident' involving the cardiovascular system, for example a heart attack or a stroke.

Arteriosclerosis and atherosclerosis. *Arteriosclerosis* means thickening and stiffening of arteries, regardless of the cause. It is popularly called 'hardening of the arteries'. *Atherosclerosis* is a more specific term referring to thickening of arteries as a result of *plaques*.

Lipid. *Lipids* are all types of molecules that don't dissolve in water and includes *fats* (triglycerides), *steroids* and *waxes*. When speaking of heart health, the most important lipids are the *triglycerides* and *cholesterol*, and when people refer to your *lipid levels*, they usually mean both these types. They don't care about your testosterone levels or how much wax you have in your ears.

Cholesterol. *Cholesterol* is a type of lipid that is chemically very different from triglyceride. Along with triglycerides, cholesterol is an important building block for cell membranes, and it is also the starting point for building important hormones, including *oestrogen* and *testosterone*. Thus some cholesterol is essential for your body. If you don't eat enough cholesterol, your body will make it. What you want is for the cholesterol to be taken up by the cells that need it, rather than having a lot floating around in your bloodstream.

Plaque. A *plaque* is a deposit of cholesterol and other substances underneath the artery wall. It can grow and grow until it blocks the flow of blood in the artery. Also, a protruding plaque can trigger the formation of clots. With time, a plaque can take up calcium from the blood. Plaques can make the arteries stiff.

Lipoprotein. This means a particle that contains both fat (*lipo*) and protein. Cholesterol can't travel around in the bloodstream by itself because, like other lipids, it isn't soluble in water, and the blood is mostly water. So the cholesterol and other lipids hitch a ride inside particles that have protein on the outside. The protein is soluble in water, and the cholesterol and triglycerides are hidden inside.

HDL. This stands for *high-density lipoprotein*. It's supposed to be the good kind of cholesterol. I always got it confused with LDL until I started thinking of HDL as *Happy cholesterol*. Just to make things more confusing, there are also subfractions of HDL called HDL2 and HDL3. HDL2 is supposed to be the best kind of HDL, and it's increased by exercise. Red wine seems to increase HDL3 levels. No one is sure if that's beneficial or not. Some people use the term *HDL-C*, meaning HDL-cholesterol. It means essentially the same as just plain HDL.

If you've ever wondered why it's called *high density*, it's because HDL contains less lipid, which floats on the top of water, than other lipid fractions. So when you spin down a solution in a centrifuge, the HDL ends up closer to the bottom of the tube.

LDL. This stands for *low-density lipoprotein*. This is the bad stuff. You can remember it by thinking of *Lousy cholesterol*. LDL, and especially *oxidized* and *glycated* LDL, contributes to the formation of *atherogenic plaques*, the deposits of lipids and other material in the arterial wall that lead to heart attacks and strokes. Again, *LDL-C* means essentially the same thing as LDL. As you can infer from the description of HDL, LDL contains more lipid and floats above HDL when centrifuged.

It is expensive to measure LDL directly, so many labs estimate the value using the formula LDL = total cholesterol − (HDL + TG/5), where TG is triglycerides.

VLDL. This stands for *very low density lipoprotein*. This contains a lot of triglyceride surrounded by protein and is the way the liver ships triglycerides out to the rest of the body to be burned for energy. When the VLDL drops off its triglycerides to the cells, it picks up cholesterol and turns into LDL.

Small, dense LDL. This is LDL that is in much smaller particles than usual. It is the worst kind of LDL we know of (so far). You can think of it as *Specially Damaging Lousy cholesterol*. Because the particles are small, they are thought to be able to get into the arterial walls more easily, starting the formation of plaques. Unfortunately, people with diabetes tend to have high levels of small, dense LDL.

Triglycerides. *Triglycerides* are fats. They consist of long chains of *fatty acids* (see Day 3) attached to a molecule of *glycerol* (see Day 3). They are often referred to as *TGs*. There are different kinds of fats, some more harmful than others.

Unsaturated fats. *Unsaturated fats* contain one (*monounsaturated fats*) or more (*polyunsaturated fats*) *double bonds*. Unsaturated fats are 'kinky', and they can't pack closely together in cell membranes. They are usually liquid at room temperature.

Double bonds are chemically reactive, and unsaturated fats can be oxidized more easily than saturated fats. This is especially true of the polyunsaturated fats. When fats are oxidized, the popular term is *rancid*. Most plant oils contain lots of antioxidants, but they may be removed during the refining process. Olive oil contains an especially high level of antioxidants.

Monounsaturated fats aren't supposed to change cholesterol levels. Polyunsaturated fats decrease total cholesterol levels, but this decrease often includes the beneficial HDL as well as the LDL, and the ratio of the two may remain constant.

Monounsaturated fats are found in olive oil, nuts, avocado, fish, chicken and wild meats such as venison and kangaroo. Polyunsaturated fats are found in most vegetable oils and some nuts.

Saturated fats. The *saturated fats* have no double bonds, so they're less susceptible to oxidation. They are usually solid at room temperature.

The saturated fats are straight chains and can pack very tightly in membranes. Some people think that tightly packed cell membranes don't work as well as they should, but this is only a theory. A diet high in saturated fat can increase LDL cholesterol levels and cause IR.

Saturated fats are found in meat, dairy foods and tropical oils such as coconut oil, palm oil and cocoa butter.

Trans fats. The *trans fats* are formed when chemists take polyunsaturated fats and partially saturate them with hydrogen gas. In this way they can turn polyunsaturated vegetable oils, which are liquid at room temperature, into partially saturated fats that are solid at room temperature and are used for margarine and vegetable shortening.

During the chemical saturation process, some of the kinky polyunsaturated fats are turned into straight rods that pack tightly into membranes just like saturated fats, and some people think that trans fats are even worse for your health than saturated fats.

Small amounts of natural trans fats are found naturally in meat and milk. Certain natural trans fats that contain kinked double bonds elsewhere in the molecule, for example, *conjugated linolenic acid (CLA)*, seem to be beneficial.

Chemically produced trans fats are contained in products that list *partially hydrogenated vegetable oils* in the ingredients list, especially cookies, crackers, solid margarine and some salad dressings.

Apolipoprotein. *Lipoprotein* refers to the whole particle. *Apolipoprotein* means just the protein part of the lipoprotein. The prefix *apo* comes from the Greek 'separated from'. There are many different types of apolipoproteins. For example, apolipoprotein A (often called just apoA) is associated with HDL, and apolipoprotein B (apoB) is associated with LDL. Sometimes people call the apolipoproteins just *apoprotein*.

Lipoprotein(a). Just to make things more confusing, there's a special kind of LDL called *lipoprotein(a)*, or just *Lp(a)*. This LDL is attached to an extra glycoprotein (a protein containing some sugar) called *apolipoprotein(a)*. It's not the same as apolipoprotein A, which is associated with HDL. The amount of Lp(a) seems to depend primarily on your genetic background, although trans fats may increase it, and high levels are associated with increased cardiovascular risk.

Keeping your BG levels low will help, but normal BG levels don't reduce the risks of macrovascular complications as much as they reduce risks of the microvascular complications of damage to the nerves, kidneys and eyes. Thus in addition to working on BG control, if you know or are pretty sure that you have IR (you can estimate this with a C-peptide test; see Day 5), you need to focus attention on the other aspects of Syndrome X – blood pressure, lipid levels and trying to eliminate that apple shape.

Dietary recommendations are controversial

People with high lipid levels are often put on a low-fat, high-carbohydrate diet. However, some think this is not the best diet for people with Syndrome X. If you have Syndrome X, you probably have high triglyceride levels, and high-carbohydrate diets often increase triglyceride levels even more.

In addition, it has been found that people with Syndrome X or type 2 diabetes often have high levels of the dangerous small, dense LDL particles. Low-fat high-carbohydrate diets usually do reduce the total LDL levels, but they seem to produce even more of the small, dense LDL particles that may be more dangerous than the total amount of LDL.

Thus some think that low-fat, high-carbohydrate diets, although they may be beneficial for people who have no IR, actually increase the risk of heart disease in those who have Syndrome X. They recommend that anyone with Syndrome X eat less carbohydrate than this diet recommends and substitute monounsaturated fat instead. Monounsaturated fat is the kind found in olive oil, avocado and nuts. Unlike saturated fat, it seems not to increase IR or LDL levels.

Not everyone with type 2 diabetes has all the symptoms associated with Syndrome X. As usual, YMMV (Your Mileage May Vary). But if you do, make sure the treatment chosen to treat your high BG levels doesn't make your risk factors for heart disease even worse. And maybe you should thank your wimpy pancreas for giving you this early warning sign. Forewarned is forearmed. Take action now and you should have years of healthy living ahead.

IN A SENTENCE:

> *Insulin resistance can cause cardiovascular problems even without high blood glucose levels.*

MILESTONE

You're now halfway through your first year. You understand the basics of diabetes care and you're beginning to understand the more subtle and controversial aspects of diabetes and its control:

○ **YOU KNOW THERE ARE MANY DIFFERENT TYPES OF DIABETES.**

○ **YOU'VE LEARNED THAT SUPPLEMENTING WITH VITAMINS, MINERALS AND HERBS IS CONTROVERSIAL.**

○ **YOUR UNDERSTANDING OF TESTING PROCEDURES AND THE PHYSIOLOGY OF DIABETES IS BECOMING SOPHISTICATED.**

○ **YOU KNOW THAT YOU MUST PAY ATTENTION TO YOUR CARDIOVASCULAR HEALTH AS WELL AS YOUR BLOOD GLUCOSE LEVELS.**

○ **YOU KNOW YOU ALSO NEED TO ENJOY LIFE, AND YOU'RE BECOMING CONFIDENT ENOUGH ABOUT YOUR DIET TO ENJOY EATING OUT AND TRAVELLING.**

As you enter the last half of the year, you understand that this learning process will always continue, but when you find a treatment and diet that work for you, your diabetes will gradually cease to be the focus of your life. In the coming months, you'll learn:

O **THE RELATION BETWEEN WEIGHT LOSS AND BLOOD GLUCOSE CONTROL.**

O **HOW TO EVALUATE VARIOUS DIETS AND FIND THE ONE THAT WORKS FOR YOU.**

O **HOW TO CALCULATE YOUR PERSONAL GLYCAEMIC INDEX VALUES.**

O **MORE SOPHISTICATED DIABETES PHYSIOLOGY, INCLUDING THE EFFECTS OF EXERCISE AND THE CAUSES OF TYPE 2 DIABETES.**

O **WHERE TO GO TO CONTINUE THIS LEARNING PROCESS.**

living

Taking Stock

YOU'VE BEEN dealing with diabetes for half a year, and some of the patterns of your diabetes care should be almost routine by now, although not all. There are still hurdles ahead, maybe your first Christmas on a diabetic diet if you were diagnosed in the spring, or your first summer holiday on a diabetic routine if you were diagnosed in the autumn.

No one is perfect, and everyone slips off the wagon every now and then. Don't despair. If you *were* perfect, all your friends would hate you. So just pick yourself back up again and climb back on the wagon. It's your *overall* control that will matter in the long term, and 90 per cent is so much better than no control at all.

Now might be a good time to sit back and reevaluate where you are, how far you've come and where you want to go in the future. You should have had at least a couple of A1c tests by now, as well as a general idea of what your blood glucose (BG) levels are at different times of the day and after different activities like walking or watching TV.

Is your diet working?

The two most important things for type 2 diabetes are diet and exercise, so that's a good place to begin. If you need to lose weight, is your diet helping you to do that? Are you losing weight as fast as you expected to lose? How about your BG levels? Is your diet keeping them under control before meals? How about after meals?

If you aren't satisfied with the answers to any of these questions, this would be a good time to schedule another meeting with a dietician, unless you're the independent type who enjoys tinkering with diets on your own. If you started out on the exchange diet and you find that your overall control is just barely OK and your BG levels have been going high after meals, maybe you should consider trying a low-glycaemic index diet or a low-carbohydrate diet instead.

Before you *do* change your diet, it's ideal if you can get a lipid (see the discussion of lipids in Month 6) and an A1c test done. Then after you've been on the new diet for about three months, you can test again to see if there are any changes in your lipid levels or average BG levels as suggested by the A1c. Labs can test for many other factors in your blood, most of which won't be affected by diet. Before you start the new diet, ask your doctor if you should have any other blood tests done.

Are you exercising?

Now take a look at your exercise programme. There's no point in having a fancy exercise programme worked out if you never bother to follow it. If you're like me, you'll probably use every excuse under the sun to put it off. It's too hot. It's too cold. It's too rainy. It's too dry. I just bruised my rib. I've got the flu. I have to visit a sick friend. My library books are due.

When I find something I enjoy doing, I can somehow find the time even if the weather is a tad too hot or too cold or too wet or too dry. So if you've found some way of exercising that you enjoy enough that you actually do it, you're in real luck. Just keep it up.

But if you're honest with yourself and admit you've been putting the exercise on the back burner, now is the time to sit down and figure out why it is you don't enjoy it. Would it help if you found some other people to join you in your daily efforts to get moving? Maybe you could find a friend who could benefit from more walking, and you could think of it as helping a friend instead of a dreaded chore for you. Or maybe you could offer to rake leaves or do other calorie-burning chores for elderly people who could use the help.

Would it help if you found some new sport to learn or some team sport to join? Would treating yourself to a brand-new portable CD player inspire you to take a walk every day while you were listening to CDs?

Go to the library and browse around in the sporting section. Maybe there's some obscure sport you've never heard about that you could try and then introduce to all your friends. One woman took up belly dancing. Or would it help if you dumped the dreaded term *exercise*? Instead of staying inside to 'exercise' tell yourself you're going out to 'play' or 'dance' or whatever it is that sounds like fun to you – and then do it.

Is your medication the best for you?

This might also be a good time to get together with your doctor and discuss your medications, if you're taking any. If your control is good, there's no reason to change. But if it could be better, maybe another drug or another combination of drugs would work better for you. By now you should have a good idea if your main problem is high BG levels after meals, high BG levels in the morning or high BG levels throughout the day. Different drugs treat different aspects of BG control, as described in Week 3. You may want to review how the drugs work so you can have a productive discussion about the options with your doctor.

Is your health care team working with you?

You may also want to think about your diabetes 'team', the medical professionals who are helping you achieve your control. Are you happy with them? Are they good listeners? Are they willing to take the time to explain things to you and pay attention to your concerns about your diabetes, or do they just rush you out the door as soon as possible after writing a prescription? Are they willing to accept A1c levels of 8 or 9 as 'the best you can do' or will they try to work with you to bring those numbers down?

If you want to test a lot, do they tell you you're being compulsive? Do they say, 'Once a week is fine for a type 2?'

If you work hard to get your BG levels close to normal and ask your doctor for help getting them down even further, into the normal range, are you brushed off with a comment like, 'Oh, you're doing fine. I have patients who'd give their right arm for BGs like yours' and then told to come back next year while they spend more time with the really 'sick' patients?

On the other hand, if you're not doing as well as they think you should, are your health care providers trying to put the blame on you, by labelling you as *noncompliant* instead of considering that maybe the most popular drugs or diets aren't the correct ones for you?

Unfortunately, this labelling is not uncommon. Barbara F. had seen a dietician who told her to eat a lot of carbohydrate, even suggesting that she put raisins in her morning porridge to 'get those carbs up'. This didn't work for Barbara. Her BG levels, which were not terribly high when she was diagnosed, kept going up and up. But instead of considering that maybe the diet wasn't working, the dietician assumed that Barbara was noncompliant and blamed her. 'After two weeks of eating the exact diet from their booklet,' said Barbara, 'my BGs were up, and I was told I really had to take my condition seriously and follow the diet. That's when I started testing after meals instead of before and discovered how high BGs were after eating all those carbs.'

When Alex E. was diagnosed with type 2 diabetes, he asked his doctor if he should get a meter and test his BG levels. 'She laughed disparagingly and said, "Sure, an occasional test wouldn't hurt anything." That's when I realized she didn't know how to treat diabetes, so I found another doctor immediately.' Some doctors accuse type 2 patients of being compulsive if they measure their BG levels a lot.

If you find that your health care people patronize you like Alex's doctor, don't respect you as an intelligent human being, or blame you for 'noncompliance' when a particular treatment doesn't work as Barbara's dietician did, don't waste your time seeing them again, if you possibly can.

Look around. Connect with other people who have diabetes and ask for recommendations. If there's a choice of potential doctors who are accepting new patients, ask for an appointment to interview them before you sign up for their care.

Explain that you want to understand your diabetes and what is being done to control it and want to be a partner in making decisions about your control. Ask if they're comfortable with this kind of approach. Ask how they feel about various drugs and diets used to control diabetes and make sure their views are compatible with yours. For example, if you want to try a low-carbohydrate diet and they tell you high-carbohydrate diets are the only way to go, or vice versa, you may not be able to work well together. If you want to try some insulin and they see insulin as a last resort for someone with type 2 diabetes, you should keep looking.

Remember, you're chairman of the board. You are choosing people to help you. You need these people. They know things that you haven't learned yet. But if you don't think they're doing the job you want them to do, don't hesitate to find someone else. There are some wonderful, caring doctors, dieticians, exercise therapists, diabetes specialist nurses out there. You just have to find the ones that are the best for you.

IN A SENTENCE:

> Take stock of your diabetes treatment programme and see if you need to make any changes.

learning

What Causes Diabetes?

ONCE YOU'VE been diagnosed with diabetes, it doesn't really make much difference what caused it. It's too late to go back and change.

Some medical people will tell you not to waste your time worrying about what caused your diabetes or what your C-peptide levels are or which variety of type 2 diabetes you may have. They're mostly interested in how to treat your diabetes and may treat different types the same, focusing on the A1c.

Of course keeping blood glucose (BG) levels down is just about the most important thing you can do to ensure a long and complication-free life. But if you're reading this, you're probably curious about your disease as well. You may want to know why you got diabetes and your overweight brother didn't or why your best friend can subsist on crisps and doughnuts and never weigh more than 54 kilograms when you just look at a pat of butter and you can feel your stomach expanding.

Both genes and environment are important

The cause of type 2 diabetes, as well as the cause of insulin resistance (IR), is not yet completely understood. What scientists do know is that for type 2 diabetes to develop, there are usually two requirements. First, your beta cells must have a genetic defect that makes them unable to cope with excessive demands for insulin. In other words, the first cause is genetic: not choosing your parents carefully.

When one of a pair of identical twins gets type 2 diabetes, the probability of the other one getting it too has been reported to be 60 to almost 100 per cent, depending on the study. Scientists have identified a gene in people of Mexican descent that predisposes them to developing type 2 diabetes, but this is undoubtedly not the only gene involved.

The second requirement is that you must have conditions that require these excessive demands for insulin, especially when they persist for long periods of time. These conditions might include the IR associated with obesity; stress-induced IR caused by surgery, infection, certain drugs or pregnancy; or many years eating more calories than you need, including a lot of saturated fat and high levels of processed 'fast' carbohydrates that quickly dump a big load of glucose into your bloodstream. In other words, the second cause is environmental.

Under low-stress conditions such as a moderate or low caloric intake; a diet in which the carbohydrate is mostly unprocessed, with a lot of fibre, and the saturated fat intake is not excessive; lots of physical work that burns off the carbohydrates that are eaten; and no stress-induced IR, genetically 'weak' beta cells may function just fine and a person will never get diabetes.

Conversely, a person born with 'strong' beta cells can undergo all these stressful conditions and just crank out more and more insulin to overcome them. Cranking out a lot of insulin is not necessarily a good thing, as discussed in Month 6. But such people will never develop high BG levels.

The Pima story illustrates environmental effects

The Pima Indians in Arizona, USA, who have one of the highest rates of type 2 diabetes in the world (closely followed by the Sunni Arabs in Bahrain), and their close relatives in Mexico, who have low rates of type 2 diabetes, are often used to illustrate how environmental factors can influence the genes we are born with.

Arizona Pima Indians. Until the 20th century, the Pima Indians in Arizona harvested wild plants and grew their own food in the harsh environment of the Sonoran Desert. They called themselves *Akimel O'odham*, the 'river people', and constructed a complex irrigation system to cultivate their crops. However, sometimes the irrigation systems failed, and periods of famine were not uncommon.

Their crops included wheat, tepary beans, cushaw squash and Pima corn, which has a lower glycaemic index than modern sweet corn. Other foods included acorns, cholla-cactus buds, honey mesquite, povertyweed and prickly pears from the desert floor; mule deer, white-winged dove and black-tailed jackrabbit as well as squawfish from the Gila River. Thus their diet had foods that had very low glycaemic index values and were high in fibre as well as low in fat.

The Pima Indians also expended a lot of energy in their farming and canal construction work and were lean, with diabetes almost unknown among them.

Then when whites moved West, they diverted the Gila River for their own farming enterprises, and the Pima Indians' way of life was destroyed. Starving, they were forced to accept government surplus food: lard, sugar and white flour; in other words they ate high-glycaemic index, low-fibre, high-fat foods and had little physical activity to burn off the extra calories they took in. Today their diet is similar to that of other Americans. A favourite food is *fry bread*, made with white flour.

As a result, obesity became the norm and rates of diabetes soared. Today, more than 50 per cent of the River Pima Indians have type 2 diabetes, which is appearing in younger and younger ages in children.

Some people feel that because of their periodic famines, the Pima Indians who survived were those with 'thrifty genes' who were able to store fat easily in better times so they could survive the times of famine. Those genes served them well under those conditions. But with modern living and permanent plenty, the genes turned out to be a liability.

Mexican Pima Indians. The Arizona Pima Indians' close relatives in Maycoba, Mexico, who undoubtedly share those thrifty genes, have not yet abandoned their traditional lifestyles. They live in a harsh mountain environment where crops are difficult to grow, and they eat primarily beans, potatoes and tortillas made from coarsely ground corn. They may have chicken once a month.

Interestingly, the Mexican Pima Indians actually take in more calories a day (about 2200 calories) than their relatives in Arizona, but the Mexican Pima Indians also expend more energy with physical work. They lack modern transportation and still walk wherever they want to go. Often they run. They spend an average of more than 20 hours a week in hard or moderate physical labour, as opposed to the two hours a week spent by the average Pima Indian in Arizona. Most Americans have to be urged to exercise only 30 minutes a day three times a week, or only 1.5 hours a week.

The Mexican Pima Indians almost surely have the same thrifty genes as their cousins in Arizona, but their lifestyle keeps diabetes at bay – at least for now.

This same situation is being found in other ethnic groups that only recently changed from a lifestyle involving a lot of physical labour and not a lot to eat to one of plentiful food and less physical labour, often when rural residents move to a city. Rates of diabetes are soaring in these groups. Worldwide, high rates of diabetes are found in the Pima Indians (50 per cent), Naurans (40 per cent), Australian aborigines (25 per cent), peninsular Arabs (25 per cent), south Asians (20 per cent) and West Africans (12 per cent). For comparison, northern Europeans have a rate of 4 per cent. In the United States, high rates are found in Native Americans, Hispanic Americans (rates in Cuban Americans are not as high), Arab Americans, African Americans and Asian Americans. Populations with high rates of type 2 diabetes often have lower rates of type 1 diabetes than northern Europeans.

Many Europeans follow a modern lifestyle that involves very little physical labour and a lot of processed foods, and they may gain weight, but they don't develop diabetes. They have the lifestyle but lack the genes.

No one knows if insulin resistance or beta cell defects come first

People who get type 2 diabetes usually show signs of both IR and defective production of insulin by the beta cells. As with the chicken and the egg, no one can yet agree on which usually comes first, the IR or the beta cell defects. From our point of view it doesn't really matter. By the time the disease has progressed enough to be diagnosed, most people show signs of both.

There is no question that obesity, and especially what is called *visceral obesity*, is associated with IR. Visceral obesity means that there's a lot of fat around your viscera, or internal abdominal organs, and it usually means that your waist is a lot larger than your hips. Men who have 'beer bellies' have visceral obesity. Another term for this is *apple-shaped*. Women who have large thighs are called *pear-shaped*, and this kind of overweight is associated with a lower risk of IR and diabetes.

There is also evidence that fat cells produce substances that cause IR. The recently discovered hormone *resistin* seems to be such a substance. When mice get obese, the fat cells secrete resistin, which causes IR in other types of cells. The interesting thing is that the glitazone drugs, which reduce IR in humans, also inhibit the production of resistin in mice. There is evidence that resistin exists in humans too.

Being overweight alone, however, is not sufficient to cause diabetes. As mentioned before, people can be quite obese and have immense amounts of IR and their beta cells will just keep spewing out more and more insulin to keep the BG levels normal.

Nevertheless, the classic view is that obesity is the *cause* of type 2 diabetes – in other words, the IR comes before the beta cell failure. In this view, you eat too much and let yourself get overweight. The overweight causes IR. Because of the IR, the beta cells have to work a lot harder to put out extra insulin to cope. They are unable to keep up the pace, some of them become 'exhausted' and die, and at that point the BG levels begin to increase and you are diagnosed with diabetes.

This view assumes that being overweight is caused by eating too much and not exercising enough and thus blames the patient for getting the disease. People with this viewpoint call type 2 diabetes a 'lifestyle disease', implying that personal lifestyle choices caused your diabetes.

However, as one researcher recently said, 'Nearly every major feature of this disease that we thought was true ten years ago turned out to be wrong.' He was referring to the molecular mechanisms of the disease. But as understanding of the mechanisms at the molecular level changes, views of the causes of type 2 diabetes will undoubtedly change as well.

One possibility is that a genetically determined IR causes obesity when sufficient food is available. The obesity would increase the IR even more, and a vicious circle would ensue.

A second possibility is that an unknown factor causes both IR and obesity independently; in other words, neither one causes the other but they just go along together. This is analogous to drinking a lot of beer and becoming intoxicated and visiting the loo a lot. Intoxication doesn't cause you to visit the loo, and visiting the loo doesn't cause you to become intoxicated (at least it doesn't have that effect on me). A third factor, the beer, just happens to cause two different effects at once.

Studies in mice have shown that a high-calorie, high-fat, high-sugar diet causes IR in muscle before any weight gain; and studies in humans put on calorie-restricted diets have shown improvements in BG control before any weight loss. This suggests that the number of calories you eat affects both your weight and your BG control, but one doesn't cause the other.

Another possibility is that the beta cell failure comes before the IR. In this view, an inherited defect in the beta cells would make BG levels rise after meals long before anyone realized anything was wrong. The high BG levels after meals would cause glucotoxicity. The glucotoxicity would make the BG levels go even higher, and this would damage the beta cells even more. Another vicious circle would ensue.

A study in thin Japanese Americans has shown that their beta cells had a secretory defect *before* there was any increase in abdominal fat and before they were diagnosed with diabetes. Five years later, those with these beta cell defects had progressed to diabetes and had more abdominal fat.

Insulin is released in two phases

To understand beta cell defects, first you should understand what is called the *biphasic insulin response* (Figure 3). When a nondiabetic person eats, the cells almost instantly release a squirt of insulin into the bloodstream. This is called the *first-phase response*, and it may be triggered just by tasting or chewing food. This insulin was probably already made by the beta cells and was sitting there in little packets waiting for a signal to be released. This short (usually about five to ten minutes) spurt of insulin is usually enough to keep the BG level from increasing a lot after the first bites of carbohydrate zip from the mouth to the bloodstream. The drug nateglinide is said to restore this first-phase response.

Then the beta cells produce a smaller but longer-lasting release of insulin called the *second-phase response*. This insulin release takes care of the rest of the carbohydrate from the meal, which is usually released over a period of time as the stomach slowly processes the food and releases it into the small intestine. The insulin release continues as long as the food keeps coming.

FIGURE 3. The two-stage insulin response. When you infuse glucose into the bloodstream, the beta cells produce a rapid burst of insulin that lasts about five to ten minutes. This is called the *phase-one response*. Then they produce a slow release of insulin (the *phase-two response*) that lasts as long as the glucose is given. If, after the first dose of glucose has been stopped, you give a second pulse of glucose, another phase-one insulin response occurs. Notice that this response is greater than the first one. This is called *priming* and means that a second carbohydrate meal may cause a smaller increase in the BG level than the first one. People with type 2 diabetes lack the phase-one response.

People with type 2 diabetes usually lack the first-phase response. Furthermore, this lack of a first-phase response is sometimes found in nondiabetic relatives of people with type 2 diabetes, which suggests that the loss of proper beta cell function precedes the IR.

However, researchers have also found IR in nondiabetic relatives of people with type 2 diabetes and say that the first-phase response is not lost until fasting BG levels reach about7.8 mmol/L.

So the jury is still out on which comes first, the beta cell defects or the IR. One possibility is our old friend YMMV (Your Mileage May Vary). Some people may have lost beta cell function first and others may have acquired IR first. Regardless of the chronology, however, once the BG levels begin to increase, this increase is amplified by glucotoxicity.

Losing weight is difficult with thrifty genes

People who are overweight tend to have more fatty acids (see Day 3) in their blood whether they consume a lot of fat or not, and there is some evidence that fatty acids coming from the visceral (stomach) area into the liver are able to increase IR. This may be another reason visceral obesity is dangerous. Losing weight may help reduce lipotoxicity as well as IR and glucotoxicity and is therefore a good thing to try to do.

Unfortunately, losing weight is difficult when, like the Pima Indians, you have thrifty genes that tell your body it wants to store fat. Just remember, in most cases, *being overweight is not your fault*. You just got genes that would have been wonderful if you were living in a time of famine. In a time of plenty, they're a liability.

But that is how it is. You've got those genes, and you can't give them back. So the only thing you can work on is controlling your environment, and that usually means losing some weight.

In a modern world filled with cars, fast food and TVs, it's not realistic to expect anyone to adopt a lifestyle as rugged as that of the Pima Indians in Mexico. But the closer anyone who was born with the 'thrifty' diabetes genes can come to their way of life, the less damaging the effects of those genes will be.

IN A SENTENCE:

> *Type 2 diabetes is caused by an interaction between your 'thrifty' genes and your food-filled, strenuous exercise-lacking environment.*

living

Losing Weight

WHEN YOU were diagnosed, your doctor probably told you to lose weight and get some exercise. Sometimes that's all the doctor tells you.

The classic treatment is weight loss

Losing weight has always been a cornerstone of treatment of type 2 diabetes because being overweight increases your insulin resistance (IR). There is evidence that overfilled fat cells secrete substances that cause IR, for example, the newly discovered hormone *resistin*. So if you have, in fact, managed to lose some weight, that's great. Your control will be easier because of it, and you may be able to keep your blood glucose (BG) levels down without tablets or insulin. But if you haven't lost weight, don't despair. Some people now think that controlling your BG levels is more important than losing weight.

You may have been told that if you would just lose a few kilograms, your diabetes would go away. In some cases, especially if you're fortunate enough to be diagnosed in the very early stages of diabetes, when it's still just impaired glucose tolerance or impaired fasting glucose (see Month 2), this may be true. Here's one success story:

'When I was diagnosed, I easily went over 10 postmeal,' said Jim D. 'But since I lost all the weight (40 kilograms) and exercise daily, my pancreas seems to have full control, again. I generally stay in a tight range, 4.5 to 5 mmol/L. Christmas dinner, I pigged out, and also ate a half-dozen chocolate chip cookies. I tracked my BGs, and the peak, at about 90 minutes, was 6, back to 4.5 by 120 minutes.'

Not always a cure. Otherwise, weight loss will reduce your IR somewhat and will make your diabetes easier to control, but it won't make it go away.

Claire M. of Australia described her experiences: 'When I was first diagnosed I read all I could, and losing weight and exercise seemed to offer the most promise of a cure, or at least regression/control. I lost 54 kilograms on a low-glycaemic index diet and a lot of walking, and my fasting glucose fell from about 11.5 to 5 mmol/L. Most of the drop in blood glucose occurred shortly after I started walking regularly and losing weight.

'Five years later I still walk one to two hours a day and my fasting blood glucose has remained about 5. I still get pronounced postprandial BG levels, and my haemoglobin A1c is slightly above normal, but I take no medication. A welcome side benefit was that my blood pressure returned to the normal range and I was able to stop medication for that. The verdict: well controlled, but not cured.'

One reason weight loss is not always curative is because once your beta cells bite the dust, they're not likely to come back to life. If you're diagnosed in the early stages, when your beta cells are still able to produce enough insulin to cope with normal demands but not enough to cope with the extra demands of IR or other stresses, then just reducing your IR may allow your still-vigorous beta cells to deal with the now-lower demands made on them.

If, however, you're not diagnosed until later in the course of the disease, or if you're diagnosed early but don't take the disease seriously and don't maintain good control, so glucotoxicity stresses the beta cells enough that many of them give up the ghost, then even with less IR, they won't be able to cope with the demand.

Another reason is that being overweight is not the only thing that causes IR. The diabetes itself also seems to cause IR; some have estimated that it causes about half. The additional IR caused by being overweight is sometimes just enough to overtax your beta cells. One man found that gaining 13.5 kilograms doubled his basal insulin requirements.

Sometimes the promise that weight loss will reverse the diabetes makes you feel guilty if it doesn't happen. 'I know that doctors are trying to be both motivational and encouraging when they say that if you lose a significant amount of weight, the diabetes may disappear,' said Lyndy B. 'But for me it turned into a statement of "It's your fault you have diabetes" and "If you would only behave, this would all go away".'

The sooner the better. This possible beta cell exhaustion is also a reason to try to lose weight as soon as possible after you're diagnosed. The sooner you can get your IR down, the less stress there will be on your beta cells and the greater the chance that you'll be able to preserve a lot of them. If you haven't made efforts in this area by now, don't put it off any longer.

Studies have shown that if weight loss is going to help with your BG control, it's most likely to start showing results after a loss of 2.5 or 5 kilograms. If you've lost this much and can't see any difference in your BG control, then you may not see much improvement even if you become as thin as a pencil.

Of course this doesn't mean you should throw your diet plan in the bin and eat pizza and cakes all day. Remember that a diabetic diet is as much for controlling your BG levels as it is for losing weight. What it does mean is that if following your diet plan gives you good control of your BG levels but doesn't make you lose weight, you shouldn't beat yourself up about it. In the long run, controlling your BG levels is probably more important than losing weight.

Restricting calories helps

In fact, some of the benefits of 'weight loss' may in fact not be as much a consequence of the weight loss itself but of the fact that when you're losing weight, you're eating less food. Some studies of overweight people with type 2 diabetes have shown improvements in BG control *even before any weight loss* when the number of calories was reduced. In other words, simply eating less can help to control your diabetes even if you don't lose any weight. As an additional benefit, eating fewer calories seems to result in fewer damaging free radicals, and animals that eat less live longer.

Even if you've had diabetes long enough that weight loss probably won't make it go away, don't give up. It will still have other health benefits. Weight loss will make controlling your BG levels easier, and it's good for your blood pressure and for your general health. When you weigh less, it's easier to exercise, and the exercise itself will reduce your IR.

Losing weight is difficult for anyone. It's often more difficult when you have diabetes and 'thrifty genes' that are especially efficient in storing fat and especially reluctant to get rid of that fat once it's safely stored away. One study showed that when put on a similar weight-loss programme, people without diabetes lost more weight than those with diabetes, even though adherence to the diet was the same in both groups.

Weight loss is usually more difficult for women than for men, because women normally have a higher percentage of fat and less muscle, and it's muscle that burns the most calories.

There's nothing more discouraging than sitting down to a meal of three peas, a tablespoon of hamburger and a portion of spinach and still staying on a weight plateau while everyone else in the family is munching on cheeseburgers with french fries, followed by huge bowls of pie and ice cream, and they're all as thin as rails.

Don't accept a 'noncompliant' label

It's even more discouraging if you stick to a strict diet and don't lose weight and then when you see your doctor, the doctor says your diabetes isn't controlled because you're not losing weight, and that's because you're 'not compliant', not following the diet the doctor or dietician gave you when you were diagnosed, implying it's all your fault. 'I was very discouraged following the exchange diet because no matter how faithfully I dieted, my BGs were always high and of course the doctor looks at you as if you are the biggest liar on the face of the earth,' said Beth H.

Unfortunately, this kind of attitude is not uncommon, but it's not entirely the fault of the medical doctors. It's the way they were trained. A lot of medical books emphasize that the only important factor in losing weight is the number of calories the patient eats compared with the number of calories burned by exercise. The books say if the patient claims to be following the prescribed diet and doesn't lose weight, the patient is either lying or isn't aware of the number of calories actually eaten – for example, eating a large dish of something when the diet specifies a small dish or figuring 'a few' peanuts aren't worth mentioning.

In addition, most doctors like to cure people. They like to write prescriptions or perform operations and solve all the patient's problems. That gives them a sense of accomplishment. Type 2 diabetes is chronic. It doesn't go away, and in most cases, especially when the disease isn't well controlled, it just gets worse. The doctors can't cure it. It may be frustrating for them to accept their inability to make you better. So unconsciously, they may shift the burden of blame onto you.

Another problem is that unfortunately some doctors simply don't like fat people. Overweight patients have more health problems and they're harder to treat. So some doctors blame the overweight patient for any medical problems that arise, no matter how small. You go in for advice on getting rid of a hangnail and they tell you to lose weight, as if you didn't already know you should.

So if you go back to see your doctor and you haven't lost any weight and your BG control isn't as good as you'd like it to be, don't be surprised if the doctor tells you the problem is that you haven't lost any weight. If this *does* happen to you, don't accept this explanation. If you're really doing everything you can to control your food intake and to exercise as much as you're able and you're still not losing weight, so be it. That doesn't mean you don't deserve excellent BG control.

Don't accept another lecture about 'If you'd just lose a few pounds, your sugars would improve.' Insist on a better treatment plan, maybe a different drug or a different combination of drugs, or ask for a referral to a dietician to see if some other diet plan would work better for you. By this time, you should have a good idea of whether your initial diet is working for you at all.

Remember that some of the diabetes drugs tend to *cause* weight gain, and they also make it more difficult to lose. It's not fair to tell a patient to lose weight, prescribe a drug that causes weight gain and then blame the patient for not losing weight. This happened to Alex E.: 'My doctor put me on glipizide. I gained 13.5 kilograms, and she reprimanded me for eating too much.' If you find your doctor simply can't understand the problems you're having with your weight, try to find another doctor.

Luckily, doctors' attitudes are changing, and if you look around, you may be able to find one who understands. As Carolyn M. said, 'The new specialist was a breath of fresh air. He said the fact that I'm fat is probably not my fault. At that point, I thought perhaps I'd somehow taken a hallucinogen, but he went on to say that in the old days we didn't know about leptin and other hormonal factors in weight and doctors routinely blamed the patient for weight gain. He then said that it certainly doesn't help anyone to lose weight to have such a punitive attitude toward the problem.' Look around and see if you can find an understanding doctor like this one.

There are many theories of weight loss and gain

If you're overweight, you probably don't need to be told what you need to do to lose. You've probably lost weight dozens of times.

'I added up all the kilos I lost separately from the ones I gained back,' said Edd A., 'and I found I'd lost over 1000 kilograms.' The problem is, of course, that most people tend to gain the weight back again, usually within five years.

Set-point theory. One explanation for a difficulty with maintaining weight loss is called *set-point theory*. According to this theory, everyone is born with a 'weight thermostat' that tells the body what weight it would prefer to be. If you're at your set-point weight and you eat a little extra food, you won't gain weight. If you eat a little less, you won't lose. If you force-feed rats, or if you starve them, they get too fat or too thin. If you then give them free access to rat food, the fat ones will lose weight and the thin ones will gain weight until they all weigh the same as control rats that weren't either force-fed or starved.

This set point clearly only operates under certain calorie ranges. Anyone will lose weight on a starvation diet. The problem is, almost no one but an ascetic can maintain a 600- or 700-calorie diet for life. And if you do lose weight by such extreme means, when you return to a more normal caloric intake, your set point will try to return you to your former weight.

An additional problem is that you may lose weight as muscle and then regain it as fat. Because muscle burns more energy than fat, the next time you try to lose weight, it's twice as difficult. This loss and regain and loss again is called 'yo-yo dieting', and it's something you don't want to do.

Uncoupling agents. Another explanation of why some people have weight problems and others don't involves uncoupling agents (proteins). These are chemicals or protein channels that uncouple the metabolism of food from the production of energy. When uncoupling agents are active, the body uses food to produce heat instead of energy that can be used to store fat. Some plants are able to use uncoupling agents when the temperatures get too low, thus sacrificing energy storage for heat.

The theory is that some thin people are also able to shunt some of their food energy into heat when they eat more calories than they need. These are the ones who can stuff themselves and never gain a kilo. Mice engineered to have more of one type of uncoupling protein (UCP-3) eat more than their littermates but weigh less. They also have less fat and lower BG levels.

In mice, at least, exercise seems to increase the amount of uncoupling proteins, yet another reason to try to get as much exercise as you can.

It's possible that people with 'thrifty genes' aren't able to use the uncoupling agents to turn their extra food into heat. They turn it into fat instead. These are the people who eat almost nothing and still don't lose weight.

Some overweight people may just have huge appetites; their problem may involve faulty hunger mechanisms more than problems with uncoupling agents. Similarly, some thin people may be thin because they just have tiny appetites; if they ate a lot they'd gain weight.

Another uncoupling protein (UCP-2) was reported in spring 2001 to be important in linking obesity, beta cell failure and type 2 diabetes, at least in mice. In this case, too much uncoupling protein seems to be the problem. Obese, diabetic mice engineered to lack UCP-2 had their first-phase insulin secretion restored and had lower BG levels.

The details of how the uncoupling proteins are linked to a tendency to gain weight and get diabetes have yet to be worked out, but they may play an important role.

Do what works for you

Like type 2 diabetes, obesity has many causes. Scientists have found more than 100 genes that may be associated with obesity. Thus YMMV (Your Mileage May Vary) applies to weight loss too. If you're overweight, you've probably already tried a lot of different types of diets throughout the years, and you should know which approach works best for you.

If you do think you eat more than you need, it may help to ask yourself why you overeat. Are you hungry all the time? It's possible that your IR or roller-coaster BG levels are contributing to your hunger. Focus on BG control instead of what the scale tells you. Some people find that once their BG levels are controlled, their appetite becomes more normal and the weight starts coming off without a lot of effort.

Are you eating because there's so much to choose from you have to try it all? Are you eating because you're bored? Because you're too polite to say no when offered food? Because you're unhappy? Because the food is put in front of you and you were raised to believe that wasting food is a sin? Are you eating even when you're not hungry because it's time to eat? Figure out what the triggers are and see if you can change them.

Enjoy your food. Think of your new diet regimen not as a temporary weight-loss plan that involves sacrifices but as a new pleasurable way of eating that you can live with for the rest of your life. *Enjoy your food*. Think of yourself as a gourmet, who eats only the best kinds of food in small amounts. Buy only the best (rather than the cheapest) for yourself. You deserve it. Don't worry about the price. If you eat smaller quantities, you can get better quality. For example, eat only 60 grams of fillet steak instead of the 220 grams of hamburger you serve to everyone else. Then enjoy every bite.

Remember that the first taste of everything always tastes the best. So savour a few bites of something – its sight, its smell, its texture and its taste. Eat slowly and pay attention to what you're eating. Don't ever eat when you're doing something else like watching TV and can't really notice – or enjoy – what you're eating.

Buy the freshest food you can. Eat a fresh strawberry, preferably just picked, and imagine you'd never tasted fresh fruit and were trying to describe its taste. A really fresh, ripe strawberry has a symphony of flavours that is much more complex than the 'strawberry flavouring' you'll get in processed or fast foods. If possible, go to farmers' markets and try different varieties of berries or vegetables. Try exotic new foods. Become a food connoisseur.

I think one reason Westerners eat so much is that our food has so little taste, so the manufacturers add a lot of salt and sugar and fat to trick us into thinking it tastes good. We eat for quantity instead of quality. Avoid that kind of food. Remember, you're a gourmet. You eat for quality, not quantity. You reject junk food.

Also – yes, I've mentioned this before – try to exercise as much as you can. Studies have shown that people who are able to keep their weight off after losing tend to be those who make exercise a routine part of their lives. Remember that muscle weighs more than fat, so don't worry if the scales don't budge even though you've taken your belt in a few notches.

Even though you probably know what kind of diet makes you lose weight, now that you have diabetes you also have to focus on the effect any weight-loss diet will have on your BG levels as well as on your weight. A fad diet that makes the kilograms come off but makes your BG levels go into the stratosphere is not a great way to go.

New way of eating. In the long run, fad diets aren't good for you anyway. So in this respect look at your diabetes as an ally, not an enemy. Having diabetes makes you look at any kind of diet in terms of a lifelong way of eating, not a temporary torture that will be over when you can fit into a new pair of trousers. Having diabetes may give you the incentive to lose that weight you've probably been trying to drop for years. In the past, losing weight was simply a question of vanity. Now it's more than that.

If you have a serious weight problem that is making you miserable and no diet seems to work, you might want to discuss the possibility of surgery, for example *gastroplasty* to reduce the size of your stomach. It's a serious decision and will mean you won't be able to eat large meals for the rest of your life, and complications are possible, but some people report that they are happier after such surgery. Others say they regained all the weight they lost and wish they hadn't had it done.

Losing weight in a society that is replete with tempting food is hard. If the only way you can keep weight off is to stick to an 800-calorie diet for the rest of your life and you decide that's simply too much to deal with, then let it be. But don't make that an excuse to give up on your BG control. Controlling your BG levels is more important than losing weight. Don't give up on that.

IN A SENTENCE:

> *Losing weight should reduce your insulin resistance, but it's not a panacea, and keeping your blood glucose levels close to normal may be more important than losing weight.*

learning

Understanding Exercise

'MY BLOOD sugar goes up when I exercise,' says Thomas. 'My blood sugar goes down when I exercise,' says Chloe. What's going on? Which person should you believe?

The fact is, the effect of exercise on your blood glucose (BG) levels is very complex and depends on many factors including the length of the exercise, the intensity of the exercise, your BG levels when you start to exercise, your insulin levels when you start to exercise, the amount of insulin resistance (IR) that you have, your level of training and other subtle variations in your own personal physiology.

Saying 'Blood sugar goes down after exercise' is like saying 'Diabetics don't produce insulin.' Both statements are correct in particular cases, but they are too general to have much meaning overall. BG levels in a trained athlete after a 100-metre dash may be quite different from BG levels in a 60-year-old computer programmer after a three-hour walk in the woods.

As I've stressed before, in the long run, exercise is one of the most important things you can do to reduce your IR, increase the mass of your BG-reducing muscles, and protect your cardiovascular health as well. But the effects of exercise in the short term are quite variable.

To understand this better, you need to understand a few basic things about the physiology of exercise.

- To get energy, muscles can burn either glucose or fatty acids.
- Insulin becomes more effective when you exercise. Or, put another way, your IR decreases when you exercise.
- Muscles can take up glucose *without insulin* when you exercise.
- Exercise opens up small capillaries. This increases the surface area of muscle that is exposed to glucose-containing blood.
- *Prolonged* exercise depletes the glycogen levels in your liver and muscles.
- *Strenuous* exercise is a form of stress and causes the release of counterregulatory hormones that tell the liver to release glucose into the blood.

ATP is energy currency

Let's start with sources of energy. The immediate source of energy for the muscles is a molecule called **ATP** (adenosine triphosphate). ATP acts as a sort of short-term energy currency for the body. When you want to store energy, for example in fat, you have to 'spend' ATP to make the fats. When you break down the fats, they pay out some ATP.

Muscles need ATP to contract, but the muscles contain only enough ATP to work for a few seconds. Then another molecule, called *creatine phosphate*, gives up its energy to make a little more ATP. However, both these molecules combined can only produce enough energy to work the muscles hard for about ten seconds, enough for a short dash, but no more than that. ATP is sort of like your petty cash account, or the money in your wallet. It's what you use to buy things, but it's not where you store most of your funds.

ATP isn't where muscle cells store significant energy. For any significant exercise, the cells have to get energy from other sources. The quickest source is glucose. Cells can quickly break down *glycogen* (the tins of glucose taped together with duct tape) to make glucose. Then they can break down the glucose (open the tins of glucose) to make more ATP. They can even do this in the absence of oxygen, so this process is called *anaerobic*. It produces *lactic acid*, which is what makes muscles ache after hard exercise.

However, even this process doesn't produce enough ATP to last very long, only about 1.5 minutes. After that, the cells need to rely on *aerobic* forms of metabolism, those that use oxygen. This they can do by oxidizing (breaking down and forming energy in the presence of oxygen) either glucose or fatty acids.

At rest, muscles use mainly fatty acids for their energy needs, and most of the glucose in the body is used by the brain. With mild exercise (about 25 per cent maximum), most of the energy in the muscles continues to come from fatty acids.

With moderate exercise (about 65 per cent maximum), the muscles begin to break down their glycogen stores and use about equal parts of glycogen, fat stored in the muscle and fatty acids shipped in from the fat cells.

With a short burst of extreme energy (85 per cent of maximum), glycogen supplies most of the energy to the muscle cells.

This gives you an idea of why it's sometimes difficult to predict how exercise will affect your BG levels: a lot depends on how rigorous the exercise is, and except for research settings, that's difficult to measure.

The more rigorous that exercise is, the more likely you are to start out burning glycogen and not fat. However, your muscle cells have another problem: the amount of glycogen in the body is limited. A 70-kilogram man has about 350 grams of glycogen in muscle and 80 grams in the liver, and about 20 grams of glucose in the blood and other extracellular fluids. After two hours of moderate exercise (swimming, skiing, running or biking), the glycogen stores are down to less than 20 per cent of their maximal level. That means that not only the intensity of the exercise but also its duration will affect your glycogen stores and your BG levels as well.

One study showed that after depleting the glycogen stores to 20 per cent, it took a full two days to restore them to their maximal levels. This means that if you can do some moderate exercise for about two hours, your muscle cells will continue to take glucose from the blood to rebuild its glycogen stores for almost two days. In addition, a single bout of intensive exercise seems to decrease IR for almost 16 hours. Seems like a good return on investment.

Exercise makes your insulin resistance go down

When you exercise, your insulin becomes more effective. This is true whether you have diabetes or not. In fact, although athletes often do something called *carbohydrate loading*, which is a way of increasing their glycogen stores so they will have more endurance, they are warned not to eat fast carbohydrates like sugar 15 to 45 minutes before they start an event. Why not? Because the carbohydrate makes their BG levels go up a little, and this triggers a release of insulin appropriate for the conditions at rest. When they start exercising, the insulin becomes more effective, and as a result their BG levels can go too low, as shown in Figure 4.

The same problem exists if you are injecting insulin or taking sulphonylurea drugs that can make your insulin levels go up. If before exercising you take a dose that would be appropriate for lounging around watching TV, it will probably be too high when you're exercising hard, and you too may go low.

On the other hand, this fact can be used to your benefit in some cases. If you find your BG levels increasing after whatever kind of exercise you usually do, try eating some carbohydrate 15 to 45 minutes before your exercise. This will make your BG levels go up, which will trigger an insulin response, and the exercise will make the insulin more effective. In addition, the insulin will put the brakes on the liver's production of glucose. Thus your BG levels should go down.

Another approach is simply to exercise *after* your meals instead of before.

FIGURE 4. The effect of eating carbohydrate before exercise. When a nondiabetic person doesn't eat sugar before exercise, the exercise may cause a small increase in the blood glucose (BG) level (see text). When the same person eats sugar 45 minutes before the exercise, the sugar triggers an insulin release. When the exercise begins, the insulin becomes more effective and the BG level drops suddenly, in this case down to almost 2.2 mmol/L, before coming back up to normal levels. In a diabetic person, the exercise-induced increase in BG levels without food, as well as the increase after eating sugar, would be greater.

Exercise has effects that don't depend on insulin

When you exercise, the muscles can take up glucose even without insulin. No one is sure exactly how this happens, although there is some evidence that nitric oxide (NO) is involved as a signalling molecule. Somehow, the exercise is able to do the same thing as insulin does: It increases the number of GLUT4 transporters (the little boats that ferry glucose across the cell membrane) in the membrane of the cell.

In addition, the exercise increases your circulation. When you're lounging around in front of the TV watching old sitcom reruns, a lot of your capillaries go on strike. The body figures it's not worth the effort to pump blood through muscles that aren't doing any work, so it shuts off some of the capillaries to those unused muscles. When you exercise, these muscles suddenly need oxygen and glucose and fatty acids, so the capillaries open up. This increases the number of cells that are competing for the glucose in your blood, and even without all the other mechanisms for increasing glucose uptake, your BG uptake would increase.

Strenuous exercise is stressful

I know, I know. For some of us, any kind of exercise at all is stressful. But that's psychological stress. I'm speaking here of physiological stress. You may recall the *fight-or-flight reaction* to stress that triggers the release of a bundle of counterregulatory hormones (they oppose the action of insulin) that make BG levels go up.

You remember that one reason the body does this is to allow the liver to produce more glucose to ship off to the muscles just in case the body the hormones are living in decides to flee or get involved in a wrestling match.

Well, strenuous exercise is really the same thing as fleeing or wrestling: The muscles need more energy, and they need it fast. So when the body gets a signal that you've started hard exercise, it secretes more stress hormones like adrenaline, growth hormone and cortisol.

These hormones help the fat cells break down fat into fatty acids, which the muscles can burn for energy. They also tell the liver to crank up its production of glucose, which the muscles can also burn. These signals to the liver are especially strong when the BG levels are not high. If there's already plenty of glucose in the blood when you start to exercise, the liver recognizes that the situation isn't critical yet and doesn't crank up its glucose production so quickly. This is another reason to eat *before* you start your exercise. The higher BG levels and higher insulin levels will slow down the stress hormone response.

With very strenuous exercise, the liver cranks out glucose, and it may produce more glucose than the muscles are able to take up, even in nondiabetic people. With short bursts of strenuous exercise, the BG levels increase about 20 per cent in people without diabetes. Then as soon as the exercise is over, the muscle cells grab the extra glucose to rebuild their glycogen stores and the BG levels return to normal. When you have type 2 diabetes, the BG levels go even higher during exercise and take longer to return to normal.

Prolonged exercise burns glucose

Although short bouts of strenuous exercise may make your BG levels go up, longer bouts of less strenuous exercise may make your BG levels go down. This is because the less strenuous exercise may not be seen by the body as stressful, so you won't get a burst of those counterregulatory hormones that tell the liver to put out glucose.

The less strenuous exercise will also burn a smaller percentage of glycogen. In fact, during low-intensity exercise, as at rest, the muscles actually prefer to burn fatty acids. However, you will burn some glycogen for a longer time. And as your muscles sense that their glycogen stores are going down, they'll do their best to take glucose out of the blood to rebuild them. So you may see your BG levels come down after this kind of exercise.

Many kinds of exercise are somewhere in between these two extremes, so it's often difficult to predict what will happen with your BG levels. You need to test before and after doing the kind of exercise you do the most and see how it affects you.

Anaerobic exercise builds muscle

The kind of exercise that makes you breathe hard, like running or playing tennis, is called *aerobic exercise* because it requires oxygen to produce the energy-currency molecule ATP. Aerobic exercise builds up your heart and the efficiency of your lungs, and it also burns glucose. It's obviously a good thing to do.

But there's another type of exercise called *anaerobic exercise*.

This is the kind you *could* do while holding your breath (although you really shouldn't; it's better to breathe while doing anaerobic exercise), for example weight lifting, push-ups or climbing a steep hill (see Day 5).

Weight lifting doesn't make you breathe hard while you're doing it, and it won't increase the efficiency of your lungs. But weight lifting will increase the strength and, especially if you're male, size of your muscles. Because the muscles are one of the main organs that take glucose out of the blood, the more muscle you have, the better you'll be able to control your BG levels in the long run.

Muscle also burns calories faster than fat cells do, so as you increase the ratio of muscle to fat, you'll make it easier to lose weight. If you *are* trying to lose weight and you're also lifting weights, remember that muscle weighs more than fat. As you lose fat and gain muscle, you may actually gain a little weight. Don't worry about it. The inches that you're losing will tell you that you're just gaining more muscle.

Exercise causes a virtuous circle

As you can see, there are many kinds of exercise, and they may all affect your BG levels and your type of fitness differently. But they're all beneficial in the long run. Exercise is a virtuous circle. More exercise creates more muscles that make more exercise easier. Short-term effects are sometimes hard to predict. But long-term effects are clear. In the long term, exercise makes the BG levels go down.

IN A SENTENCE:

> *In the long run, both aerobic and anaerobic exercise will help keep your blood glucose levels low, but in the short term, the effects of exercise are sometimes difficult to predict.*

living

Tracking
Your Progress

WHEN YOU started out managing your diabetes, the important thing was to get into the habit of testing your blood glucose (BG) levels. Now you may want to get a little fancier in the way you keep track of your BG levels so you can spot trends and see how different foods and exercise patterns affect your control.

Start with log books

You probably already have a few *log books* designed for this purpose. They come with meters and include spaces to enter your BG readings at standard times, usually before meals and at bedtime, sometimes more, as well as insulin dosages and comments.

These log books are a good place to begin, and maybe they're all you'll ever want. But you may find them limiting and want to document more information; for example some log books don't have space for fasting or postprandial readings. Or you may want the information in a different form.

Even before I was diagnosed with diabetes, I'd written down everything I ate in a little notebook, because I thought I might be allergic to wheat. This method continues to work for me. Each day takes up a page, and I can write down what I eat and my BG levels as well as other pertinent information like weight, blood pressure, illness, exercise or starting or stopping medications.

I also graph some of my results. For instance, when I measure BG levels after trying a new food (see the Learning section), I graph the results in a spiral graph paper notebook so I don't end up with a mess of sheets I'd probably lose. I also graph my fasting BG levels, which I no longer measure daily, but several times a week unless there's a reason to do so more often, for example if I'm sick or taking a new drug.

I note on the graphs any different conditions like starting a new drug or not getting exercise because I'm sick or injured, and I find it easier to see patterns this way. Others might find the log book presentation simpler to analyze.

Everyone has different needs, and as time goes on, you may figure out your own log book form that tells you what you want to know. Richard H., who had type 1 diabetes, designed his own graphlike BG-tracking forms with a fresh sheet for every day. There were spaces at the top to plot his BG and ketone levels throughout the 24-hour period. He also entered his food intake and his insulin doses. At the bottom, he plotted both his activity level and the way he was feeling, using codes from zero to 6. For example, activity code zero was sleeping, 1 was 'inactive, watching television, reading', 3 was 'intermittent activity, driving tractor, walking', and 6 was 'heavy work, lifting, digging, carrying, shovelling'. Feeling code 1 was 'quite low [BG level], dull, tense, poor eyesight', 4 was 'slightly high, feel safe', 5 was 'moderately high, tired, some aches', and 6 was 'very high, tired, aches, thirsty, frequent urination'. There was also room for comments.

You may not want to devote that much time to documenting daily activities. But if you did it occasionally, you might learn a lot about how various factors do affect you.

Computer programs may help

If you have a computer, much of this documentation and manipulation of data can be done on it. All kinds of computer software are available, from *spreadsheet* programs with which you can design your own system, to simple free programs that work like logbooks, to fancy Windows- or Macintosh-based graphics programs that let you graph and print your data in myriad ways. Some of these programs can be downloaded from the Internet, sometimes free and sometimes for a fee. In the latter case, you can usually try out an abbreviated form of the program before you buy it.

In most programs, you can enter the data two ways. You can type in your results every day, or you can download your meter directly into the computer. If you think you'll be interested in downloading a meter, you'll obviously need a meter that allows this feature. Ask if the meter has a *data port*. You'll also need a cable that plugs into the meter and into a port on your computer. Sometimes the cable comes with the software and sometimes it's an additional expense.

Not all software will accept downloads from all meters. So before you buy, make sure the meter you want and the software you want are compatible.

Work with your doctor

If you decide you want to get your own software and print out your results to bring to your doctor, it's a good idea to check first to see what kind of data the doctor wants to see. Some people take fancy graphs and analyses to their doctors and find that the doctors are thrilled. They don't have to deal with difficult handwriting in cramped log books, and the graphs and analyses provide additional information.

Other people spend hours printing out fancy graphs and analyses but their doctors don't want to see all that. They just want to look at the log book or the A1c. In fact, some doctors don't even want to look at your daily BG numbers; if you have type 2 diabetes, they often only care about the A1c. This can be discouraging if you've gone to a lot of work to manage your data.

Most of the programs produce the same types of information, but they all display it in a slightly different form, and it may be easier for a doctor to spot trends if all the patients present the data in the same way. So if you think a computer program would help you understand what's going on, discuss it ahead of time and see what kinds of information the doctor wants to see and make sure that's included as well as the fancy charts and graphs.

Diabetes programs usually show similar things

Software is constantly changing, so I won't discuss specific programs. Most of them do basically the same thing. They usually have a log book, which is like the paper versions. Before you buy a program, make sure its log book works for you. Some of them have only a limited number of spots for entering BG levels, and if you lead a rather unregimented life and eat lunch at 11 a.m. one day and at 3 p.m. the next, or if you don't test for several days and then you test 15 times the next day, some of the programs' log books wouldn't be suitable.

Most allow you to input your target levels at various times, and they'll tell you what percentage of the time you were at or above or below your targets. They also usually plot a *modal day*, which is a graph of your BG levels throughout a 24-hour period for a certain length of time, for example for the last week or month or year (usually you can choose the time period). That makes it easy to spot if you're always high in the morning or always low before dinner, so you can take steps to correct the problem.

In some of the programs you can also sort the data by the day of the week, so you can find out additional factors. For example, if you find you're off target every Wednesday, you could look at what you do on Tuesdays and Wednesdays that might cause the problem. Is there an office treat every Wednesday morning? A stressful staff meeting? Do you play poker late into the night on Tuesdays?

In various programs you can also sort by events or by the time of day and so forth and view and print line graphs or bar graphs or fancy pie charts in many colours.

Nutritional programs are useful

Some of the commercial programs also include nutritional analyses, in which you can type in what you eat and the program will tell you how many calories and the amount and percentages of selected nutrients you've eaten so far. Some will even warn you when you've reached your daily limit. If the nutritional analysis is *all* you're interested in, there are hand-held nutritional tracking gizmos that are small enough that you can take them with you to work or to restaurants. You punch in what you eat and they give you daily totals and percentages. One of them includes diabetic exchanges.

Before you invest a lot of money in any of these programs, make sure the program matches your needs. Sometimes too much data is worse than not enough. If you think you'll get swamped with too much information, start out with one of the simpler free programs. If you find it useful, you can upgrade later to one of the fancier ones.

Internet sites will analyze your data

There are also sites on the Internet where you can type in your results or download your meter and their software will analyze it for you. This raises questions of security, whether you care if your BG data is out in cyberspace somewhere, presumably secure, but not really under your control. Also, the sites might cease to exist and then your data would no longer be available. These sites are also not free.

The more data you have, the better idea you'll have of what you can do to improve your control. The trick is not to become so over-whelmed with data that you don't know what to do with it. Maybe just writing down the daily BG levels and foods eaten in a log book would be just fine. That alone is a tremendous advance from the old days in which people with type 2 diabetes had their fasting levels checked at a doctor's office every six months or so. No wonder they often got complications.

But if you enjoy playing around with numbers and charts and graphs, go for it. The software is probably out there. Find what fits the bill and use it. If you can't find what you want, a customized spreadsheet program might work for you. If you're familiar with computer programming, design your own program and then share it with others. Several people with diabetes have done that and offered the programs free via the Internet.

The important thing is not how you keep track of your progress, but the fact that you do. Thinking you're now fine and you don't need to test and keep track anymore often leads to gradually rising BG averages, which may lead to complications. Keeping track keeps you on track for complication-free years in the future.

IN A SENTENCE:

Keeping track of your blood glucose levels – whether in a logbook or on a computer – helps you maintain good control.

learning

Estimating Your Personal Glycaemic Index Values

BY NOW, you should be comfortable measuring your blood glucose (BG) levels regularly. If so, you're probably controlling better than most people with type 2 diabetes. Simply accepting that you have the disease and being willing to invest the little time it takes to do BG tests is a giant step toward good control. But you can do even more with your meter than just test your BG levels at various times of the day.

Although these little home meters aren't as accurate as expensive clinical lab equipment, they can provide sophisticated information. You can even measure your own *glycaemic index* values, which estimate how much a particular food will raise your BG levels.

A first step in understanding how food affects your control is to measure your BG levels immediately before and two hours after you eat. That gives you a general idea. But it doesn't tell the whole story. Different foods raise BG levels at different speeds.

The BG level after eating glucose or another simple sugar usually peaks at about 30 minutes, and the level after eating white bread peaks a little later, at about 60 minutes. But if both foods contained the same amount of carbohydrate, the overall increase in the BG level would be about the same with both foods. This is shown in Figure 5. If you measured only at 30 minutes, you would conclude that glucose causes a much greater increase in BG levels than bread. But if you measured at 90 minutes, you would conclude that bread causes a much greater increase in BG levels than glucose (see Figure 5). This illustrates the problems when your diabetic specialist nurse (DSN) says to keep your BG levels under 7.8 mmol/L after meals. You might have a different definition of 'after meals' than the DSN.

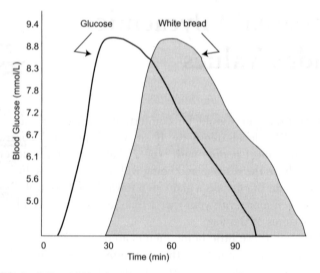

FIGURE 5. Different blood glucose responses to different carbohydrates. Glucose tablets (left) usually peak in about 30 minutes. Starch (white bread) peaks at about 60 minutes.

Testing More Often. The way to overcome this problem is to test more often after eating a particular food, enough to produce a real *BG curve*, meaning you can see when the BG level goes up, when it peaks and when it comes down to baseline again, as shown in Figure 5. Of course this takes more test strips than simply testing once or twice a day. If money is no problem, you can buy extra strips for this purpose. Otherwise, if your control has been pretty steady, you can test fewer times for a few days, or even every other day, for a while, save up the strips, and then do a good curve on a new food.

When measuring BG curves, first you need to decide what time of day you're going to do the tests. The effect of a particular food can sometimes depend on what you ate at the previous meal. For example, a soluble-fibre-filled meal for breakfast may result in lower BG level increases after lunch. A BG curve can also depend on how much exercise you had before the test. If you're one of those people who always has the same breakfast and the same lunch and pretty much the same dinner and always exercises at the same time of day for the same length of time, then it won't matter much when you decide to do your tests as long as it's always the same time.

If your daily schedule differs a lot, however, it's probably safer to do your tests in the morning, before you eat. The problem here is the *dawn effect* (see Day 6). If your BG level increases before you get up in the morning and then stays the same until you eat, this won't be a problem. But if your BG level starts increasing when you get out of bed and increases different amounts on different days, then you might want to postpone your testing until the level becomes steady.

This kind of testing requires more than one reading

Let's assume you've decided to test the effect of eating a slice of bread, and you want to start first thing in the morning. What do you do? First, of course, you measure your BG level at time zero. Then you eat a slice of bread as quickly as you can. Five minutes to eat a test food won't matter, but it's obviously not a good idea to savour it for a half an hour or so. If you know that coffee or tea (with no milk or cream and obviously with no sugar – not even sugar substitutes that contain bulking agents) won't affect your BG level, you can drink them. Otherwise drink water.

Then you start measuring. As a general rule, a reasonable amount of glucose tablets will peak in about 30 minutes. Processed carbohydrate like bread will peak in about 60 minutes. A slower carbohydrate, or starch with fat added, will peak even later, at about 90 minutes. Some very slow carbohydrates won't increase BG levels much until about four or five hours, the same as protein foods.

If you're measuring a simple sugar like glucose, you'll probably want to do the first test at 15 minutes. When you're testing something that you expect to peak at 60 minutes, you can wait until 30 minutes to do your first test.

How often should you test? Again, that depends on how many strips you can afford to use and how many finger-pricks you can stand to endure. I usually measure at 30 minutes, 1, 1.5, 2 and 3 hours, or until the numbers return to baseline. If for some reason I really want to know exactly where the peak is, I might measure at 30 and 45 minutes, 1, 1.25, 1.5 and so forth, assuming the peak is around 1 hour. The more points you measure, the more accurate the curve. The more tests you do, the better sense you get of what times you should test. If you plot your results on graph paper as you go along, you'll see what's happening, and if one point seems unreasonable, you can take a second reading.

Figure 6 is an example of what you can learn by doing this type of test. In this test, I ate a piece of French bread with sugar-free jam and then took a 30-minute walk up and down a steep hill. When the BG level had returned to baseline, I ate another piece of bread and jam and worked at my computer. You can see from the figure that without the exercise, my BG level went about twice as high.

FIGURE 6. Effect of exercise. When exactly the same food was eaten (French bread and sugar-free jam), the blood glucose level rose almost twice as much when I sat at my computer compared with hiking up a steep hill immediately after eating the bread and jam. The food was eaten at 9.45 and 11.30 a.m. Between 8 and 9.45 a.m., the slight rise from 4.7 to about 5.6 mmol/L is due to the dawn effect. The point marked A is where I started feeling ravenously hungry.

You can do your own mini-glucose tolerance test

This method can even be used to do what I call a *mini-glucose tolerance test (GTT)*, using glucose tablets. A real GTT (see Day 5) done in a lab to diagnose diabetes usually uses a whopping 75 grams of glucose. I don't like to subject my system to such huge doses, so I use 12 grams, which means quickly eating three of the 4-gram glucose tablets washed down with water. Bread and jam tastes a lot better, but manufacturers often change their recipes or suppliers. Glucose tablets tend to be more uniform. I stick with one brand when I can.

Then when you have a baseline glucose curve, you can try different things to see how they affect it. For example, Figure 7 shows the effect of fat. Fat delays the emptying of the stomach, and if you have some insulin production, as you usually do with type 2 diabetes, sometimes your beta cells are able to cope better when little spurts of carbohydrate come out of the stomach instead of a huge carbohydrate dump all at once.

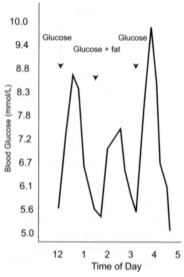

FIGURE 7. Effect of fat. When I eat fat, the blood glucose (BG) peaks are smaller. In this case I first ate glucose tablets (curve on left), then glucose tablets mixed into whipped cream (centre curve), and then pure glucose tablets again (right curve). In each case the pure glucose caused a greater BG-level increase than the glucose mixed with fat. Note that some people find that fat *increases* their BG levels.

To test this idea on myself, first I measured a curve after eating 12 grams of glucose. Then I ground up the glucose tablets and mixed them into whipped cream (no sacrifice too great in the name of science; this was really good). You can see that in my case, the fat actually reduced the BG level. Then, just to make sure the second curve wasn't lower because of some residual effect from the first curve (for example, maybe the first dose of glucose had induced enough insulin to carry over into the second curve), I did another 12-gram glucose curve without any fat. This was very similar to the first curve, suggesting that the effect of the fat was real. In order to *prove* it, I'd have to do a lot more tests. But this suggested that *for me* a little fat will reduce my BG levels, at least in the short term.

But YMMV (Your Mileage May Vary). Some people say fat *increases* their BG levels after a meal. It's possible that fat would decrease the BG level in the short term and increase it in the long term. Several people with type 1 diabetes have remarked that when they eat a lot of fat, their insulin requirements go up later, from six hours to several days after eating the fat.

One interesting thing I've discovered when doing these mini-GTT curves is that I often get ravenously hungry shortly after the BG peak, when the BG level is falling rapidly, as shown in point A in Figure 6. I don't know if this is a universal phenomenon or not, but others have said they've found similar things. 'Most of my food cravings occur when my blood sugar changes, either up or down. If I can hold it constant, or near constant, I eat less and feel better,' said Jim D.

I also discovered that no-sugar-added ice cream raised my BG level just as much as the same amount of regular ice cream (same brand). The real stuff also tasted better.

The area under the curve gives you a number

Now that you know how to measure a BG curve, you might like to get a number that would let you compare the results of eating one food or trying one exercise with the results of another. How do you do that? You measure the *area under the curve*, often called just the *AUC*. This means the area on the graph that has increased as a result of trying a particular food or exercise, as shown by the shaded area in Figure 5. If the food didn't make the BG level go up at all, then the AUC would be zero.

If you happen to have a computer with sophisticated graphing software, you're in luck. Otherwise you'll have to use approximations of the AUC. One way is simply to look at two curves and get an idea of which food causes a greater increase. When the curves are the same shape, this is pretty simple. But sometimes if one food causes a high peak that comes down quickly and another one causes a lower peak that extends for a longer time (Figure 8), it's more difficult to compare them.

One method of doing a rough estimate is simply to count the number of squares under the curve on a sheet of graph paper. This gives you a numerical estimate, but it's rather tedious. If you are mathematical or have a mathematical friend and a computer, you can set up a spreadsheet to calculate the AUC for you.

The haemoglobin A1c depends on the cumulative AUCs throughout the day. As shown in Figure 8, you could have two different foods with the same AUC, one of which gave you a high peak that quickly returned to baseline and the other of which gave you a low, long-lasting peak. Which would be more damaging? Not everyone agrees on the answer to this question. Some people say that short peaks, even high ones, are no problem, as long as they don't last very long, that the only important factor is the AUC. Others think high peaks can be damaging.

FIGURE 8. Areas under the curve (AUCs). The hypothetical curve at the left shows a high peak but a short duration. The hypothetical curve at the right has a low peak but a long duration. The AUCs are approximately the same. The haemoglobin A1c values are thought to reflect the AUCs. If so, it wouldn't matter if you ate a food that caused a high, short spike or one that caused a lower peak if that lower increase persisted for many hours.

The glycaemic index measures blood glucose increases

This approach (using sophisticated computer integrations) can be used to get the AUC of various foods, and this is what is done by researchers when they measure the *glycaemic index* of food. They give both diabetic and nondiabetic people an amount of food that contains 50 grams of carbohydrate. Then they test the BG level every 15 minutes for the first hour and every 30 minutes for two hours in nondiabetic and three hours in diabetic volunteers, and from this they calculate the AUC. They test each food two or three times with each person and then average the results from eight to ten people to get an official glycaemic index number, which describes how much a particular food will raise the BG level relative to glucose or white bread. Glycaemic index results compared with glucose are always a little lower than the glycaemic index results compared with white bread.

Researchers have found that although the BG levels rise different amounts in different people after eating the same food, the *relative* amounts are usually the same. In other words, Dennis's BG level might go up 100 points with rice cakes and 40 points with a pear, and Chanelda's BG level might go up only 30 points with rice cakes and 15 points with a pear. The effects of the carbohydrates are quite different in these two different people, but in both cases the rice cakes raised the BG level a lot more than the pear.

Foods with a large particle size, high fibre and fat content, and high acidity have lower glycaemic index values than highly processed foods with very little bound-up fibre and small particle sizes. Raw foods have lower glycaemic index values than cooked.

Substance glycaemic index includes noncarbohydrate foods

Researchers working with the glycaemic index have measured only foods containing carbohydrates, and the glycaemic index gives you a good idea of how much two different high-carbohydrate foods will raise your BG level, for example white bread compared with wholemeal bread. But there are no glycaemic index values for low-carbohydrate foods like steak or cheese.

Furthermore, the glycaemic index researchers have tried to standardize the foods relative to the same amount of carbohydrate in each food. The glycaemic index values tell you only that 50 grams of carbohydrate in carrots will raise your BG level more than 50 grams of carbohydrate in chickpeas. But carrots contain a lot of fibre; a half cup of raw carrots contains only about 3 or 4 grams of nonfibre carbohydrate, and you'd have to eat 6 or 8 cups of carrots to get those 50 grams of carbohydrate. Chickpeas contain about 15 grams of nonfibre carbohydrate per half cup, so you'd have to eat only 1.7 cups of chickpeas to get the same amount of carbohydrate.

Thus although the glycaemic index provides a lot of useful information, it can sometimes be misleading. For this reason, Derek Paice, a former RAF pilot who is now an engineer with type 2 diabetes, came up with a concept he calls the *substance glycaemic index*, or *SGI*. This is similar to the glycaemic index except that instead of comparing foods with the same amount of carbohydrate, he compares foods with the same total weight.

This means he can get SGI numbers for noncarbohydrate as well as carbohydrate foods. He's also comparing weights of foods one might actually eat (60 grams are about 2 ounces) instead of amounts that contain 50 grams of carbohydrate, which can be enormous with foods that don't have a lot of carbohydrate. As his standard he uses 60 grams of whole-wheat bread, and he expresses the numbers as a percentage of the AUC for a similar weight of whole-wheat bread.

For example, with his sample size of one person (himself) and using a home BG meter, he finds that if whole-wheat bread has an SGI of 100, some sausage rolls made with wheat flour have an SGI of 56, steak has an SGI of 17 and a cheese omelette has an SGI of 6.

Your results can provide useful information

Doing tests like this can be quite tedious and time-consuming. Some people just measure the AUC for the first two or three hours, as the glycaemic index researchers do. I don't like to test a substance without doing a complete test, waiting until the BG level returns to baseline. In some cases, this can take hours. For example, some foods containing protein or slowly digested carbo-hydrate that acts almost like protein cause very little BG increase until five or six hours after you eat them. If you stopped your test at three hours, you might conclude they had almost no effect at all.

Because exercise can affect the results, I also like to avoid any kind of exertion when I'm testing, and of course I can't eat anything else when I'm doing a test. This means every test curve requires a real investment of hunger and effort, not to mention holes in the fingers. Some of you may not want to invest this much time and energy in getting AUC numbers for all your foods.

If not, doing just a few curves so you'll understand more about when the various foods you eat will peak might make sense. Then you could always measure at those times. Even just always measur-ing one or two hours after a meal or a new food will give you a rough estimate. As shown in Figure 5, it can give some erroneous results, but it's better than not testing at all. The continuous monitors that are being developed will be a godsend for this type of testing.

Even the AUC method can give inconsistent results. Type 2 diabetes is complicated, and many different things can affect how much your BG level will go up after a meal. For example, an unknown infection, a telephone call saying a close friend or relative is sick, having to get a cat out of a tree or other stressful events could affect the results of a test. This doesn't mean they're not worth doing.

Figure 9 shows some of the variations that can affect an AUC test. I was trying to find out if I could eat some of the supersweet local cantaloupe being sold at a local farm. So first I ate 180 grams of melon first thing in the morning, which is when I do AUC tests. As you can see, my BG level went quite high, too high for me. Then I wondered if I could tolerate slightly less cantaloupe with other food, so I had lunch of beef, broccoli, pepper and 120 grams of melon. This time, my BG level hardly moved.

Then, to see if the lower BG rise had to do with the food I ate with the melon or to other factors, I had another 210 grams of melon with no other food. You can see that the BG level didn't rise nearly as much as it had in the early-morning test, even though I ate more melon.

This lower rise with more melon could have been caused by several factors. (1) Most people are more sensitive to carbohydrates in the morning. Maybe the large rise early in the day was just part of the dawn effect.

FIGURE 9. So many variables, so little time. When you're trying to figure out how a particular food affects your BG levels, you have to remember that many factors can be involved. This shows how my BG levels responded to three different meals containing cantaloupe. In the curve at the left, I ate 180 grams of melon with no other food, and my BG level went quite high. Then I had 120 grams of melon along with meat and vegetable (beef, broccoli and pepper), and my BG level hardly increased at all. Finally, I had 210 grams of melon with no other food, and the BG level increased just a little. Measuring after only one melon-containing meal might have led to an erroneous conclusion. The time of day, accompanying food and previous meals, as well as exercise and stress, can all affect the response.

(2) I had other food before the 210 grams of melon. Even though the BG level had returned to normal, some food might have remained in my stomach and could have slowed down the digestion of the melon. (3) Some people show what is called a *priming effect*. This means that if you eat a lot of carbohydrate at one meal, you produce more insulin the next time you eat carbohydrate (see Figure 3 in Month 7). This seems to be true for me. A second mini-GTT usually shows a lower BG peak than the first one.

So it's difficult to know what caused the difference. But it does suggest that if I want to eat a little bit of fruit, I'm much better off eating it along with some protein and fibre-rich vegetable, especially later in the day.

What's true for me might not be true for you. If you do have the time and energy to invest, testing this way and getting AUC numbers for your favourite foods will give you a much, much better idea of which foods and activities you can choose for maximal control.

IN A SENTENCE:

> With a little extra work, you can use your home glucose meter to get approximate values for your own personal glycaemic index values.

MONTH **10**

living

Complications

I HOPE that by keeping your blood glucose (BG) levels close to normal, you will avoid ever developing any diabetic complications. As discussed in Day 6, there is now real evidence that the lower your average BG level is, the smaller the risk of complications, especially the *microvascular* ones.

Unfortunately, however, because you may have had diabetes for many years before being diagnosed, you may already have had early signs of complications when you were diagnosed. If not, you should at least be aware of what kinds of complications can occur so you can be alert for their early signs and insist that your periodic health examinations test you for their presence.

Microvascular complications are serious

Microvascular complications are the ones caused by problems in your small blood vessels and include *retinopathy* (eye problems), *nephropathy* (kidney problems) and *neuropathy* (nerve problems): the 'Three O'Pathy Sisters'. They are more common in people with long-standing type 1 diabetes, but people with type 2 diabetes are not immune. Microvascular complications usually occur only after about 10 years of high BG levels.

Eye problems can be detected with regular eye examinations

Glaucoma and cataracts are not limited to people with diabetes, but if you have diabetes, your chances of getting glaucoma and cataracts are increased.

Glaucoma. *Glaucoma* means the pressure in your eyes is greater than normal. This pressure can damage the optic nerve, the one that sends messages from your eyes to your brain. Uncontrolled, glaucoma can cause blindness, usually starting with a loss of peripheral vision. When caught early, however, glaucoma can be controlled with eyedrops, and your chances of losing sight are small. Make sure your *intraocular pressure* is measured when you have your regular eye examinations. Ask your ophthalmologist or optician about the symptoms of acute glaucoma, which include pain, nausea and halos around lights, and seek medical attention immediately if they occur.

Cataracts. *Cataracts* result from clouding of the lens of the eye and are common in elderly people. If you have diabetes, you're more likely to have cataracts and to get them at a younger age. These days, the lens can be removed and replaced with an artificial lens in a fairly routine outpatient procedure, and some people report that their vision is much better after this operation than it ever was before.

Retinopathy. *Retinopathy* is the eye condition that is limited to people with diabetes, and it's the one that has been shown to be reduced in frequency when BG levels are lowered. When BG levels have been elevated for 10 or 20 years, most people show signs of early retinopathy. About 20 per cent of people diagnosed with type 2 diabetes show such signs when they're diagnosed.

This early stage of retinopathy is called *nonproliferative* or *background retinopathy*, and it doesn't usually cause any loss of vision. For some reason that is not completely understood, when BG levels are elevated, the capillaries become more fragile and leaky. Some of the capillaries in the eyes form *aneurysms*, or outpouchings, that can be seen when a doctor examines the *retina* of your eyes, the part of the back of your eyes that is responsible for detecting light and converting it into nervous signals that are sent to the brain. Sometimes the capillaries also leak fluid, and fats from the fluid can condense and form what are called *hard exudates* because their borders look sharp.

As long as the retinopathy doesn't proceed any further, your vision should remain normal, unless some of the fluid leaks into the *macular* area of the retina and causes swelling, called *macular oedema*. The macula is the part of your eyes responsible for central, detailed vision, so when this area is swollen, your vision may be reduced.

If BG levels aren't controlled, retinopathy can proceed through several other stages to *proliferative retinopathy*, which can cause loss of vision. As in the rest of the body, when circulation through capillaries is slowed down or stopped, the body tries to fix the problem by making new capillaries. If this happens in your heart, it's a good thing. When it happens in your retina, it's not.

The new blood vessels can obstruct your vision or, worse, because they are even more fragile than normal, they can leak blood into the clear fluid in your eyeball (called the *vitreous humour*), causing clouding of your vision. If they bleed and then clot, the clot can contract and pull the retina away from its attachments. This is called *retinal detachment* and is a serious condition that can lead to blindness.

These days, laser surgery can be used to seal the leaky capillaries before serious damage occurs. The procedure does hurt; most books say a little, some patients say a heck of a lot. But it works. Studies have shown significant reduction in serious vision loss when laser surgery is used this way.

A better way to save your sight is to keep your BG levels down so you'll never need the surgery. Early retinopathy has no symptoms, so it's important to get an annual eye examination (see Week 2) to detect retinal changes early, before they've done any damage. It's also important to keep your blood pressure down, as high blood pressure increases the chances of bleeding throughout the body.

Nephropathy can be detected with lab tests

Diabetic nephropathy, or damage to the kidneys, usually goes along with retinopathy. So if there are no signs of damage to your eyes, your kidneys are probably OK. Conversely, if you have signs of early retinal problems, you probably have early kidney problems as well, so make sure your doctor checks you carefully for this (see Day 5) and continues to do so in the future.

Early nephropathy can be reversed by maintaining BG levels at near-normal levels, but if you wait until there is a lot of protein in the urine, the damage probably can't be undone. If you keep your BG levels in the normal range, or close to that, you probably won't get either kidney or retinal damage in the first place. However, the risks of both problems are partly genetic, and if you're of Indian or West Indian origin, the risks of these complications are greater even with good control.

How kidneys work. The kidneys are the body's waste collectors, including an efficient recycling centre. They basically filter metabolic waste products, toxins, some drugs and extra fluids out of the blood, producing urine, while retaining proteins and anything else that the body can reuse.

Here's how they work. The kidneys have a lot of structures called *nephrons*, each of which consists of a pompon-like tuft of capillaries (called a *glomerulus*) inside a balloon-like pouch. When healthy, these capillaries have small pores in them, and they are surrounded by a mesh of material called *basement membrane* that also acts like a filter. Both the pores and the basement membrane have a negative charge.

Blood flows through the capillaries, and much of the liquid and small molecules like glucose and sodium chloride can go through the pores and the basement membrane and are secreted into the pouch and then down a series of tubes into the bladder. Large molecules like proteins usually can't fit through the holes. Even when the proteins are small enough, the negative charge on the pores and basement membrane tends to keep them out.

On the way to the bladder, through a complicated series of steps, many of the beneficial small molecules are reabsorbed into the blood and recycled by the body, so only the stuff the body really doesn't want ends up in the urine.

How damage occurs. Even when BG levels are normal, some nephrons become damaged with age; after the age of 40 years, we lose about 10 per cent of our nephrons every 10 years. But that doesn't make much difference because we have a lot more nephrons than we really need, so the damage is often not apparent until 80 per cent of the nephrons have been damaged.

When BG levels remain high for a long time, this degeneration is much faster than normal. It is thought that *AGEs* (advanced glycation end products; see Month 4) contribute to the changes. The basement membrane gets thicker. The negative charges are lost. Just as happens in the retina of the eye, the capillaries become leaky, and they start letting proteins escape into the urine. When tiny amounts of the protein *albumin* can be detected in the urine, a state called *microalbuminuria* (meaning 'tiny amounts of albumin in the urine'), this is a sign that the nephrons are showing damage.

Cells between the capillaries called *mesangial cells* begin to proliferate until they squeeze the capillaries and increase the capillary blood pressure. Eventually the capillaries become completely blocked and can't do their job at all. Essentially, what was formerly an exquisitely engineered waste-processing plant has been turned into a mass of scar tissue.

High blood pressure makes the damage to the nephrons worse, so controlling blood pressure, especially with drugs called **ACE** (angiotensin-converting enzyme) **inhibitors**, is a good way to reduce the probability that you'll ever develop nephropathy and a good way to minimize the damage if it's already begun. High cholesterol levels and smoking also increase the damage. The other important thing to do is to bring your BG levels to normal levels as soon as the microalbuminuria is detected.

Neuropathy can be painful

Neuropathy means damage to the nerves. Like damage to the kidneys and eyes, neuropathy is much more likely to occur when your BG levels have been high for many years. However, about 20 per cent of people with type 2 diabetes already have signs of early neuropathy when they're diagnosed, and sometimes the neuropathy is what brings them to the doctor in the first place.

Peripheral neuropathy. No one is sure exactly how the nerve damage occurs. It may be from direct damage to the nerves or from damage to the blood vessels supplying the nerves, or both. What is called **peripheral neuropathy** is the most common form and involves damage to the nerves of the hands and feet, especially the feet. You may feel tingling, burning or prickling in your feet, especially at night and in the winter. Drinking alcohol can make the pain worse. Sometimes the feet are so sensitive that even the pressure of the blankets causes pain.

Luckily, this early stage of neuropathy can usually be reversed by bringing your BG levels back to near-normal levels. As you improve your control, the pain in your feet may get worse at first. Don't worry about this. It just means the nerves are healing and are better able to feel pain. This increased pain should be temporary.

If you don't improve your control, the neuropathy will progress, the pain will eventually subside, and your feet will become numb, unable to feel pain at all. At this point, the nerves are probably dead and bringing your BG levels back to normal probably won't make the feeling return. You might think this would be a relief, but actually it's a great danger. Without feeling in your feet, things like splinters or calluses can go unnoticed and turn into ulcers that are difficult to heal.

Note that if you do have neuropathy and the pain is so bad that you need medication, the doctor may prescribe a type of antidepressant. Don't worry. The doctor isn't implying that your pain is psychological. Some antidepressants reduce the pain of neuropathy by a mechanism unrelated to their antidepressant effect.

Having diabetes makes all your nerves more sensitive to damage from other causes. For example, people with diabetes are twice as likely to have *carpal tunnel syndrome*, which is caused by pressure on the nerves going into the hand, often by repetitive actions. People without diabetes also get carpal tunnel syndrome, but not as easily.

Motor neuropathy. The damage I've mentioned so far is damage to *sensory nerves*, the nerves that allow you to feel sensations of hot, cold, pain and so forth. The *motor nerves*, which make your muscles move, can also be damaged, although this is less common.

Autonomic neuropathy. High BG levels can also damage what are called autonomic nerves, the nerves responsible for all the actions that the body carries out automatically, without conscious effort, for example breathing, beating of the heart and digestion. This is called (surprise) **autonomic neuropathy**. It can cause problems with bladder emptying, sexual function, digestion, sweating and control of the heartbeat. Autonomic neuropathy usually occurs after sensory neuropathy, but if you have a lot of neuropathy in your extremities, you may have some autonomic neuropathy as well.

When autonomic neuropathy affects the heart, it may not speed up or slow down properly, or the rhythm may be out of whack. Sometimes the typical symptoms of heart attack are absent, so you might think a heart attack was something else.

Gastroparesis. A common result of autonomic neuropathy to the *vagus nerve* is **gastroparesis**, or slow emptying of the stomach. This is especially dangerous if you're taking sulphonylureas or injecting insulin, as you take a certain amount based on when you expect the food to be digested. If the food doesn't leave the stomach on time, the drugs will make you go low. If then the food is suddenly dumped, you'll go too high.

Even if you're not using insulin, gastroparesis can cause what appear to be random fluctuations in your BG levels that you can't explain. If you also feel full after eating very small meals and have a lot of indigestion, nausea and maybe constipation or diarrhoea that you can't explain, ask your doctor about the possibility of gastroparesis. There are drugs that help with this, as does eating small meals with very little fat or fibre.

If you have neuropathy in your extremities, there's a good chance you have some early signs of gastroparesis, so be alert for them.

Other neuropathies. Autonomic neuropathy can also cause changes in the way you sweat, with very dry feet that tend to crack and increased sweating in the face.

Unfortunately, another possible type of neuropathy in men is impotence. Because there are many other possible causes of impotence, including psychological ones, you can't assume that it stems from neuropathy without excluding those other causes. Again, high BG levels increase the probability of impotence, so do what you can to keep them in the normal ranges. In women, autonomic neuropathy can cause a decrease in lubrication.

Some complications are not unique to people with diabetes

Some conditions are not unique to people with diabetes, but they are more common. These include yeast and other fungal infections; thickened skin; Dupuytren's contracture, a thickening of tendons in the hand that causes a finger to refuse to straighten out, and frozen shoulder. Some skin conditions include a flushed face that returns to normal when BG levels are controlled and yellowish skin that may result from AGE formation.

Macrovascular complications can be lethal

Macrovascular complications are those related to the larger blood vessels and include heart attacks, strokes and *peripheral vascular disease*, which can be lumped together as *cardiovascular disease*. Most people with type 2 diabetes will eventually die from cardiovascular disease. If this sounds grim, remember that most people will eventually die from something or other; your high risk factors for cardiovascular disease are like an early warning system, letting you know where you should focus your preventive actions.

Macrovascular complications can be somewhat reduced by keeping your BG levels close to normal, but not as much as microvascular ones. One reason may be that much of the damage from the insulin resistance (IR) that is usually the cause of type 2 diabetes has already occurred by the time you are diagnosed and can't be easily reversed.

Cardiovascular disease is not limited to people with diabetes. When you have all the symptoms associated with type 2 diabetes except high BG levels (IR, an 'apple shape', high blood pressure, high levels of triglycerides, low levels of HDL, normal or only slightly elevated levels of LDL), this is called *Syndrome X*, or *insulin-resistance syndrome*, and I discussed the details in Month 6. Treatment for cardiovascular risk factors is similar in diabetic and nondiabetic people. However, because of the increased risks, it's a good idea to try to keep your cholesterol levels and blood pressure a little lower than you would if you didn't have those additional risks.

Plan ahead for pregnancy

Pregnancy isn't really a complication of diabetes, unless you happen to meet your partner at a diabetes support group. But it can complicate your control.

Because type 2 diabetes is usually diagnosed in older people, most of you probably won't have to deal with this complication. But more and more young people are being diagnosed with the disease and need to know of the potential problems.

The important thing to know is that high BG levels or high ketone levels *early in pregnancy* can cause birth defects, so it's essential to plan your pregnancy ahead of time and make sure you're in excellent control before conception and in the early months. This would be a good time to see an endocrinologist if you haven't already done so, or an obstetrician who is experienced treating people with diabetes.

The other important thing to keep in mind is that many drugs can harm the foetus, so if you're taking oral diabetes drugs, you need to switch to insulin before you become pregnant. IR goes up two or three times in late pregnancy, so you may need insulin at that time even if you were controlling with diet and exercise alone before you became pregnant. Once the baby is born, the IR returns to prepregnancy levels.

Some other drugs such as ACE inhibitors for kidney problems may also damage the foetus, and other drugs should be substituted. Again, plan ahead and stop taking any potentially damaging drugs *before* you get pregnant. This includes caffeine and alcohol.

If you already have any eye or kidney damage, it may become worse during the pregnancy but usually returns to former levels after the baby is born.

With planning and normal BG levels, you should have just about the same chances of having a normal baby as someone without diabetes. If you're male, your diabetes shouldn't affect the outcome of the pregnancy. Type 2 diabetes has a strong genetic component, so your children will be at increased risk. However, knowing that ahead of time should help them keep their diabetic genes under control by exercising regularly and moderating their consumption of processed carbohydrates and saturated fat.

There may be several causes of complications

No one is sure exactly what causes diabetic complications. However, it's quite clear that high BG levels are a major factor. As mentioned in Day 6, several long-term studies of people with both type 1 and type 2 diabetes proved without a doubt that keeping your BG levels down will reduce the statistical probability that you will develop diabetic complications.

Table 1 in Day 6 shows the relationship between BG levels and retinopathy. Risks of other complications are reduced in a similar way. It's quite clear that keeping your BG levels down gives you just about the same risk of developing complications as someone who doesn't have diabetes. Letting your BG levels stay high almost ensures that you will eventually have problems. And remember that type 2 diabetes develops slowly, so you may already have had high BG levels for several years, or even more, before you were diagnosed.

It's not very surprising that scientists haven't figured out the exact mechanisms of diabetic complications yet even though so many people develop them. They haven't figured out the exact mechanisms of aging yet either, and 100 per cent of people age, if they live long enough. In some ways, diabetes simply accelerates the normal aging process.

One way high BG levels are thought to cause complications is by means of AGEs. Everyone's blood contains some glucose. If you heat glucose with proteins at a very high temperature, you get what is called *browning*. That's what happens when you brown beef in a frying pan. Even at normal BG concentrations and normal temperatures, glucose reacts slowly with many of the proteins in your body in a similar reaction, forming AGEs. When your BG levels are high, more AGEs are formed.

AGEs may be one cause of aging, and thus when your BG levels are high, you're causing accelerated aging. Some chemicals that can break some of the AGE bonds seem to help to reverse some complications, but such drugs have not yet been approved by the relevant authorities.

In diabetic cataracts, it is believed that high glucose levels inside the lens of the eye cause the formation of the sugar alcohol *sorbitol*. This reaction is catalyzed by an enzyme called **aldose reductase**. The sorbitol can't get out of the lens again and draws in water, so the lens swells. Note that eating sorbitol isn't apt to cause cataracts. When you eat sorbitol, it is converted to fructose in the liver.

There is some evidence that sorbitol in nerve tissue contributes to nerve damage, but not primarily by causing swelling. In this case, the sorbitol may somehow keep a compound called *myo-inositol*, which is important for membrane function, from entering the nerve cell, which doesn't conduct current as well as a result.

Free radicals may contribute to diabetic complications. Other mechanisms may cause complications, but they are not well understood. One seems to involve a particular form of a protein called *protein kinase C*.

No one understands why some people get complications and others do not. Some people can have high A1c results for years and never have serious complications, whereas others have much lower A1cs and still develop complications. Some ethnic groups, for example those of African or Hispanic origin, seem to be more prone to developing complications.

Be in charge

When discussing complications and testing for early signs, many books on diabetes say things like, 'Your doctor will check you for this regularly.' But in fact, many doctors *won't* check you regularly, due to time limitations and cost-cutting pressures.

So it's up to you to understand which complications you think you're at most risk for and to make sure your doctor orders the appropriate tests.

It's also up to you to make sure you keep your BG levels close to normal so the risks will be low or, if you already had some complications when you were diagnosed, the complications can be reversed as much as they can.

IN A SENTENCE:

> High blood glucose levels can cause diabetic complications, but microvascular complications can usually be controlled or even reversed if you are alert for their symptoms and seek early treatment.

Diet Wars: Getting Beyond the Hype

DIET AND EXERCISE are the cornerstones of treatment of type 2 diabetes, even if you are also using oral drugs or insulin. Everyone agrees that if you have type 2 diabetes you should 'eat healthily'. The problem is, no one can agree on what healthy eating is. No topic raises more passion than a discussion of dietary prescriptions for people with diabetes – or, for that matter, without.

Diet gurus push their agendas

Some of the popular diet books would have you believe that if you follow their diet, you'll cure everything that ails you. The authors tend to cite all the evidence that supports their point of view and ignore all the evidence that doesn't.

For example, it has been found that many groups of people who switch from a traditional way of life that includes a lot of hard work and an adequate but not excessive diet develop diabetes when they move to the city and adopt a so-called civilized way of life. This usually includes a lot less physical labour and a varied diet that includes a lot more calories, including both more fat and more processed carbohydrate.

Proponents of low-fat diets cite people like the Bantu, from southern, eastern and central Africa, who traditionally had a low-fat, high-carbohydrate diet and say, 'See, these people didn't eat a lot of fat until they moved to the city and adopted Western high-fat diets and got diabetes. Therefore, fat causes diabetes.'

Proponents of low-carbohydrate diets cite people like the Eskimos or Yemenite Jews, who traditionally had a high-protein, low-carbohydrate diet, and say, 'See, these people didn't eat a lot of carbohydrate until they adopted Western high-carbohydrate diets and got diabetes. Therefore, carbohydrates cause diabetes.'

Like politicians, various popular diet authors sometimes seem so busy pushing their own agendas that they don't have time to listen to each other or cooperate in trying to reach the truth. For example, in February 2000 the American government sponsored what was called The Great Nutrition Debate, at which authors of the leading diet books and representatives from government agencies were given a few minutes to present their cases. Reading a transcript of the debate, I got the feeling they were all wearing earmuffs when the other people were speaking.

However, both extremes in the diet wars now seem to be moving towards the middle. Advocates of high-carbohydrate diets are now saying that if your triglycerides go up too much on their diet, you should substitute monounsaturated fats for some of the carbohydrates. Advocates of low-carbohydrate diets say if your lipids go up too much on their diet, you should substitute monounsaturated fats for the saturated ones.

What people with type 2 diabetes desperately need is a formal study showing which dietary approach works best not just for weight loss but for long-term control of blood glucose (BG) and lipid levels. Unfortunately, such a study has yet to be done.

This means it's very difficult to learn the truth about which diet works best for diabetes from reading the popular literature. To get somewhere near the truth, you have to read a great variety of books, some preaching one doctrine and some preaching the other. Then try them yourself and see which works best for you.

Don't rely on just one author's interpretation of the limited studies that have been done so far.

Evaluate blood glucose and lipid control as well as weight loss

When you read about various types of diets, keep in mind that when the writers in the media discuss a *diet*, what they usually mean is a *weight-loss diet*. When they evaluate a diet, they are evaluating how well it works to make you lose weight. They are not evaluating how well it controls diabetes.

One standard criticism of the more extreme diets, for example, very low fat or low-carbohydrate diets, is that 'no one could stick to a diet like this for more than a month or so.' Although that might be true for someone dieting simply to get into a smaller size of jeans by the next work party, for anyone with serious health problems, those criticisms are no more valid than saying a person with high blood pressure wouldn't be able to give up salt for more than a month or so. Giving up butter or giving up bread is better than giving up your eyesight and your feet. In the old days, people with diabetes had to weigh their food, and they followed such rigid regimes for years.

Weight loss usually does reduce insulin resistance (IR). However, you should never forget that controlling your BG levels is more important than losing weight. If you found some fad diet that made you lose weight but also made your BG levels stay around 16.7 mmol/L all day, this would not be a good diet for you. The reduction in IR from the weight loss would not balance the damage you'd have from the high BG levels.

Because you are at increased risk for heart disease, you also need to evaluate the effects of any diet on various lipid levels, including LDL, HDL and triglycerides. As tests for new heart-disease risk factors become common, you must evaluate the effects of the various diets on these factors as well.

So if you want to try a new dietary approach, keep testing your BG levels before and after meals and keep track of your A1c and blood lipid levels before you settle on a particular diet for life.

Don't rely on the media.

Keep in mind amounts versus percentages

Most diets are described in terms of the percentages of carbohydrate, fat and protein (see Day 3) that they allow, and they are often labelled according to these percentages as *high this* or *low that*.

But percentages aren't the same as amounts. Most national heart associations, for example, the British Heart Foundation, recommend a diet that contains 30 per cent fat or less. You've probably always been a big eater, and let's say that before your diagnosis you were eating 3000 calories a day. That means you could have been guzzling 900 calories (100 grams) of fat a day.

Now let's say you go on a strict diet and eat only 1500 calories a day, limiting your fat intake to 675 calories (75 grams) a day. In this case, you'd be eating less fat, but it would represent 45 per cent of your total caloric intake. So even though you'd now be eating less fat than before, some people would castigate you for your 'increased' fat intake.

The same is true of protein. When people are limiting calories, some so-called **high-protein diets** actually contain smaller *amounts* of protein than the average Westerner eats, yet because the *percentage* of protein is higher, the diets continue to be criticized on the theory that eating a lot of protein could damage the kidneys (see later).

This is also true of carbohydrate foods. If you're not eating a lot of calories, even though the carbohydrate percentages may be high, on a 'high-carbohydrate' diet, the amounts may be relatively low compared with what you were eating before. This is particularly true if you're eating low-glycaemic index foods that are rich in fibre.

Don't be swayed by popular labels such as 'high-carbohydrate diet' or 'high-protein diet'.

All the diets make you eat less

I described various diet approaches on Day 4. Despite claims about their miraculous properties, most weight-loss diets work by tricking you into eating fewer calories, and some studies have shown that people lose weight at about the same rate no matter which approach they take. Let's look at how this works.

Exchange diets. The *exchange diets* are the most obvious. You are given a certain number of exchanges that total a certain number of calories, depending on your size and goal weight. As long as you stick to the prescribed exchanges, your calories will be controlled.

Low-fat diets. With the *low-fat, high-carbohydrate diet*, sometimes you don't need to count calories, but because carbohydrates have only four calories per gram and fats have nine calories per gram, when you eat a lot of carbohydrate, you're eating fewer calories with an equal amount of food. You feel full sooner and tend to eat less.

Low-glycaemic index diets. Low-glycaemic index foods are usually high in indigestible fibre. Most *low-glycaemic index diets* also emphasize substituting the low-glycaemic carbohydrates for fats, and the low-glycaemic index foods have even greater bulk for the number of calories they contain and fill you up even sooner. Again, the net result is eating fewer calories.

Low-carbohydrate diets. *Low-carbohydrate diets* work another way. Eating a lot of fat makes many people slightly nauseous. Most people can imagine downing stacks of pancakes or bagels, but the thought of eating several packets of butter or drinking a cup of olive oil doesn't have the same appeal. So when you're allowed to eat all the fatty meat and cheese you want, most people automatically limit the amount they eat, especially after a few days. In addition, low-carbohydrate diets cause *ketosis*, and ketones in the blood also cause people to lose their appetite. The mild ketosis caused by eating very few carbohydrates or burning a lot of fat occurs when BG levels are normal and is not the same as *ketoacidosis* (see Month 2), which is a serious condition that occurs when BG levels are high. As long as your pancreas is able to produce some insulin, the insulin will slow down the production of ketones before they cause acidosis.

Food-combining diets. Weight-loss diets that prohibit combining certain foods also result in eating fewer calories. For instance, one such diet says not to eat protein and starch at the same meal. So instead of eating meat and potatoes for lunch and dinner, you eat meat and green vegetables for lunch, and potatoes and green vegetables for dinner. Net result: You've substituted low-calorie green vegetables for high-calorie potatoes and meat.

One-food diets. Real fad diets such as those that limit your intake to one or two foods make you eat less because you quickly become bored with those foods. It's having a variety of foods available that makes most people eat too much. You probably remember trying to explain to your mother when you were a child why it was that you were too full to finish your spinach but as soon as she brought out the chocolate cake, your appetite miraculously reappeared.

Apparently rodents have the same problem. Some studies have shown that mice that are genetically engineered to gain weight easily do so only when offered 'cafeteria diets', meaning foods with different tastes. When offered nothing but ordinary mouse food, they don't eat as much and remain normal weight. This is a good example of the fact that like type 2 diabetes, obesity often has both a genetic and an environmental component. In order to be overweight you usually need both the genes that predispose you to easy weight gain and an environment in which there is a bountiful, varied food supply.

Complex theories. Diet books may cite complicated theories of why their diets allow weight loss with no effort on your part, but in general they simply get you to eat less food. Eating less food is a good thing. As I discussed in Month 8, often simply reducing your caloric intake will help reduce your BG levels, even if you don't lose weight. So if one of the popular approaches works for you *and doesn't result in an increase in your BG levels*, that's the way for you.

Don't be influenced by complex theories of how a particular diet will let you lose weight while eating all you want.

Dietary misunderstandings are common

Many things you'll read in diet books are based on truth. But sometimes they're only half-truths that have become garbled with time. Following are a few examples of this.

If a carbohydrate isn't a sugar, it's 'complex'. For many years, doctors and dieticians urged people with diabetes to eat a lot of so-called *complex carbohydrates* (meaning *polysaccharides;* see Day 3). They explained that 'simple sugars' like sucrose were quickly broken down by the body and raised the BG level quickly. Instead they told people to eat a lot of complex carbohydrates like potatoes and rice, because the big molecules were supposed to be broken down slowly and raise the BG levels slowly.

Why no one thought to test this idea is beyond me, but they didn't. Then someone realized that in fact starch is digested so quickly that it raises the BG level as fast as sucrose (table sugar) – in fact a little faster, because starch is all glucose, and sucrose is only half glucose, the other half consisting of the sugar fructose, which doesn't raise BG levels as fast.

Nevertheless, many health care people continued to urge people to eat more complex carbohydrates, and a few still do. Some dealt with this situation by redefining *complex carbohydrate* to mean slowly digested (low-glycaemic index) carbohydrates such as those bound up with a lot of fibre, and not high-glyacemic index carbohydrates such as the starch found in potato or white bread. Others urge that we dump the term *complex carbohydrate* altogether and refer to dietary carbohydrates by their formal names: *monosaccharides* and *disaccharides* (which can both be called *sugars*) and *polysaccharides* (or, more specifically, *starch* and *fibre*, depending on whether or not it can be digested by humans).

Protein is bad for kidneys. Another oft-cited half-truth concerns the effect of low-carbohydrate diets on kidneys. Many dieticians frown on low-carbohydrate diets because they say high-protein diets (meaning high *percentages*) are damaging to kidneys.

Almost everyone agrees that a high-protein diet is not good for kidneys that show some signs of damage. But in those without kidney damage, there is no published evidence that a high-protein diet causes damage. Body builders eat large amounts of proteins, and there is no evidence that their kidneys are harmed by doing so.

The Food Pyramid gives you licence to eat all the carbo-hydrate you want. Another misconception concerns the famous Food Pyramid. If you look at the pyramid, it might appear that you should spend all day guzzling down huge mounds of pasta and bread. In fact, they suggest '6 to 11 servings' of carbohydrate foods. If you're small, that means only six servings, and each serving is pretty small, for example one piece of bread or two biscuits. Six servings really isn't that much at all, only 90 grams a day. Some people look at the pyramid and think, 'If I don't eat fat, I can eat all the carbohydrate I want.' In fact, followed exactly, the Food Pyramid is a calorie-restricted exchange-type diet. That is, if you follow the Food Pyramid, you'll probably lose weight because you're eating fewer total calories, not because you're eating a lot of carbohydrate.

A low-carbohydrate diet gives you licence to eat all the fat you want. If you are large and need a lot of calories to main-tain your weight, you may be able to eat all you want on a low-carbohydrate diet and still lose weight, because you may lose your appetite after eating a lot of fatty foods. But if you're small and your caloric needs are also small, you may have to pay attention to how much you eat on this kind of diet if you want to lose weight as well as keep your BG levels down. One of the popular low-carbohydrate diets (*Protein Power*) even mentions this, but they do so in a footnote, in tiny type, so some readers may not notice.

Carbohydrate is good for diabetes. Some dieticians prescribe a 'heart-healthy' low-fat diet with about 60 per cent of the calories coming from carbohydrate, as approved by the various professional groups. You may recall the rationale for this diet. Having diabetes, you are already at increased risk of heart disease. Standard Western diets containing a lot of fat are associated with a higher risk of heart disease.

Hence the real reason for promoting this diet is to *reduce your fat intake, not increase your carbohydrate intake*. The carbohydrate content is high because you have to replace the fat calories with something, and many dieticians are taught that too much protein is bad. The only thing left is carbohydrate. The carbohydrate *does* increase your *postprandial* BG levels, but people endorsing this diet think that's not as important as eating less fat.

Unfortunately, the basic message is sometimes garbled. Instead of telling you to eat less fat, some dieticians may tell you to eat more carbohydrate. Some people say they go to their dietician complaining that their BG levels are too high and the dietician tells them to add more carbohydrate to the diet. After getting this type of advice, Bobbie K. used to eat the same dinner she'd always eaten and then *add* extra bread or potato. 'Have to get my carbs.'

Another problem is that the Food Pyramid and some dieticians don't distinguish between 'fast', or high-glycaemic index carbohydrates like white bread and white flour and low-glycaemic index carbohydrates like whole grains or broccoli. Early studies that showed that low-fat, high-carbohydrate diets could reduce IR in people with diabetes used lowglycaemic index, high-fibre carbohydrates. Somehow the message that 'carbohydrates are good' got through and the message that 'they should be unprocessed and high in fibre' got lost.

If it's popular, it's a fad diet. After years of being told to avoid fat like the plague, many people are now going to the other extreme and avoiding carbohydrates to try to lose weight. These diets are now very popular, and in that sense they are fad diets.

Critics say things like, 'The only reason people try these diets is because they give them an excuse to eat the fatty foods they love, like roast beef and whipped cream.' This makes as much sense as saying, 'The only reason people go on low-fat diets is to give them an excuse to eat the starchy foods they love, like spaghetti and freshly baked bread.'

When you have diabetes, you need to choose the diet that will do the best job of keeping your BG and lipid levels close to normal. If a low-fat or a low-carbohydrate diet or some mixture of the two does this for you, it's a medically necessary diet for you. It's not a fad diet. Don't let the knee-jerk critics influence your choice.

Low-carbohydrate diets lack nutrients. Critics of low-carbohydrate diets for weight loss often say they are devoid of the important nutrients you get in fresh fruits and vegetables. The media often describe these diets as consisting of nothing but fatty meat, cheese and whipped cream.

Those using such diets simply to lose weight might, in fact, take them to these extremes. If you have diabetes, you are in this for the long run and should be more interested in nutrition and variety than in superquick weight loss.

Such diets do not usually prohibit fruits and vegetables, just those that are high in sugar and starch. You can eat nutritious green leafy vegetables and reasonable amounts of high-fibre vegetables such as broccoli and cauliflower and even small amounts of fibre-rich fruits such as berries. In fact, the produce eaten on such diets is often more dense in nutrients than the starch-filled ones prescribed in low-fat diets.

Learn to analyze the claims

When you have diabetes, you need to understand diet and nutrition better than most people, even some experts. With experience, you can evaluate the effect of a particular diet on *your own particular physiology* better than any diet analysts.

IN A SENTENCE:

> *Diet book authors don't agree on what is the best diet for people with diabetes, so you'll have to learn to find the truth beyond the hype.*

Burnout

MANY PEOPLE work through a period of depression after their diagnosis (see Week 4) and then move on, focusing on the positive things in their lives.

Unfortunately, however, this does not mean that depression has gone from your life forever. After many months, or years, of dealing with diabetes, many people suffer a bout of secondary depression, or 'diabetes burnout'. You probably won't reach this point in your first year, but you should know that it may lie ahead and not be surprised if it occurs.

You can't sell out

One problem with diabetes is that it's relentless. Like the farmer who has to milk the cows twice a day 365 days a year whether healthy or sick, whether holiday or none, you never get any time off. You have to deal with controlling blood glucose (BG) levels 24 hours a day, seven days a week. It never stops. And unlike the farmer, you have no choice. You can't sell your diabetes at an auction.

Some people quickly accept the diagnosis and the challenge ahead and work incredibly hard to control their BG levels. They go on a strict diet and lose a lot of weight. They start exercising and develop muscles they hadn't used in years. Their A1c levels drop into normal levels. They are enthusiastic and preach the rewards of taking charge to the newly diagnosed.

Then one day after several years of this good control they just get tired of it all: the constant testing, the constant deprivation, the tantalizing treats they can't have, all those medical appointments and most of all, the fact that there are no holidays from this rigid routine.

'Mostly I'm just kind of, for lack of a better word, *disenchanted* with the whole thing,' said Fran R. 'For all practical purposes I'd have to honestly say I've back-burnered the diabetes and lost the desire to test, and exercise has gone by the wayside in my busy life with work, kids, dog etc. I keep thinking I'll "snap out of it", but I think I felt really discouraged with the months of 10 plus morning highs and that kind of thing. I KNOW all about the horrendous complications that can happen, and it just seems getting the routine of exercise and trying to lose weight have been, well . . . so damned hard.'

Remember the second fantasy in Day 2, that your diabetes would suddenly disappear. Many people carry this fantasy for years. Unfortunately, this tendency is encouraged by some members of the medical profession, who tell you that if you would just lose a little weight, your diabetes might go away. 'Sometimes just two to five kilograms will make a difference.'

As described in Month 8, in some cases, weight loss *does* return BG levels to normal, especially if the diabetes is diagnosed in the very early stages. But that's not the universal situation, because most people aren't diagnosed until their BG levels are fairly high. Weight loss can help with insulin resistance (IR), but usually once your BG levels get high enough for you to be diagnosed, about 80 per cent of your pancreas has been destroyed, and no matter how much weight you lose you'll always have trouble with BG control. Feeling betrayed, promised something that didn't happen after you worked so hard to do what they said would help, can contribute to burnout.

Diabetes doesn't show

Always feeling different, always having to explain can also cause you to suffer burnout. Diabetes doesn't show. It's not like you are in a wheelchair or have a cast on your arm. If you've lost weight and taken a lot of exercise, you probably look a lot healthier than before you were diagnosed. It's difficult for people to remember that you have a disease.

'I just got some delicious cheesecake from a friend in London. Why don't you come over and share it with me?' or 'Would you like a biscuit? I baked them myself.' Even your best friends may make offers like this, and once again you have to explain that you can't (or won't) have those things. 'Oh yes, I forgot.'

Each time a friend describes in tantalizing detail the extra-rich chocolate cake someone made for a birthday, you are reminded once more that you are different. You can't eat that stuff. You know they don't do it on purpose. Diabetes doesn't show, so they forget you're sick.

'We don't look or most of the time act as though anything is wrong with us,' said Barbara F. 'Plus, most of the time we don't even notice what other people are eating, and they don't notice what we're eating. Just once in a while it hits. Chet invariably comes to wherever I am to eat his afternoon snack. Most of the time I don't notice or it doesn't bother me. But once in a while it really gets to me. This afternoon he was eating a chocolate brownie, which he consumed in about three bites, hardly tasting it. I had to get up and walk away. I *really* wanted just a bite and I'd have let it roll around in my mouth just to enjoy the flavour. At the moment it seemed to me he was doing it on purpose just to make me suffer. I know that's not true. If he knew how it made me feel he'd never do it again. The next time he eats a brownie, I won't even notice he's eating it.'

Even those who remember that you have diabetes often don't understand the realities of the disease. Well-meaning friends or relatives may suggest that if you'd just take the right vitamins or supplements, 'your little sugar problem' would go away. Or they'll say, 'I saw on the news last night that eating fibre prevents diabetes,' not realizing that what might statistically reduce the chances of getting diabetes is not going to cure it once most of your pancreas has been destroyed.

Others won't understand the reality of being on a restrictive diet for the rest of your life. 'I did Weight Watchers for six months, and it wasn't so bad,' someone might say when you are feeling down about having to yet again miss out on an exotic Asian rice dish at a dinner party. Of course diets are never fun, but most people dieting for weight loss expect to see light at the end of the tunnel. Your diet will never end.

Sometimes it all seems overwhelming

Sometimes all these little things seem to happen all at once, and suddenly the depression that you overcame after the diagnosis returns. It all just seems overwhelming. You want the diabetes to go away.

Again, the solution is time, getting in touch with people who understand, and venting your frustrations. I tend to be like Mary Mary, Quite Contrary. If someone tries to tell me diabetes is no big deal, it's better than having brain cancer, I'll feel they don't understand, get grumpy and go home and whine a lot. But if they do something thoughtful, like making sure there's something I can eat at their party, then I'm so touched by their caring that I realize diabetes really isn't that much of an extra burden and many of my friends *are* dealing with things that *are* much worse. Then I can get on with my life.

As with so many other aspects of life, you want to be understood. If your friends and relatives take the time to listen and understand, you may be able to minimize the number of times you are blue. If they won't, try to find people who *do* understand, and share with them. 'Maybe I just need to whine and let off steam now and then, then turn around and just get on with it, eh?' Betty G. concluded after letting off steam on an e-mail list.

Set an example

If things suddenly seem like too much and you can't get motivated to keep good control even though you know it will make you feel better, think of the others in your life. Taking care of your diabetes will set a good example in case they ever develop the disease. We all know someone who had a diabetic Uncle Denial who refused to change his diet or drinking habits and lost both his legs and went blind and sat in a wheelchair listening to the radio until kidney failure did him in. The fear that you'll end up like Uncle Den may be one reason for denying your diagnosis at first or feeling it's not worth the effort to control your diabetes because his fate is inevitable.

Now you have a chance to change that image for your children and your grandchildren and all your friends as well. Imagine that one of your nephews is diagnosed with diabetes in 20 years. Maybe instead of feeling that things are hopeless, he'll think of Uncle Moderation, who took good care of his diabetes and had no side effects and kept active and healthy for a long time – and still is. Instead of denying his disease, he might come to you for advice, ask how it is that you are managing to control so well and to lead such a normal, active life.

Others often aren't interested

When you find out what a bother it is to have diabetes, you most likely want to do what you can to prevent the disease in other people, especially close friends and relatives. You may often think, 'If only I'd known then what I know now about the dangers of "slightly elevated" BG levels and diets high in processed carbohydrate and fat, I could have done something to prevent this thing from ever progressing so far.' You'd like to educate others, to warn them.

Unfortunately, in most cases, you'll find they're not interested. In teenagers, this is no surprise. Teenagers almost always think they're immortal, that nothing bad will ever happen to them. But you'll probably find pretty much the same reaction in others you try to warn. Diabetes is your problem. It won't happen to them. If you keep preaching and talking about it, they'll get bored with the topic and tell you to get a life.

Whatever you do, don't nag. If you tell young people that if they eat too many sweets they'll get fat and get diabetes when they're older, then if they *do* get diabetes when they're older, they'll always feel guilty about it. They'll feel that it's all their fault, even though they know it's partly genetic and eating sugar doesn't cause the disease.

That happened to Natalie S. 'I was raised with the admonishment (from ALL of the older generations) "Don't eat that, you'll get fat and you'll get diabetes!" I remember thinking, as a teenager and young adult, "The hell you say!!" And when I was indeed diagnosed with diabetes, I could hear all those voices saying, "I told you so!!!!!" I spent my whole first visit with a diabetologist and dietitian crying my eyes out. The ironic thing is that, in my family, diabetes is NOT associated with obesity. But the voices had done their dirty work, and I still struggle with feelings of guilt and self-blame. The media certainly tries to reinforce the guilt trip too, implying that by keeping your weight down, or losing weight, you can prevent diabetes.'

The only thing you can really do to help is to be there if they do ask, and to stick to your diet and your exercise plans even when you're feeling blue. Who knows. Maybe if they notice that you're losing weight and feeling more energetic when you eat more vegetables and less pizza, they'll be tempted to try it themselves.

Don't stop testing

Another form of burnout is simply getting tired of pricking your fingers all the time. If you've done a lot of testing and you have a good idea of which foods keep your BG levels at near-normal levels and which kinds of exercise help you the most, and if your BG tests are usually where you'd expect them to be, you may decide it's not worth the trouble to test.

Then there's the trick of having something you know isn't good for you and 'forgetting' to test afterwards because you really don't want to know how much it made your BG level go up. This is human nature. Everyone does it. 'I had a piece of chocolate and as far as I know, my blood sugar didn't go up at all – of course that could be because I didn't test.'

As long as you do occasional spot checks at different times of the day, not testing as often after you've learned how different foods affect your control is usually OK. It's avoiding the spot checks too that can be dangerous.

Sometimes, without realizing it, you'll start eating just a little more of 'problem foods' and then a little more, and a little more, until you've returned to your former eating patterns.

'I've gone through a couple of periods of no testing,' said Alex E. 'I thought I might save some money by not testing every day. I was doing okay, so I skipped a day here, a day there. Then a few days at a time, and then all of a sudden, I'd gone three months without testing. And sure enough, my BGs had drifted back up. Once wasn't enough. I had to go through that twice.'

Just be alert for this and try to do spot checks now and then. It's always easier to get back on the wagon when it isn't moving too fast.

Don't despair

Diabetes burnout and having the blues is, unfortunately, probably going to be an occasional companion as you learn to deal with this new way of life. Just understand that some initial mourning is normal, and burnout may crop up occasionally in the future. Don't despair. This is also normal. Take time out. Reevaluate. Spoil yourself. Connect with fellow travellers. This mood should pass, and you should soon be back in the saddle of diabetes control. Once you get control, it's really not as bad as it seemed at first. Life goes on. Enjoy it.

IN A SENTENCE:

> *You may occasionally have to deal with 'diabetes burnout',*
> *but don't despair, the mood should pass.*

Diet Wars: Finding What Works for You

IN THE last Learning section I discussed how you can learn to get beyond the hype in the diet books. Now you need to learn how you can evaluate any particular diet's effect on your diabetes and weight loss.

Evaluate both short-term and long-term hunger

The high-carbohydrate diet supporters say that carbohydrate will fill you up sooner, and indeed, studies have shown that a boiled potato makes you feel full sooner than an equivalent number of calories eaten as fat. Some people have even worked out a *satiety index* that classifies foods according to how fast they fill you up, and carbohydrate foods lead the list. *Low-glycaemic index* carbohydrates tend to fill you up even more than other carbohydrates because they have more bulk and take longer to digest.

When you're taking hunger into consideration in choosing a diet, remember to consider how long that feeling of fullness will last. Some people find that high-carbohydrate diets (especially high-glycaemic index *processed carbohydrates*) make them feel stuffed for an hour or so, but then they get ravenously hungry. This may be especially true of people who have fluctuating blood glucose (BG) levels, that is, people with diabetes. Rapidly rising and falling levels of glucose or insulin or both may trigger hunger pangs as well as surges of *adrenaline*, which also stimulates hunger.

In Jennifer L.'s experience: 'I could eat half a kilogram of pasta (with the "regulation" fat-free sauce) and an hour later be standing in the kitchen in front of the fridge, starving. Needing to eat something, anything. Unable to stop thinking about food. Feeling very very very hungry, even though my stomach was full.'

Protein and fat leave the stomach more slowly and may keep the hunger pangs away for a longer period of time than carbohydrate, even if they don't fill you up quite so quickly. The same is true of low-glycaemic index carbohydrates such as lentils, high-fibre vegetables and some beans. They are digested slowly and may keep your BG levels on an even keel.

'I chose to follow a lower-carb plan to control my BG,' said Jennifer. 'It worked. But more amazing to me was that those almost daily crave attacks disappeared completely. Entirely. At least for the last year and a half. I have had NONE. It is the first time in my 40 years that I have not had these cravings. And for a person that had them daily, it's amazing.'

Also try to figure out if your main problem is starting to eat (eating more often than usual because you're hungry all the time) or stopping eating (eating only at the normal times but eating a lot because you don't feel full). A diet that fixed one of these problems might not be as good for the other.

Pay attention to other short-term versus long-term effects

Sometimes when you try a new type of diet, you'll find that your

BG or lipid levels change. If so, don't make any decisions right away. Sometimes it can take days, weeks or even months for your body to adapt to a new way of eating.

For instance, some people find that when they start on a low-carbohydrate diet, their lipid levels go down at first. But after six months they may go back up again. Others may find the exact opposite. Still others find their lipid levels go in one direction and stay there.

Some people report extreme fatigue when they suddenly switch from one type of diet to another. One reason for this is that the body is a very adaptable, efficient machine and doesn't waste energy producing enzymes it doesn't need. So if you've been living on a low-fat, high-carbohydrate diet for a long time, your body has been producing the enzymes it needs to process carbohydrates, but not many of the enzymes that are needed to process fat. If you switch suddenly, it doesn't have the 'machinery' it needs to get energy from fat and ketones, and you may feel tired for a while until the body has time to 'manufacture' enough of the enzymes needed to process the new type of diet.

The same is true if you go the other way. If you've been living on a low-carbohydrate, high-fat diet, your body hasn't been producing many of the enzymes it needs to process carbohydrate. If you suddenly eat a lot of carbohydrate, your BG levels will go very high. In fact, people who have been on low-carbohydrate diets or who have been starving (the ultimate low-carbohydrate diet) will test diabetic even when they're not. This is called *starvation diabetes*, and it's the reason you're usually asked to eat 150 to 300 grams of carbohydrate a day for several days before taking a glucose tolerance test.

These enzymes that are only produced in the presence of the substances that they process are called *inducible enzymes*.

This means that you should never make any decisions on a new way of eating after just a day or so. Try it for at least a week. In terms of lipid levels, a few months is better. Then keep testing every six months or every year to make sure.

Low-carbohydrate diets make you more sensitive to carbohydrate

When you go on a low-carbohydrate diet, you may find that as long as you avoid carbohydrates, your BG levels will stay fairly low. But if you give in to temptation and eat more carbohydrate, your BG levels will go higher than they used to.

This is because, as explained in the previous section, your body stopped producing a lot of the inducible enzymes that process carbohydrate. What this means is that if you don't think you'll be able to stick to a low-carbohydrate diet most of the time, you might be better off with one of the other diet approaches. An occasional spike when temptation is overwhelming probably won't hurt you, but high BG levels on a regular basis could.

Let's look at how some of these diet changes might work. Assume you're starting from a standard Western diet with plenty of calories, fat and carbohydrate. Just reducing calories, as on an *exchange diet*, usually brings your BG levels down. You're eating less food, so even when BG levels rise after eating, they don't rise as far.

Now let's say you decide to try the high-fibre, high-carbohydrate, low-fat diet instead. Let's say on the exchange diet, after eating 57 grams of carbohydrate (two starch exchanges, one fruit exchange and one milk exchange), your BG level went up to 11 mmol/L. On a high-fibre, low-fat diet, you might be eating even more carbohydrate than that, say 70 grams per meal. When you began such a diet your BG level might go even higher than 11 mmol/L, maybe to 13.9 mmol/L.

But after a few days, your body would adapt, and you might find that even when eating 70 grams of high-fibre carbohydrate, your BG level wouldn't go over 10 mmol/L. Your glucose tolerance would have improved, because both the machinery needed to process carbohydrates was stimulated and your insulin resistance (IR) was reduced.

Now let's see what would happen on a low-carbohydrate diet. In this case you'd be eating only about 6 to 20 grams of carbohydrate per meal, preferably 'slow' low-glycaemic index carbohydrates, along with more protein and fat. In this case, your BG level might not go above 6.7 mmol/L because you simply weren't eating a lot of carbohydrates and the increased fat meant that your stomach emptied more slowly. As long as you stuck to this diet, your BG levels would remain low.

The trade-off would be that if one day you gave in to temptation and ate the same 57 grams of carbohydrate that sent you up to 11 mmol/L on the exchange diet, you might go even higher, maybe 16.7 mmol/L now, because your body would no longer be accustomed to processing carbohydrates and your IR might have increased if you were eating a lot of saturated fat.

So again, consider which diet you think you could maintain in the long haul, and wait a few weeks before evaluating its effects.

The effects of different diets on your postprandial lipid levels are not so easy for you to see as the effects on postprandial BG levels, because cholesterol levels don't change as quickly as BG levels and home meters that measure lipid levels are just beginning to become available in the United States. So in the near future, you'll need to rely on fasting lipid panels to see how these various diets affect your lipids.

What does it all mean?

All this means that when you're trying to decide which diet will be best for your diabetes, you shouldn't just read one popular diet book and think that it's the only possible way. No one diet is best for every person with diabetes. Try to understand the science behind the diets and figure out which one would work best for your own particular type of diabetes, lifestyle and reasons for eating. Then try it, test your BG levels, your lipid levels and your weight before you decide which one is for you.

Ask yourself a lot of questions:

     ○ Does this diet keep my BG levels close to normal?
     ○ What is the effect of this diet on my lipid levels?
     ○ Does this diet provide me with enough energy to do the activities I like to do?

- O Am I losing weight on this diet?
- O Does this diet include the kinds of foods I like best? Does this diet control my hunger? Could I stick with this diet for the rest of my life?
- O Am I an active person who needs a lot of carbohydrate to burn for energy when I run or ski? A low-fat diet might work best if you could control your BG and triglyceride levels.
- O Am I a pretty sedentary person who nibbles a lot when I'm hungry? A hunger-controlling low-carbohydrate diet might be better for you.
- O Can I face not eating a particular kind of food for the rest of my life? If not, a calorie-restricted diet that lets you eat a variety of foods might be best.
- O Is IR my main problem? Some people with a lot of IR find that saturated fat (see Month 6) increases their BG levels. In that case, a low-fat diet might work for keeping your BG levels down. However, be aware that some people feel that *very low fat diets* increase cardio-vascular risks in people with a lot of IR and recommend substituting monounsaturated fat for saturated fat instead.
- O Do I think I don't have much IR but I just don't produce enough insulin? In that case, a low-carbohydrate diet might match your needs.

If you decide to try a low-fat diet, which means eating the bulk of your calories as carbohydrate, make sure to measure your BG levels one or two hours after meals. Physicians used to think that postprandial BG levels didn't make any difference as long as they came back to normal before the next meal, but more recent evidence has shown that postprandial BG levels are an important factor in predicting your A1c levels and risks of complications. Also keep track of your triglyceride levels, as high-carbohydrate diets sometimes make triglyceride levels go up.

If you decide to try a low-carbohydrate diet, which usually means more saturated fat, make sure to keep track of your lipid levels. Most people on such diets see their lipids improve, even when they're eating a lot of saturated fat, but some find their cholesterol levels get worse. If you're in the latter group, substitute lean for fatty meats and monounsaturated fats such as olive oil, avocado and nuts for saturated fats like butter and cheese.

If you decide a more varied diet like one of the exchange diets is what you need, you should also measure postprandial BG levels and keep track of your lipids as well. Keeping records on each diet you try lets you decide if another one is working better or worse.

A good dietician will work with you to answer these questions and come up with a diet that satisfies your own particular needs. If the dietician simply hands you a prepared 'diabetic diet' sheet or says only one kind of diet works for people with diabetes, say good-bye and try to find one who will treat you as the individual you are.

Understanding the effects of different diets on diabetes control is difficult. As Edd A. said, 'So which road do we take? None of them seem safe. Unfortunately, we each have to choose a path even if none of them are adequately illuminated.' Sometimes a dietary theory sounds great but it doesn't work for you. The important thing is not to get caught up in the diet wars, to look beyond the diet rhetoric and try to find the truth behind all the hype.

Sometimes the simplest theory of all may be just what you need. Linda C.'s mantra is to simply 'eat less and move more'. In a more poetic mood she added, 'As my Irish grandmother would say, "If you dance with the devil then you have to pay the piper." So I stopped dancing with French fries and chocolate bars, and now I just dance alone for movement.'

IN A SENTENCE:

> *You may have to do some experimenting to find out which diet works best for you, but you should believe your own results more than what anyone else tells you.*

living

Finding
More Resources

YOU'VE COME through almost a year with this blinking disease, and I hope you've learned enough that you're starting to feel comfortable taking charge of your diet, your exercise and anything else you need to stay in control.

Regardless of the type of diabetes care you're getting and no matter how much you've learned already, continuing to learn should be a part of your diabetes care for a long time to come. Type 2 diabetes is an incredibly complex disease, and research into its causes and treatment is going on at a furious pace. New drugs and new theories are announced almost every week, it seems. Only a decade or so ago, doctors treating patients with type 2 diabetes had a choice of only insulin or first-generation sulphonylurea drugs, in addition to diet or exercise. Today there is a plethora of drugs, working in many different ways. Many more are working their way through the long process of testing by the pharmaceutical companies in an effort to receive approval by the authorities.

You'll probably want to keep up with these advances as they occur. And you may want to delve deeper into the science behind the disease and its treatment, subjects I could only summarize briefly in this book. Where should you go to look?

Magazines are useful

Newspapers and TV and radio news programmes usually announce major advances in diabetes research as they occur, but news stories are necessarily brief. Furthermore, the job of the news media is to present an interesting story, so they tend to overplay the importance of each tiny step that is made in solving the diabetes puzzle. They'll tell you that a new drug or a new way of administering insulin has been found and then rehash a description of what diabetes is and the difference between types 1 and 2, with a few statistics thrown in to fill the space. The headline often implies that the problem of diabetes has been solved.

To get more information than this, you might want to start with *Balance*, the bi-monthly journal of Diabetes UK, which is free to members but can also be ordered from newsagents. Diabetes UK tries to have an upbeat tone and provide basic diabetes education at a simple reading level. They produce many free pamphlets as well as *Balance for Beginners* (type 2), which is straightforward and cheap.

Balance, like its American equivalent *Diabetes Forecast,* tries to have something for everyone. So you'll usually find inspirational stories of people who have triumphed over their diabetes, games for children, recipes, a feature article on some aspect of diabetes care such as the feet or insulin pumps and an article on some aspect of current research. *Balance* also produces guides to what diabetic products are available. The problem with *Balance* is that by trying to have something for everyone, they can't have a lot for any specific interest group.

Make use of libraries and bookshops

If you don't want to subscribe to a diabetes magazines, check with your local library for availability.

If you want to go to the next level and take a look at some of the professional diabetes magazines, ask if your local hospital has a medical library. If they do, you may be able to use it if you talk to the librarian and explain why you need to do so, although you might not be able to check out books unless you're a member of the staff.

The local hospital library probably carries major journals such as the *New England Journal of Medicine*, and diabetes journals like *Diabetes Care, Diabetes, Diabetologia* and *Diabetic Medicine*.

If you live in a city with a medical school, check with the school to see if they have a library that is open to the public. If they say you have to be on staff, explain your need to get information and see if you can get special permission at least to read books and journals in the library.

If you can't find a specialized medical library near you but you're close to a college or university, see if you can use the libraries there. They may not have as many specialized medical journals, but they may actually have more journals of basic science such as *Nature* and *Science*.

If you want more general information on a specific aspect of diabetes care, there are popular diabetes books that focus on particular areas, for example books for diabetic men, diabetic women and diabetic children, books focusing on sports, complications, diabetic burnout and different types of diabetic diets.

When you're ready to start delving into textbooks, you might want to start with a medical physiology text. They usually have a chapter or two on the control of carbohydrate metabolism in nondiabetic people as well as a discussion of diabetes. Another good source is endocrinology textbooks. They usually go into a little more detail. Even if it's more than you want to know at the time, there are often useful figures and tables. You can always go back to them later.

If you don't want to read that much background science, look for textbooks on diabetes and thumb through them until you come on a topic that interests you. Sometimes just seeing colour illustrations of what can happen to your feet if you ignore your control is enough to inspire you to stick with your diet for another month.

Other things you might want to check out would include books on nutrition, books on exercise physiology or, if you're really dedicated, biochemistry books. Books written for nursing students are usually a little easier going than more comprehensive texts.

If you just won the lottery, you might want to buy some of these books yourself, but be warned, they *are* expensive. Some of the major tomes on diabetes cost hundreds of pounds. If you live near a medical school, there's undoubtedly a medical bookshop somewhere on the campus or nearby, and the shops should be open to the public. That lets you at least scan any books before you decide to buy.

You can often get good discounts on the previous edition of a science textbook when the new edition comes out, for example, £10 for a textbook that costs £100 in the latest edition. Some aspects of science change quickly, but others don't, and some chapters don't change much from edition to edition, so you can learn a lot from the older books. In fact, most science textbooks were written at least a year before their publication date, sometimes more, and stay in print for several years after that. So by the time you buy even the current edition of a professional book, some of the information may be out of date.

If you have access to a computer (and if you don't have one at home, you can usually find one at your local library), you can easily see what's available at online bookstores. Amazon.co.uk often has reviews by both professional reviewers and customers who bought the books.

The Internet offers breaking news

I find books and magazines much more efficient than computers for getting background information about the science of diabetes. I prefer reading curled up in a comfortable chair to staring at a screen, and I can read a page in a book faster than scrolling down a screen, especially when the web page has a poorly chosen typeface or a background pattern that obscures the print. But if you have a computer and online access, the Internet is a good way to keep up to date with breaking news in the diabetes field. In the Learning section, Internet expert Rick Mendosa will guide you through 'surfing' the Internet for diabetes information.

Finding the truth takes work

When a book or journal cites another article to support a statement, you can usually assume the author has summarized the results of that article correctly. But if it's a crucial topic and you're especially interested in it, you're better off locating and reading the cited article yourself. When you do, there are a few things you should look for:

- ○ What group was studied? Many papers refer simply to 'diabetics'. You know by now that this is a vague term that could mean different types of diabetes, different degrees of control and different age groups. Sedentary middle-aged type 2 subjects with A1cs of 10 might react differently from athletic type 1 university students with A1cs of 7.
- ○ Improved (worsened) control means improved compared with what? The titles of many papers say that some treatment or other 'improved control' without saying what they're comparing the treatment with. This is especially important in papers concerning diets.
- ○ Is there interesting information here not mentioned in the title? Often a paper contains fascinating information that is not the central finding of the paper and hence is not mentioned in either the title or the abstract. For example, some of the studies done on alpha-lipoic acid were done with intravenous infusions, not oral pills, but this isn't mentioned in the title.

Sometimes it takes a long time to locate a paper, and when you find it, you discover it doesn't say very much. But sometimes it tells you just what you were looking for. It doesn't take a PhD to be able to get something out of most published papers. With a little work, you can learn a lot.

Keep learning

Today, opinions about the best way to treat type 2 diabetes can be very different. In the coming years, research into the causes and treatment of type 2 diabetes will continue to be intense. For this reason, instead of just giving you 'the answers', which of course would be *my answers*, I've tried to give you enough background information about the science of diabetes that you can make your own decisions about which treatments will be best *for you* and so you will also be able to understand the new developments as they occur.

Type 2 diabetes is a very complicated disease that can be very frustrating to understand. Sometimes you do exactly what you did yesterday, eat exactly the same foods, think you've had almost exactly the same emotions and still your BG levels after a meal are different. Don't despair. This is normal. But the more you understand about this disease, the more you will gradually learn to identify stresses, foods or exercise patterns that affect you in a particular way. The best way to understand your diabetes is to keep on learning.

I've emphasized in this book that diabetes is not your fault. But taking control of your diabetes *is* your responsibility. Part of taking control means continuing to educate yourself.

After only a year with diabetes, no one expects you to know everything there is to know about this disease. But I hope you're well on your way to understanding what normal reactions to foods and physical and emotional stresses are, how to learn, where to get more information, when to seek help from professionals and when to look for fellow patients with whom you can discuss your experiences.

In type 2 diabetes care, knowledge is power. Seek it and use it. Then share it with others. Never stop seeking. Knowledge is the key to control.

IN A SENTENCE:

There are many resources for learning more about diabetes, and you should learn to use them.

learning

Searching the Internet

by Rick Mendosa

IMAGINE THAT they built a huge library containing billions of documents. You walk up the steps, open the door and look around for the card catalogue.

You can't find it. You can't even find the steps, the door or a librarian. There aren't any.

That library actually exists, but what it lacks is not a problem. It happens to be the world's largest and has something even better than a card catalogue. This library is called the World Wide Web,

After earning a BA with honours from the University of California, Riverside, and an MA from Claremont Graduate University in government, Rick Mendosa went to work for the US government. During a 15-year career as a Foreign Service officer with the US foreign aid programme, he served 11 years in Washington and 4 years in Africa. Subsequently he became a journalist, initially specializing in writing about small business.

After he was diagnosed with type 2 diabetes in February 1994, he segued into writing about that condition. He started his 'Online Diabetes Resource' website in February 1995 when there were only two other websites dealing with diabetes. It now lists and links more than 800 sites with substantive information about diabetes.

or just the web when we get to know it better. It's the Internet's electronic document depository.

Instead of a card catalogue, the web has search engines, directories and hyperlinks to help you find your way around its vast resources. While card catalogues index their library's holdings by author, title and one or two subjects, these web tools take cross-referencing to a higher dimension.

Search engines let you do keyword searches for information

Wouldn't it be great to have a huge index of essentially every significant word in every document? We don't have that yet, and because the Web is growing so fast, perhaps never will. But what we do have isn't that far removed – search engines of almost unimaginable breadth, speed and precision.

The search engines are so important to the web that it's hard to imagine life in the 21st century without them. Experts estimate that we use a search engine about 85 per cent of the time we go looking for information on a website we haven't previously visited.

Search engines are themselves websites. So before you can even start searching the web, you need to know the Internet address – the Uniform Resource Locator (*URL*) – of at least one search engine.

That's why the next few words are the most important part of this chapter: *http://www.google.com.*

That is the URL for Google, which is the best search engine invented, at least so far. Before Google exploded onto the Internet in the late 1990s, there was a whole line of good search engines with names like Lycos, Excite, AltaVista, Inktomi, AllTheWeb and NorthernLight. You can still use them and dozens of others. There are even services like Dogpile that will let you use several search engines at the same time. But for almost all searches Google is best.

A couple of tips about web addresses: With most browsers you can omit the 'http://' and the beginning of the address and the '/' at the end. So Google comes up whether you type *http://www. google.com/* or *www.google.com*.

That's optional. But what is mandatory when you find a web address in print like this is to be sure not to include the punctuation that's there just because it's in a sentence. For example, http://www.google.com/. doesn't work.

Google indexes far more web pages than any other search engine. In 2001, Google says that it indexed more than 1.3 billion web pages. That's most of what is known as the *visible web*. A year earlier the most recent NEC Research survey said that the number of visible web pages had reached 1 billion. A recent study says that the web is growing at the rate of 1.5 million documents per day. Google is also fast. When, for example, I searched for *diabetes*, it reported in 0.10 seconds that there were about 5.2 million pages that mentioned that term. And it is intelligent. What sets Google apart the most from other search engines is its PageRank software, which uses the web's link structure as an indicator of an individual page's value. In essence, Google interprets a link from page A to page B as a vote by page A for page B. But Google also analyzes the page that casts the vote. Votes cast by pages that themselves get a lot of votes help the pages they are linked to get more votes.

Then Google combines PageRank with sophisticated text-matching techniques to find pages that are both important and relevant to your search. This means that the first pages that Google returns are usually the best ones on that subject.

Google has many special features. It groups different pages at the same site together. One that I use all the time are *cached* links, which is what the page looked like when Google found it by crawling the web. If the page is unavailable when I find it through a Google search, I click on *cache* to see the page as it looked when Google found it. Another is that it is also the first search engine to index Adobe Portable Document Format (PDF) files.

It doesn't matter how you capitalize your search terms. But it often helps focus in on just what you want when you use quotation marks ('like this') in a search for a phrase or a person's name.

It may sound like I own stock in Google, but I am sorry to say that I don't. It is privately held, and I'm not a holder.

The invisible web includes MEDLINE

While Google is clearly the best tool to search the visible web – at least until something better gets built – what about the so-called *invisible web*?

The invisible web consists of information stored in databases. Unlike pages on the visible web, the software *spiders* and *crawlers* that automatically retrieve documents from the web can't get at the information stored here.

The most important part of the invisible web for health care professionals and people with diabetes is probably MEDLINE. It contains more than 12 million bibliographic citations and abstracts from more than 4500 biomedical journals. MEDLINE is a service of the US government's National Library of Medicine (NLM) in Bethesda, Maryland. In the early 1960s it established the Medical Literature Analysis and Retrieval System (MEDLARS) for health professionals to search the literature. MEDLINE is the on-line version of MEDLARS (MEDlars onLINE).

Several web sites offer free access to MEDLINE. The easiest to use is the Medscape Medline Search at *http://www.medscape. com/server-java/MedlineSearchForm*.

Directory searches use human intelligence

Lots of people think of Yahoo, *http://www.yahoo.com*, when the subject of search engines comes up. But until 2002 it was a place where human editors organize websites into categories. Since then it has been using Google to provide its main results. You can still use its directory – a list of relevant web pages compiled by humans. To do that, search from the *http://dir.yahoo.com* page rather than the regular *yahoo.com* page. Yahoo is the largest human-compiled guide to the web, employing about 150 editors.

Perhaps a disadvantage, perhaps not, is Yahoo's relatively small size. While it lists well over 1 million sites, that's a small percentage of the available web pages. But by focusing on the best sites, a Yahoo directory search should be able to save you time.

Yet it doesn't always work that way. If, for example, you drill down from *health* to *diseases and conditions* to *diabetes*, it will return the links for several hundred sites. Some of these are the best you will find anywhere, but in my judgment the first 50 or so listings that a regular Google search returns are generally higher-quality sites.

If Yahoo can't find it, it turns to Google. Google, however, doesn't return the favour. It has its own directory at *http:// directory.google.com*.

The web also has many specialized directories. In fact, I have one that lists, links and annotates what I think are the 800 or so websites with substantive information about diabetes. My Online Diabetes Resources consists of 15 web pages starting at *http://www.mendosa.com/faq.htm*.

Hyperlinks are the key to the Web

The key to the web is *hyperlinks*, or just *links* for short. The search engines use them to crawl around the web to find anything linked to the starting page. Likewise, the humans who develop directories follow the links the same way as investigators follow the money.

You could do worse than to start with the Diabetes UK website, the operating name of the British Diabetic Association. The URL is *http://www.diabetes.org.uk*. It links 50 or so of the best diabetes sites at *http://www.diabetes.org/internetresources.asp*.

Evaluating web sites requires judgement

Choosing reliable diabetes websites is a lot trickier than picking the right search engine or directory. Be especially careful of those sites that want to sell you something. These are the hundreds or thousands of sites offering cures in exchange for your money. Medical quacks have, of course, been buzzing around people with diseases even before the days of Hippocrates. The Internet simply makes their pitch easier. A famous *New Yorker* cartoon shows two dogs talking, as they do in cartoons. One dog sitting in front of the computer turns to the other and remarks, 'On the Internet, nobody knows you're a dog.'

That's all too true. A website costs very little and yet offers a forum for the most vicious animals to sell their wares. The real dogs of the Internet are the cyberquacks.

All of us have to understand the playing field and make our own evaluations. As in all research, the key is consistency. Is the information on the site internally consistent? Is it consistent with what you know of the world otherwise?

For example, you know that a site offering eternal life devices for £10 to £100 including shipping stretches credibility beyond reason. But even less outrageous claims should not pass your smell test. Does the author of the web page have some authority in the field? Here an endocrinologist can generally be trusted, but not necessarily an emergency room doctor, several of whom have sites. Can you communicate with the site? Does it provide a physical address as well as email? Is the information current? If there are a number of broken links or no news for several months, what does this say about the credibility of the information?

Remember as you read that if it sounds too good to be true, it probably is. If it claims to cure many diseases, it probably won't cure any. And if it claims to cure diabetes, it won't.

Keep up to date with diabetes news

If you remember, you can read the latest news about diabetes on-line on several websites every week or so. The American Diabetes Association shows some of the top news articles at *http://www.diabetes.org/News/default.asp.*

But once you sign up to get an e-mail newsletter sent to you, it will come automatically. Many people think this is an even better way to stay up to date on diabetes news. Four of the best diabetes e-mail newsletters are as follows:

Diabetes E-alert. Diabetes UK sends out regular email updates to keep you informed of the latest news and developments in diabetes and Diabetes UK. You can subscribe at *http://www.diabetes.org.uk/webreg.nsf/DHlegislation?openForm*.

Diabetes E-News Now. This is the electronic newsletter of the American Diabetes Association. The Consumer Edition is the one that most people will want to sign up for, but the organization also has an Advocacy E-News Newsletter and a Health Care Professional Edition. The URL is *http://www.diabetes.org/emaillist2.asp*.

Diabetes Newsletter. The Diabetes Newsletter from About Diabetes will go to your e-mail inbox each week after you subscribe. You can subscribe at *http://home.about.com/health/newsletters.htm?PM=59_208_T*.

Diabetes Update. My own newsletter is free and will go to your email inbox once a month after you subscribe. You can subscribe by sending an email message to me at mendosa@mendosa.com with the subject 'Subscribe Diabetes Update'.

These are the tools that you need to start exploring the wealth of information on the web. There's so much on the web to find out about diabetes and anything else that interests you that the only limits are your time and imagination. Go to it.

A1c: See **haemoglobin A1c**

ACE INHIBITOR: Angiotensin-converting **enzyme** inhibitor. The **hormone** *angiotensin* constricts blood vessels. By inhibiting the formation of angiotensin, ACE inhibitors reduce blood pressure. They also help prevent kidney complications, may improve insulin sensitivity and may even slow down the appearance of type 2 diabetes in prediabetic people.

ADA: American Diabetes Association. Diabetes UK is the British equivalent.

ADA DIET: An old term referring to a low-fat **exchange diet.** The ADA now says that no one diet is good for everyone with diabetes, so this term should be avoided.

ADRENALINE: A **counterregulatory hormone** that is secreted by the adrenal glands and raises **BG** levels by increasing **insulin resistance**. Adrenaline contributes to the '**fight-or-flight' response** in several ways and also helps prevent **hypoglycaemia**. It is also called *epinephrine*. One trade name is Adrenalin.

-AEMIA: A suffix meaning 'in the blood'. For example, *glycaemia* means 'glucose in the blood' .

AEROBIC EXERCISE: Exercise that requires oxygen and increases your heart rate, for example running more than a quick dash. Aerobic exercise is good for your **cardiovascular** health.

AGE: Advanced glycation end product. These are substances, usually proteins, that have been modified by the addition of **sugar** molecules, making them not work as well as they should. AGEs are thought to be one cause of aging.

ALBUMIN: The major protein in your blood. It is used to transport other molecules, for example **fatty acids**. The **fructosamine** test measures how much glucose is attached to albumin. When your kidneys are beginning to fail, they may allow albumin to leak into the urine.

ALCOHOL: Usually refers to *ethyl alcohol*, or what is sometimes called *booze*. May also refer to *isopropyl alcohol*, which is used as *rubbing alcohol*. It is also the name of a type of chemical with a hydroxyl group, as in **sugar alcohol**.

ALDOSE REDUCTASE: An **enzyme** that converts glucose to **sorbitol**. The *aldose reductase inhibitors* are a class of drugs that inhibit this enzyme and may prevent diabetic complications caused by sorbitol.

ALPHA CELLS: The cells in the **pancreas** that produce **glucagon**.

AMINO ACIDS: The building blocks for **protein**.

ANAEROBIC EXERCISE: Exercise that can be done in the absence of oxygen, for short periods of time. Examples are weight lifting and a 100-metre dash. Anaerobic exercise causes short-term increases in blood pressure and long-term increases in muscle strength.

ANTIBODY: A **protein** produced by the body's immune system to help get rid of infections or other substances it thinks don't belong there.

ANTICOAGULANT: A substance that keeps your blood from clotting, popularly called a *blood thinner*.

ANTIOXIDANT: A substance that neutralizes **free radicals**.

ARTERIES: The blood vessels that bring oxygenated blood from the heart out to the rest of the body.

ARTERIOSCLEROSIS: Thickening and stiffening of the walls of **arteries**, regardless of the cause. Popularly known as *hardening of the arteries*. See also **atherosclerosis**.

ATHEROSCLEROSIS: Thickening of the walls of **arteries** as a result of the formation of fatty **plaques**. See also **arteriosclerosis**.

ATP: Adenosine triphosphate. It is the 'energy currency' of cells.

AUTOANTIBODY: An **antibody** produced against your own tissues.

AUTOIMMUNE DISEASE: A disease in which your immune system mistakenly attacks your own tissues. Type 1 diabetes is thought to be an autoimmune disease. Rheumatoid arthritis is another.

AUTONOMIC NERVE: A nerve controlling an 'automatic' function you don't have to think about in order to perform, for example breathing or the beating of your heart.

AUTONOMIC NEUROPATHY: A form of **neuropathy** that affects your **autonomic nerves**.

BETA CELL: The cells in your **pancreas** that produce **insulin**.

BLOOD GLUCOSE (BG): Usually means the concentration of glucose in the blood in millimols per litre (mmol/L).

BLOOD THINNER: See **anticoagulant**.

BORDERLINE DIABETES: An old term referring to the early stages of diabetes. The term is misleading, can delay treatment and should not be used.

CAPILLARY: A tiny, thin-walled blood vessel that allows nutrients, waste products and gases to be exchanged with the surrounding tissue.

CARBOHYDRATE: A type of food consisting of **sugar** units, from one (**monosaccharide**) to many (**polysaccharide**). Carbohydrate has the greatest effect on your **BG** levels. It contains 4 calories per gram.

CARBOHYDRATE COUNTING: A dietary approach in which you calculate the amount of carbohydrate you eat at every meal and don't keep track of calories, protein or fat.

CARDIOVASCULAR: Referring to your heart or blood vessels. A *cardiovascular event* is an incident involving your heart or blood vessels, for example a heart attack or a stroke.

CHOLESTEROL: A **lipid** that is a building block for cell membranes and a precursor for certain hormones. Too much of certain types of cholesterol, for example, **LDL**, in the circulation can contribute to the formation of **plaques**.

CONTINUOUS MONITOR (METER): A monitoring device that measures your **BG** level every few minutes without requiring you to get a sample of blood. Some use implanted sensors and some measure **interstitial fluid**.

CONTROLLED TRIAL: A way of testing a new treatment by comparing one group of people who get the treatment with a matched group who do not.

CORTISOL: A **counterregulatory hormone** released from the adrenal glands when you are stressed. It can raise **BG** levels by increasing **insulin resistance**.

CORTISONE: A synthetic hormone used as an anti-inflammatory agent. The body converts it to **cortisol**.

COUNTERREGULATORY HORMONE: A hormone that opposes the action of **insulin**, causing **insulin resistance (IR)**.

C-PEPTIDE TEST: A test that measures the approximate amount of insulin that you are producing.

DAWN EFFECT or **PHENOMENON:** The normal rise in **BG** levels that occurs in the morning, often before rising.

DCCT: Diabetes Control and Complications Trial.

DEXTROSE: Another name for **glucose**, often used in food labels.

DIABETES UK: The British equivalent of the ADA.

DIABETES SPECIALIST NURSE (DSN): A nurse who specializes in the outpatient management of diabetes. Equivalent to the American Diabetes Educator.

DIABETIC KETOACIDOSIS (DKA): A serious short-term complication that occurs mostly in people with type 1 diabetes when their insulin levels get extremely low. See also **ketosis**.

DIABETOLOGIST: A doctor, usually an **endocrinologist**, who specializes in diabetes.

DIETICIAN: A person trained to devise nutritionally balanced meals. A *state registered dietician* is one who has a specified amount of training and has passed a special examination. See also **nutritionist**.

DIPSTICK: A chemically treated strip of material that changes colour when it is dipped into a solution containing a particular substance. Different dipsticks detect different substances, for example **glucose** or **ketones**.

DISACCHARIDE: A **carbohydrate** containing two sugar units.

DIURETIC: A drug that increases elimination of fluids from the body.

DOUBLE-BLIND: Referring to a study in which neither the patient nor the medical people involved with the study know which patients have received the study drug.

EFFECTIVE CARBOHYDRATE: The amount of **carbohydrate** that is digested and can raise your **BG** levels, that is, the total carbohydrate minus the indigestible **fibre**.

EFFECTIVE INSULIN: The amount of **insulin** that is actually active in your body, that is, the total amount of insulin you produce or inject minus the amount that is 'inactivated' by **insulin resistance**. This is a concept only, as one can't actually measure it.

ENDOCRINOLOGIST: A medical doctor specializing in disorders of endocrine (hormone-releasing) glands, including diabetes.

ENZYME: A protein that makes a chemical reaction go much faster. Many of the body's control systems involve increasing or decreasing the levels or activities of enzymes.

EXCHANGE DIET: A type of diet in which each food is assigned to a category, the amount of each food that represents one exchange is specified, and you are allowed a certain number of exchanges in each category. Within each category, you can choose between different foods, as they all have *approximately* the same amount of protein, fat and carbohydrate.

FASTING: Referring to a test done in the morning before eating any food. Sometimes defined as after eating no food for at least 6 to 14 hours.

FAT: A type of food consisting primarily of **triglycerides**. It contains 9 calories per gram. By itself, fat will not raise your **BG** levels, but it may cause **insulin resistance (IR)**. The body uses its own fat for long-term energy storage.

FATTY ACIDS: The building blocks of fats. Fatty acids are long, acidic molecules, mostly insoluble in water. Like **glucose**, they can be burned for energy.

FIBRE: A **carbohydrate** that is not broken down by human **enzymes**. Fibre is classified as both **soluble fibre** and **insoluble fibre**.

FIGHT-OR-FLIGHT RESPONSE: A complex response to stress that activates all the bodily systems that would help a person react in a stressful situation, for example releasing extra **glucose** into the blood for energy. It also suppresses systems that aren't needed, for example the digestion of food.

FOOD PYRAMID: A general guideline for eating developed by the US Department of Agriculture that puts **carbohydrate** foods at the base of a pyramid, **fats** and sweets at the top and other foods between. You're supposed to eat foods in amounts relative to their position in the pyramid, that is, lots of carbohydrate and relatively little fat and sweets.

FREE RADICAL: A chemical with an unpaired electron that is extremely reactive and can cause damage to cells. Free radicals can be neutralized by **antioxidants**, which are usually found in fruits and vegetables.

FRUCTOSAMINE: The name of a test that measures your average **BG** level for the past two weeks.

FRUCTOSE: A **monosaccharide** found especially in fruits that does not raise your **BG** level as fast as **glucose** does. However, it can be converted to glucose in the liver and contains the same number of calories.

GALACTOSE: A **monosaccharide** that is part of the milk sugar **lactose**. It can be converted to glucose in the liver and contains about the same number of calories.

GASTROPARESIS: A form of **autonomic neuropathy** that causes the stomach to empty slowly and sporadically, resulting in unpredictable **BG** levels and nausea or bloating.

GESTATIONAL DIABETES: A form of diabetes that can occur during pregnancy and usually goes away after the baby is born.

GLUCAGON: A hormone produced by the **alpha cells** in the pancreas that makes **BG** levels increase.

GLUCONEOGENESIS: The formation of **glucose** out of nonglucose substances, especially **protein**.

GLUCOSE: A **monosaccharide** that is the main source of energy for most cells. The **BG** levels are normally kept within a small range. When this control is lost, you have diabetes.

GLUCOSE TOLERANCE TEST (GTT): A test of your ability to keep **BG** levels in normal ranges after being given a large dose of **glucose** on an empty stomach.

GLUCOSE TRANSPORTER: An apparatus in the membrane of most cells that 'ferries' **glucose** into the cell. The number of glucose transporters in the membrane increases when insulin levels are high, or when you exercise.

GLUCOTOXICITY: A reduction in the production of **insulin** by the **beta cells** and an increase in **insulin resistance**, both caused by high **BG** levels.

GLYCAEMIC INDEX: A measure of how quickly a **carbohydrate**-containing substance will raise your **BG** level.

GLYCATED HAEMOGLOBIN: A form of **haemoglobin** in which a **sugar** molecule has become attached. This is the substance measured in the **haemoglobin A1c** test. Also called *glycohaemoglobin*. Sometimes the term *glycosylated haemoglobin* is used interchangeably with *glycated haemoglobin*, although some people define the terms slightly differently.

GLYCEROL: A small *E*-shaped **sugar alcohol** to which **fatty acids** can become attached, forming **fats**. Glycerol can be converted to **glucose** in the liver. Also called *glycerin*.

GLYCOGEN: Long chains of **glucose** that are used for medium-term storage of energy in liver and muscle.

GLYCOHAEMOGLOBIN: See **glycated haemoglobin**.

GLYCOGENOLYSIS: The breakdown of **glycogen** to form **glucose**.

GROWTH HORMONE: A **counterregulatory hormone**.

GTT: See **glucose tolerance test**.

HAEMOGLOBIN: The protein in **red blood cells** that transports oxygen from your lungs to your tissues.

HAEMOGLOBIN A1c: The fraction of haemoglobin that contains most of the **glucose** that has been attached to haemoglobin.

HDL: High-density lipoprotein. The 'good' cholesterol that takes extra cholesterol from the bloodstream and returns it to the liver.

HIGH-CARBOHYDRATE-AND-FIBRE DIET: A diet that emphasizes carbohydrate foods that are high in fibre and minimizes fats.

HIGH-CARBOHYDRATE DIET: A term often used for **low-fat diet**s. Depending on your caloric intake, a low-fat diet does not necessarily have a large *amount* of carbohydrate.

HIGH-PROTEIN DIET: A term often used for **low-carbohydrate** diets. Depending on your caloric intake and whether you replace carbohydrate with fat or protein, a low-carbohydrate diet does not necessarily have a large *amount* of protein.

HORMONE: A substance produced in one part of the body that can act in another. **Insulin** is a hormone produced in the **beta cells** of the **pancreas** that acts throughout the body.

HYPER-: A prefix meaning 'more than normal'.

HYPERGLYCAEMIA: A higher-than-normal amount of **glucose** in the blood.

HYPERINSULINAEMIA: A higher-than-normal amount of **insulin** in the blood.

HYPO-: A prefix meaning 'less than normal'.

HYPOGLYCAEMIA: Less than normal amounts of **glucose** in the blood, popularly called *low blood sugar.*

IDDM: Insulin-dependent diabetes mellitus. An older name for **type 1 diabetes**. A person with **type 2 diabetes** may become insulin dependent but will still not have type 1 diabetes, which is **autoimmune**.

IMPAIRED GLUCOSE TOLERANCE: An abnormal condition (but not diabetes) in which your **BG** levels are normal when fasting and are between 7.8 and 11.1 **mmol/L** at the two-hour point in a **glucose tolerance test**.

INSOLUBLE FIBRE: Fibre that is not soluble in water, for example cellulose. There is a lot of insoluble fibre in fruits, vegetables and whole grains, especially wheat bran, rice bran and corn bran.

INSULIN: A hormone produced by the **beta cells** of the **pancreas** that has many actions, including helping cells take up **glucose** and thus reducing **BG** levels.

INSULIN RECEPTOR: A structure in the membrane of cells that binds **insulin** and triggers a cascade of events leading to an increase in the number of **glucose transporters** in the membrane. The net result is that more glucose can get into the cell.

INSULIN RESISTANCE (IR): A condition in which, for a yet-unknown reason, insulin doesn't work properly.

INTERSTITIAL FLUID: The nonblood fluids that are between your cells.

ISLET CELLS: The cells in the **pancreas** that produce **insulin** (the **beta cells**) and **glucagon** (the **alpha cells**). The full name for the islet cells is the *islets of Langerhans.*

KETOACIDOSIS: See **diabetic ketoacidosis**.

KETONE: A breakdown product of fat that can be burned for energy by some types of cells.

KETOSIS: A condition in which the level of ketones in the blood is higher than normal. This can be the result of very low insulin levels or a very high fat intake.

LACTOSE: Milk sugar, consisting of **glucose** and **galactose**.

LANCET: The needle used to draw blood for home **BG** testing.

LDL: Low-density lipoprotein. The 'bad' cholesterol that can contribute to **plaques** in the walls of the arteries.

LIPID: A general term for fatty substances that are not soluble in water. It includes **triglycerides** and **cholesterol**.

LIPOTOXICITY: A reduction in the production of **insulin** by the **beta cells** and an increase in **insulin resistance (IR)**, both caused by high **lipid** levels.

LOW-CARBOHYDRATE DIET: A diet that limits the amount of **carbohydrate** you eat and allows increased levels of **fat** or **protein**, or both.

LOW-FAT DIET: A diet that limits the amount of **fat** and fatty meats and emphasizes **carbohydrates**. Such a diet may or may not emphasize the **glycaemic index**.

LOW-GLYCAEMIC INDEX DIET: A diet emphasizing carbohydrate foods that have **low-glycaemic index values**. It is similar to the **high-carbohydrate-and-fibre** diet, but some foods such as potatoes and beets that would be considered good choices on that diet have high-glycaemic index values and would be avoided on the low-glycaemic index diet.

MACROVASCULAR: Referring to the large blood vessels. *Macrovascular complications* are those resulting from damage to the arteries, for example heart attacks, strokes and peripheral vascular disease.

METABOLIZE: Convert into something else. *Catabolism* means breaking something down into smaller parts and *anabolism* means building something up, as with *anabolic steroids*. *Metabolism* is the sum of the anabolic and catabolic processes in your body.

MG/DL: Milligrams per deciliter, the units usually used in America when measuring **BG** and lipid levels. European countries use **SI** units (**mmol/L**).

MICROVASCULAR: Referring to the small blood vessels. *Microvascular complications* are complications result from damage to the capillaries, for example, **retinopathy**, **nephropathy**, and **neuropathy**.

MODY: Maturity-onset diabetes of the young.

MONOSACCHARIDE: A **carbohydrate** containing one **sugar** unit.

MONOUNSATURATED FAT: Fat containing one double bond. Monounsaturated fat is considered a 'good fat' that does not increase **cholesterol** levels.

NEPHROPATHY: Damage to the kidneys.

NEUROPATHY: Damage to nerves.

NIDDM: Non-insulin-dependent diabetes mellitus. An old term for **type 2 diabetes**. Some forms of diabetes, for example, gestational diabetes, may not require you to use insulin, but they are no longer classified as type 2 diabetes.

NUTRITIONIST: A general term for someone specializing in nutrition. A nutritionist can be a registered **dietician** or a self-educated person.

OPHTHALMOLOGIST: A medical doctor who specializes in eye diseases rather than in prescribing lenses.

PANCREAS: An organ behind the stomach that contains the **beta cells** that produce **insulin**. It also contains **alpha cells** that produce **glucagon** and several other types of cells that produce other hormones. The pancreas also produces digestive enzymes.

PERIPHERAL NEUROPATHY: The **neuropathy** that occurs in your hands and legs.

PERIPHERAL VASCULAR DISEASE: Clogging of the arteries in your hands and legs.

PHYSIOTHERAPIST: A person who has a degree in physiotherapy.

PLAQUE: A deposit of fatty substances including cholesterol in the wall of an artery, resulting in narrowing of the arterial cavity.

PLASMA: The part of blood that remains after you've removed all the blood cells and **platelets**.

PLATELET: Small disk-shaped structures in the blood that are required for clotting.

POLYSACCHARIDE: A **carbohydrate** containing many **sugar** units.

POLYUNSATURATED FAT: A type of fat containing more than one double bond. Polyunsaturated fats are found in vegetable oils and tend to lower the 'bad' **LDL** levels but may lower beneficial **HDL** levels as well.

POSTPRANDIAL: After a meal.

PREPRANDIAL: Before a meal.

PROCESSED CARBOHYDRATE: A **carbohydrate** that has been finely milled or otherwise separated from its natural fibre, resulting in faster digestion and a higher **glycaemic index**.

PROTEIN: A type of food made of **amino acid** building blocks. By itself, protein contains 4 calories per gram, but most protein foods such as meat also contain fat. Protein may or may not raise your **BG** levels.

RED BLOOD CELL: A type of cell in the blood that contains **haemo-globin**, the compound that transports oxygen.

RETINOPATHY: Disease of the *retina*, the back part of the eye that senses light.

SATURATED FAT: Fat containing no double bonds, usually solid at room temperature. Saturated fat is thought to increase **cholesterol** levels and **insulin resistance (IR)**. Saturated fats are found in animal products and tropical oils.

SI (SYSTEME INTERNATIONALE) UNITS: The unit of measurement for glucose, lipids and other blood constituents in Europe and Australasia. Blood glucose is expressed in **mmol/L**. To convert to mg/dL multiply by 18.

SMALL, DENSE LDL: A type of **LDL** that is supposed to be more apt to cause arterial **plaques**.

SOLUBLE FIBRE: The kind of fibre that forms a gummy solution in water. It can delay the emptying of the stomach and slow digestion, resulting in smaller increases in **BG** levels after a meal. It is also thought to lower **lipid** levels. Soluble fibre occurs in fruits, beans and oat bran.

SORBITOL: A **sugar alcohol** often used to replace table sugar in diet desserts. When glucose is converted to sorbitol within cells, this may contribute to complications.

STARCH: A **carbohydrate** food consisting of long chains of **glucose**. There are different types of starches, and some have higher **glycaemic index values** than others.

STATE REGISTERED DIETICIAN: See **dietician**.

STEROID: A class of compounds derived from **cholesterol** and including the sex hormones *oestrogen* and *testosterone* as well as anti-inflammatory drugs such as **cortisone** and *prednisone*.

STRESS HORMONE: A hormone released when you're stressed, for example, **cortisol** and **adrenaline**.

SUCROSE: Table sugar, a **disaccharide** consisting of **glucose** and **fructose**.

SUGAR: Any of a **carbohydrate** class of sweet water-soluble compounds. The degree of sweetness depends on the particular sugar. The term is often used to mean **sucrose**. A 'simple sugar' is a **monosaccharide**, but the term is often loosely used.

SUGAR ALCOHOLS: Derivatives of sugars that don't raise **BG** levels as much but contain almost as many calories and can cause diarrhoea.

SULPHONYLUREAS: A class of compounds that reduces **BG** levels by increasing the output of **insulin** by the **beta cells.** They were the first tablets used to treat type 2 diabetes.

SYNDROME X: A syndrome of symptoms including high **insulin** levels, high blood pressure, high **triglyceride** levels, low **HDL** levels and **impaired glucose tolerance**.

THRIFTY GENES: Genes that make you tend to gain weight when food is plentiful.

TRANS FAT: A type of fat produced by the industrial treatment of oils to make them solid at room temperature. The trans fats are supposed to be more detrimental to health than **saturated fat**. They are found in biscuits, crackers, solid margarine and some salad dressings.

TRIGLYCERIDE: Fat. Triglycerides are composed of a molecule of the *E*-shaped **glycerol** plus three **fatty acids**.

TYPE 1 DIABETES: An autoimmune disease in which the body, for unknown reasons, destroys the **beta cells**, resulting in a total or almost-total lack of **insulin**.

TYPE 2 DIABETES: A disease caused primarily by **insulin resistance (IR)**, in which a person may actually produce more **insulin** than normal but it may not work very well.

UKPDS: UK Prospective Diabetes Study.

UNSATURATED FAT: Fat containing double bonds, usually liquid at room temperature. Unsaturated fats either lower **cholesterol** levels or have no effect. They are found in plant oils.

VEIN: The blood vessels that bring carbon dioxide from the tissues to the lungs, where it is exchanged for oxygen.

VITAMIN: A carbon-containing substance present in food, or manufactured in the body, that is required in small amounts for good health.

VLDL: Very low density lipoprotein. The form in which the body ships **triglycerides** from the liver to the tissues to be burned for energy or stored as fat. When the VLDL has dropped off its fat, it turns into **LDL**.

WHITE BLOOD CELLS: Cells in the blood that fight infection and perform other useful chores.

YMMV: Your Mileage May Vary, meaning that what works for me might not work for you, and vice versa.

For Further Reading

Basic diabetes care

Diabetes for Beginners (Type 2). (An inexpensive 94-page pamphlet published by Diabetes UK that is easy to read and a useful introduction for the first few weeks.)

Diabetes UK has a number of other pamphlets that are listed on its website: www.diabetes.org.uk

Day, J.L., *Living with diabetes: The Diabetes UK Guide for those treated with diet and tablets.* John Wiley & Sons, London, 2001. (Written by a leading UK authority on diabetes.)

Fox, Charles, Sue Judd, Peter Sonksen. *Diabetes at Your Fingertips.* Class Publishing, London, 2003. (An excellent reference book that answers most questions you might have. Written by an endocrinology professor, a practising doctor and a former diabetes specialist nurse, this book has received enthusiastic reviews by health care professionals and patients.)

Hillson, Rowan. *Diabetes: The Complete Guide: Essential Introduction to Managing Diabetes.* Vermilion, 2002. (Written by a diabetologist in cooperation with Diabetes UK.)

In-depth reading about diabetes

Gill, G., J.C. Pickup, G. Williams. *Difficult Diabetes*. Blackwell Science, London, 2001. (A useful discussion of the areas of doubt in clinical diabetology.)

Krentz, Andrew J. *Insulin Resistance*. Blackwell Science, London, 2002. (A comprehensive survey.)

Pickup, J.C., G. Williams (eds). *Textbook of Diabetes*. Blackwell Science, London , 3rd edition, 2003. (The easiest to read of the half dozen or so large textbooks of diabetes. The illustrations are particularly outstanding.)

Watkins, Peter. *The ABC of Diabetes*. BMJ Books, London, 2003. (Intended for general practitioners but relatively easy for the general reader.)

Diets

LOW-CARBOHYDRATE

Atkins, Robert C. *Dr. Atkins' New Diet Revolution*. rev. ed. New York: Avon, 1999.

Eades, Michael R., Mary Dan Eades. *Protein Power*. New York: Bantam Books, 1996.

Bernstein, Richard K, *Dr Bernstein's Diabetes Solution: The Complete Guide To Achieving Normal Blood Sugars, Revised and Updated*. Little, Brown, 2003.

Ezrin, Calvin. *The Type 2 Diabetes Diet Book*. Contemporary Books Inc, 1999. (An endocrinologist's low-fat, low-carbohydrate approach.)

Goldberg, Jack, Karen O'Mara. *GO-Diet: The Goldberg-O'Mara Diet Plan: the Key to Weight Loss & Healthy Eating*. Niles, Ill.: GO Corporation, 1999.

LOW-FAT HIGH-CARBOHYDRATE-AND-FIBRE

Goor, Ron, Nancy Goor. *Choose to Lose: A Food Lover's Guide to Permanent Weight Loss*. 3rd ed. Boston: Houghton Mifflin, 1999.

McDougall, John A., *The McDougall Program for Maximum Weight Loss*. New York: Plume, 1995.

Ornish, Dean, *Eat More, Weigh Less: Dr. Dean Ornish's Advantage Ten Program for Losing Weight Safely While Eating Abundantly*. rev. ed. New York: Quill, 2000.

Pritikin, Robert. *The Pritikin Principle: The Calorie Density Solution*. Alexandria, Va.: Time Life, 2000.

LOW-GLYCAEMIC INDEX

Brand-Miller, Jennie, Thomas M.S. Wolever, Stephen Colagiuri, Kaye Foster-Powell. *The New Glucose Revolution: The Authoritative Guide to the Glycemic Index*. New York: Marlowe & Company, 2003.

Montignac, Michel. *Eat Yourself Slim . . . and Stay Slim*. London: Montignac Publishing, 1999.

Steward, H. Leighton, Morrison C. Bethea, Sam S. Andrews, Luis A. Balart. *Sugar Busters!: Cut Sugar to Trim Fat*. New York: Ballantine, 1998.

EXCHANGES AND CARBOHYDRATE COUNTING

Most of the 'diabetic cookbooks' you see in bookshops follow the official Diabetes UK approach of a low-fat, high-carbohydrate diet. Recipes are followed by nutritional information including carbohydrate counts and sometimes by exchanges. There are many, many of these books on the market, ranging from fast cooking to gourmet cooking to ethnic cooking. Browse in your local bookshop or look around on the Internet to find a cookbook that appeals to you.

Franz, Marion J. *Exchanges for All Occasions with Carbohydrate Counting: Pocket Guide to Healthy Food Choices Anytime*. Minneapolis: International Diabetes Center, 2000.

Myers, Azmina Govindji, Jill Myers. *Diabetes (Recipes for Health)*. Harper Collins, London, 2001. (Written by a former dietitian for the British Diabetes Association, this low-fat, low-sugar cookbook lists calorie and carbohydrate counts for all recipes. However, carbohydrate counts may be high for those following a limited-carbohydrate diet.)

CALCULATING NUTRITIONAL CONTENT

Bender, A.E. and D.A. Bender. *Food Tables and Labelling*. Oxford University Press, Oxford, 1999.

See also USDA Nutrient Database for Standard Reference online at *http://www.nal.usda.gov/fnic/cgi-bin/nut_search.pl*

MEASURING SGIs

Paice, Derek. *Diabetes and Diet: A Type 2 Patient's Efforts at Control*. Available from Paice & Associates, 114 Rosewood Court, Palm Harbor, FL 34685. (A disk containing a DOS program for measuring areas under the curve is also available. A free download is currently available at http://diabetes.about.com/library/mendosagi/DiabetesAndDiet.pdf – if the URL is unavailable, you can contact Derek Paice by email at Dpaice@ieee.org)

Syndrome X and insulin resistance

Challem, Jack, Burton Berkson, Melissa Diane Smith. *Syndrome X: The Complete Nutritional Program to Prevent and Reverse Insulin Resistance*. New York: John Wiley, 2000.

Insulin Resistance: The Metabolic Syndrome X. Ed., Reaven, Gerald M., Ami Laws. Totowa, NJ: Humana Press, 1999. (Very technical.)

Reaven, Gerald M. *Syndrome X: Overcoming the Silent Killer That Can Give You a Heart Attack*. New York: Simon & Schuster, 2000.

Herbal medicine

Your bookstore or health food store should have a selection of popular books on herbs and supplements. The following books provide the medical community's views.

Bailey, C. J., Day, C. 'Traditional plant medicines as treatments for diabetes.' *Diabetes Care* 12:553, 1989.
Blumenthal, Mark, ed. *The Complete German Commission E Monographs: Therapeutic Guide to Herbal Medicines.* Newton, Mass.: Integrative Medicine Communications, 1998.
Blumenthal, Mark, Alicia Goldberg, ed. *Herbal Medicine: Expanded Commission E Monographs.* Newton, Mass.: Integrative Medicine Communication, 2000.

Exercise

Colberg, Sheri. *The Diabetic Athlete: Prescriptions for Exercise and Sports.* Champaign, Ill.: Human Kinetics, 2000.
Nelson, Miriam E. *Strong Women Stay Young.* New York: Bantam Books, 1998.
Wilmore, Jack H., David L. Costill. *Physiology of Sport and Exercise.* 2nd ed. Human Kinetics, 1999.

Other special focus

Henry, Walter L., Kirk A. Johnson. *The Black Health Library Guide to Diabetes: Vital Health Information for African Americans.* New York: Kensington, 1999.
Jovanovic-Peterson, Lois, June Biermann, Barbara Toohey. *The Diabetic Woman.* rev. ed. New York: Tarcher, 1996.
Jovanovic-Peterson, Lois, Morton Stone. *Managing Your Gestational Diabetes: A Guide for You and Your Baby's Good Health.* Minneapolis: Chronimed, 1994.
Levin, Marvin E., Michael A. Pfeifer, ed. *The Uncomplicated Guide to Diabetes Complications.* Alexandria, VA.: American Diabetes Association, 1998.

Lodewick, Peter A., June Biermann, Barbara Toohey. *The Diabetic Man: A Guide to Health and Success in All Areas of Your Life*. 3rd ed. Los Angeles: Lowell House, 1999.

Polonsky, William H. *Diabetes Burnout: What To Do When You Can't Take It Anymore*. Alexandria, VA.: American Diabetes Association, 1999.

Rubin, Richard R., June Biermann, Barbara Toohey. *Psyching Out Diabetes: A Positive Approach to Your Negative Emotions*. 3rd rev. ed. Los Angeles: Lowell House, 1999.

Resources

American Diabetes Association
1701 North Beauregard Street
Alexandria, VA 22311
001-800-342-2383
(800-DIABETES)
www.diabetes.org

Diabetes UK
10 Parkway
London
NW10 7AA
Tel: 020 7427 1000
Fax: 020 7424 1001
www.diabetes.org.uk

European Association for the Study of
   Diabetes (EASD)
Rheindorfer WEG 3
D 40591
Düsseldorf
Germany
Tel: 49 211 7584690

International Diabetes Federation (IDF)
Avenue Emile de Mot 19
B-1000 Brussels
Belgium
Tel: +32 2 538 55 11
Fax: +32 2 538 5114
www.idf.org

MedicAlert®
1 Bridge Wharf
156 Caledonian Road
London
N1 9UU
www.medicalert.org.uk

National Institute for Clinical Excellence
(NICE)
Midcity Place
71 High Holborn
London
WC1V 6NA
Tel: 020 7067 5800
Fax: 020 7067 5801
www.nice.org.uk

Acknowledgements

I THANK all those who helped me in this endeavour, directly or indirectly, especially my fellow diabetic 'passengers' in this voyage of diabetes, who shared their knowledge, their experiences, their feelings, their failures, their successes, their hopes and their fears, as well as their wit, which made me laugh. I especially thank those who allowed me to quote their thoughts in this book.

I also thank Rick Mendosa for putting me in touch with Marlowe & Company, and for his contribution to the 'Month 12' chapter of this book; Rhoda Martin for her contribution to the Week 3 chapter; Mark McCarthy for the Foreword; Virginia Rose Page for her intelligent interpretation and precise rendition of the rough drawings that I sent to her; Elizabeth Smith for her magical camera work; and Bill Tomczak for wise computer advice when I thought my Big Black Box had gone south.

I also thank Marlboro College for allowing me to audit Todd Smith's biochemistry course; Derek Paice and Rick Mendosa for reading the entire manuscript and offering useful suggestions and Randie R. Little for clarifying some haemoglobin A1c terms for me. Any errors are, of course, my own.

I thank my mother, Ellen V. Becker, for giving up daughter-prepared meals as I approached the deadline; June Biermann and Barbara Toohey for their encouragement and Nancy Humeniuk for listening to my cyberspace whining when I was feeling overworked.

In addition, I thank Dr Allison Goldfine for her caring treatment of patients (and research subjects); for devoting her keen mind to the study of diabetes. I also thank Professor Robert Tattersall for reading the UK edition of this book and making helpful suggestions.

Finally, I thank my editor, Matthew Lore, who has the gift of guiding with a gentle nudge. The overall shaping of this book is his.

FIGURE CREDITS

Figure 1 (page 79) adapted from Y. Tasaka, M. Sekine, M. Wakatsuki, H. Ohgawara and K. Shizume. 'Levels of Pancreatic Glucagon, Insulin and Glucose during Twenty-Four Hours of the Day in Normal Subjects.' Hormone and Metabolic Research, 1975: 7:205-206.

Figure 2 (page 118) adapted from DeFronzo R.A., Bonadonna R.C., Ferrannini E. 'Pathogenesis of NIDDM.' *Diabetes Care*, 1992: 15:318.

Figure 3 (page 254) adapted from Grodsky G.M., Landahl H., Curry D., et al: In Faulkner S., Hellman B., Taljedal I-B (eds). 'The Structure and Metabolism of the Pancreatic Islets.' Wenner-Gren Center International Symposium Series. Oxford, Pergamon Press, 1970, pp 409–422.

Figure 4 (page 271) adapted from Wilmore J.H., Costill D.L. 'Physiology of Sport and Exercise.' *Human Kinetics*, 1994, p 353.

Page numbers in italics refer to the Glossary; those in bold refer to Tables and Figures.